American Man-Killers

True Stories of a Dangerous Wilderness

Don Zaidle

Safari Press, Inc.

American Man-Killers

Zaidle, Don

Second edition

Safari Press, Inc.

1997, Long Beach, California

ISBN 1-57157-056-X

Library of Congress Catalog Card Number 96-70226

10 9 8 7 6 5 4 3 2

Readers wishing to receive the Safari Press catalog, featuring many fine books on big-game hunting, wingshooting, and sporting firearms, should write to: Safari Press, Inc., P.O. Box 3095, Long Beach, CA 90803, U.S.A. Tel: (714) 894-9080, or visit our web site at http://www.safaripress.com.

CONTENTS

Chapters

FOREWORD

Like most kids I used to enjoy a good ghost story. Surely you can remember feeling your skin prickle to classics like *August Heat* and The *Monkey's Paw*. Of course, those were just stories. This fact made the unavoidable shivers of horror all the more delicious, for there was really nothing to be afraid of.

I still love to read, and I still enjoy a good bedtime story—partly because it's usually those last few minutes before I go to sleep that I can find a few quiet minutes to read. If this is the kind of reading you enjoy, then I recommend caution as you begin Don Zaidle's book, for this is not a bedtime story that will lull you to sleep. You will find it terrifying and disturbing in the best traditions of classic tales of horror. But with a chilling difference: Don Zaidle's things that go bump in the night (or at noon) are real, as are the screams of the victims and the sounds of breaking bones and rending flesh.

This book might not be the best reading matter for the dark, quiet hours—and you might use some discretion as to where you read it. Don sent me a copy of his manuscript on the eve of departure for an African safari, and I read much of it by flashlight with Africa's night sounds for accompaniment. Reading about close encounters with bears, cougars, and wolves while listening to hyenas and lions was not the proper recipe for dreamless sleep!

Over the past thirty years I have been fortunate to have spent a good deal of time in the wild country of literally all the continents, each of which has its own deadly denizens. In spite of the genuine threat posed by assorted nasties, I do not regard the wilds as particularly scary or threatening, although I've had my share of close encounters with some of Nature's toothier creatures. The first such episode was about 1965, on a hiking trip on the Philmont Scout Ranch in New Mexico.

We had a bear come into camp early in the evening, and we drove it off by the approved method of banging on pans and "loud vocalizations" (about which, in due course, Mr. Zaidle will have more to say). Much later I awoke from a deep sleep to find the stars blotted out and a great weight on my chest. I was lucky; the bear had me pinned. The boy sleeping next to me was equally terrified but not so fortunate. He sat up and the bear swatted him back down, removing much of his scalp. It was a long night.

Since then I've had a number of other encounters with bears, but never another so terrifying. I've also had close encounters with all of Africa's dangerous game. Like everyone who has spent much time outdoors, I've got my share of snake stories and I've caught my share of insect-borne ailments. I've never dwelled on these things in my writing, and I'm not likely to start now. This for a couple of reasons. First, I don't go to Africa looking for a lion charge. Second, with the kind of writing I mostly do, it's part of my job to make people want to experience the outdoors—not scare them into staying home!

Still, bear encounters, lion charges, and other assorted wrecks have occurred and probably will again. If they do, I'll deal with them as part of the experience, but it's not my "thing" to dwell upon them or sensationalize them. I continue to believe that America's wild country (and suburbs!)—as well as Africa's bush—are much safer than most highways, and that the greatest danger to man is always man himself.

That's my philosophy, whether sound or not—but that doesn't mean we should ignore the other very real dangers that await the unwary. In this regard, I owe a debt to Don Zaidle and his *American Man-Killers*, for he offers an honest, well-researched wake-up call to me and to all of his readers. Nature is neither benevolent nor cruel—she simply *is*. Zaidle's message that her denizens bite is clearly one that needs broadcasting.

Zaidle is, of course, not the first author to dwell upon this unpleasant subject. My library holds several volumes of grisly grizzly tales, and no collection of Africana is lacking in tales of man-eaters and hair-raising charges. As a boy I thrilled to Patterson's *Man-eaters of Tsavo* and Jim Corbett's tales of pursuing man-eating tigers and leopards. Fifteen years ago I had the privilege to edit Peter Capstick's *Maneaters*, a wonderfully scary book about the world's people-eaters—written, of course in classic Capstick prose.

Don Zaidle's *American Man-Killers* is a fitting addition to this genre and tradition, incorporating sound and detailed research with good—if downright scary—storytelling. It's a timely addition, too, for I fear we are heading into an Orwellian era when, indeed, some animals are more equal than others. Right now the predators are quickly becoming the most equal of animals.

I live in California, where much of Zaidle's well-documented cougar mayhem has taken place. I do not yet fear for my children in their backyard—but I fear for a vast-vanishing deer herd and must ponder what will happen when the fully protected predators run out of prey. Now the wolves are coming back as well. I think all of this is wonderful in that I want cougars, coyotes, wolves, and even grizzlies to have a place in my world—but today, under the myth that such animals are cute and cuddly, we have created an entire class of sacred cows out of the greatest predators that live in America's wilderness. These animals are all beautiful, but they are not cuddlesome. I'd like to think that at least some of those who think they are will read this book.

Realists will applaud *American Man-Killers*. Its explicit examples of predation upon humans clearly portray these messy, gory true-life encounters. While some of the images may be disturbing, they should not produce any lasting trauma. The nature Nazis, bunny huggers, fern fairies, and such will hate this book, for it suggests that those cute Teddy bears, adorable wolf pups, and "endangered" mountain lions might be more than mere harmless ornamentation in our ecosystem. The fanatics in these groups won't be impressed with Zaidle's research or logic; one can only hope it's they—and not their children—who jog unconcerned in cougar country and camp at will where grizzlies roam. Perhaps, however, there will be some well-meaning but ill-informed souls who will read this book and ponder its contents—with the result, just perhaps, that these souls might wonder if we are going too far in creating sacred cows of our American man-killers.

Craig Boddington
Mulobezi River, Zambia
September 1996

INTRODUCTION

Regardless of what may be inferred from the title, this is not a book about the relative deadly merits of blondes, brunettes, and redheads, nor is it a treatise on the sanguinary arts as practiced by Henry Lee Lucas, Jack the Ripper, Ted Bundy, and the rest of the morally challenged. This book is about things that go bump in the night, that breathe somewhere out in the darkness, watching and waiting until the moment is right to come for you.

If you are lucky, you will never know what hit you, instantly dead from a snapped neck or crushed skull. If you are not so lucky, you may get to watch yourself bleed to death or see your flesh ripped away and eaten one piece at a time. You may be crushed beneath pounding hooves, or battered into something that would clog a garbage disposal by a set of wrist-thick horns or antlers. Or you could simply drown, anchored beneath dark, chilly water in the jaws of a saurian nightmare.

If none of these fits your particular death wish, you may opt to be poisoned or infected with a fatal disease by something small and crawly. Other options include decapitation, disembowelment, limb removal, and, if you really want to stretch out the fun, gangrene and secondary infection. For the weak of heart, simple maiming is also available.

In an era when lasers, moon landings, home satellite systems, computers, cellular phones, and biogenetic engineering are as commonplace as dirty dishes, it is hard to imagine that people in America still die on a near-daily basis in attacks by wild animals. In Africa, sure. Asia, unquestionably. Heck, I'll even buy Australia, no matter how fancy its opera house is. But right here in the most advanced civilized nation in the world? No way!

I used to think that way too, but then I started noticing the reports that kept cropping up in the newspaper about campers and hunters killed by bears, joggers slain and eaten by cougars, children dying in gang assaults by wild dogs; it just never seemed to end. When I started checking into this seemingly emergent phenomenon, I got an even bigger surprise.

You would think that any state's police agency, health department, or wildlife-management office could punch a few buttons on a computer and get an instant printout of the number of deaths and injuries resulting from attacks by animals in their jurisdiction. Nope. All reports are lumped into a common database with no utility for cross-checking, so unless you have a specific name, date, or report number, forget it. The same is pretty much true of the national agencies, like the Centers for Disease Control and Prevention, which has two general "bites" categories, one each for animals and insects, but can no more tell you whether somebody died as a result of having their insides pulled outside by a bear or bled to death after their Yorkshire terrier bit them on the ankle.

Most of the national parks keep very detailed and well-organized records on their wildlife's shenanigans, and the administrators thereof are willing to share what they know, and are darn nice about it to boot. Who says government paperwork is worthless!

The game departments of a few states do keep animal-related death ledgers, but most are anything but complete. Some states only recently began keeping attack records after their wildlife started showing an increased propensity to eat taxpayers, so historical accounts are severely lacking. Some lists do not even include all of the modern-day deaths, the record-keepers being very choosy about who they allow onto the hallowed pages.

In California, for instance, political pressure resulting from the recent upsurge in cougar attacks and deaths fairly forced the Department of Fish and Game to start to at least appear to keep close tabs on the situation. Yet at least one confirmed cougar death plus several "probables" remain unlisted. The same is pretty much true of Florida and its alligators. When I contacted the wildlife departments of these states and requested the pertinent data, I got the same standard-issue packages sent out to all "journalists"—a collection of ambiguous, incomplete, and mostly useless information in terms of research value. Going through official channels proved useless; nobody in administration wanted to tell me anything. Only the subterfuge of contacting biologists and wardens directly in the field yielded any meaningful information.

I ran into similar resistance from other agencies; some wouldn't return my phone calls, and a few got downright hostile. Two things gradually became clear: (1) I was pretty much on my own research-wise, and (2) there seemed to be what I could only interpret as a conspiracy among some wildlife officials and "experts" to downplay, obfuscate, and deny whenever possible the existence of man-killing wildlife.

The specific reasons for this vary somewhat with locale and species, but they mostly boil down to two rather simple principles: It is difficult to garner popular support for a dubiously "endangered" species if it is known to habitually kill and eat its supporters. Similarly, it is hard to attract tourists with the enticement, "Come vacation among our scenic vistas and killer wildlife."

Whatever the reasons, it became apparent that the general public was not being told the whole truth about the carnage taking place in what was often its own literal back yards, and was in fact being outright lied to in some cases. Hence, this book.

In its production, I turned over one helluva pile of reference rocks in an effort to offend just about everybody. The wolfmen will no doubt clamor for my head for suggesting their monarch *might* be a man-killer, while the cattlemen prepare a bonfire and suitable stake in my honor for intimating the wolf is anything less than the Antichrist. The Disney crowd will probably hire a Sicilian hit man to avenge my vicious and unrepentant denigration of Bambi. I don't want to even think about what the dog and cat lovers might come up with.

For the sensitive reader, a word of warning is in order: Herein are graphic descriptions of gruesome, bloody human deaths under the indelicate fangs, claws, and horns of animals: infants dead in their blood-soaked cribs, chewed into shapeless lumps by the family pet; women dragged away screaming in the darkness, eaten alive by bears; men pummeled and torn into mattress stuffing by an assortment of horned and fanged beasts. If books were subject to the same rating system as movies, this one would be stamped "XXX" for violent content. Parental discretion is advised.

This violence is not gratuitous, but rather serves a definitive purpose. It is intended to undo a half-century's worth of damage to the average person's understanding of what the term "animal" really means, and to instill in the reader's mind that the half-baked "warnings" about the dangers posed by wild and domestic animals should not be taken lightly.

In the same manner that a mutilated corpse viewed in the morgue makes a more lasting impression than platitudes like "Alcohol Kills," reading about a young woman screaming "Mommy!" while a grizzly eats the flesh from her arms is more convincing than "Don't Feed the Bears." The press is more inclined to tell you that a young boy was "mauled" or "badly bitten" by a Rottweiler than to describe how his genitals and lower intestines were torn out. TV "nature" shows may make ambiguous references to the fact that it is "unwise" to keep wild animals for pets, but rarely will they tell you about ferrets eating off the faces of infants in their cribs, or monkeys killing and partially eating their owners' children. But I will.

I think it prudent to invest a few words regarding my literary approach to death, which some in the past have labeled "insensitive" and severely lacking in the reverence department.

Americans in general harbor some strange ideas about death. Doctors often underprescribe pain medications for terminally ill patients lest they become addicts. If you are dying anyway, why should it matter if you die addicted to morphine? In some states, terminally ill children remain subject to compulsory education laws, it being somehow better to die with a head full of information, no matter how unlikely you are to make future use of it. And Lord forbid that anyone about to cash in from cancer should fail to pay his Social Security!

I have seen quite an assortment of death in my lifetime, and have even had a few personal encounters with it that were far closer than I would have liked. Through this exposure, I long ago came to the conclusion that death is the logical and inevitable conclusion to life, and even though it can be put off for a while, as the late George Burns conclusively demonstrated, in the end we must all deliver our salts back to the earth from whence we came. Since death is inevitable, I see no more reason to be maudlin about it than to lament the creak of my aging bones or weep over the handfuls of hair that daily clog my shower drain. Yes, I feel sorrow for the mother whose child was killed by a speeding car. Yes, I wish I could kill cancer with a bullet. No, I do not enjoy paying taxes. But, like it or not, the inescapable reality of death is that there is nothing you, I, or anyone else can do about it—least of all after the fact. Therefore, if I can lighten the load of the living with a bit of applied gallows humor, I am gratified. Any seeming disrespect for the dearly departed is merely a reflection of the fact that the dead care not one whit for my respect, making it a commodity best reserved for the deserving living.

In closing, it is my hope and intent that your experience within these pages leaves you with one or more of the following iconoclastic impressions:

Mother Nature is a cruel, calculating old bitch who will kill you given half the chance.

Man's position at the top of the food chain does not exempt him from active participation in the lower links.

Adventure in America's wild places is not dead, even if quite a few of the adventurers are.

You are never so alive as when something is trying to kill you.

ACKNOWLEDGMENTS

The author wishes to express his appreciation to the following persons and agencies whose assistance made this manuscript possible:

Todd Malmsbury of the Colorado Division of Wildlife, for sharing from his personal files. And Michelle Ancell, the Phantom Phaxer.

Sheri Edwards, for all the legwork and not complaining about photocopier's elbow.

Sam Burr, lion hunter, friend, and a true gentleman, for his thoughts on things that bite.

Don Donaldson, for keeping me informed on the California mountain lion.

"Nevada" Jim Ornellas, my friend in the desert.

David Vaught and his mother, Kim Brown, for sharing their story.

Dave Fjelline and Cliff Wylie, for sharing their thoughts and observations on, and photographs of, mountain lions.

"Mary Castle" and all the others who wish to remain anonymous.

Don Neal, for putting up with my incessant questions.

Lee Whittlesey of Yellowstone Park, for his invaluable assistance on just about everything in this book.

Ed Wiseman, for telling his story one more time.

Steve Frey, chief ranger of Glacier National Park, for his willingness to answer endless questions about bears.

Dr. Walter E. Howard, for answering my leopard questions.

Larry McNease of the Louisiana Department of Wildlife and Fisheries, who taught me more than I thought it possible to know about alligators.

Nick Gilmore of Game & Fish Publications, who taught me to be a writer.

The Alaska Department of Fish and Game, for baring the bear facts.

Larry Bozka, one of my old magazine editors, for all the encouragement and kind words.

Gary Enkowitz, friend and fellow outdoor writer, and his wife Hazel, all-round good egg, for letting me bend their ears.

My publishers, Ludo Wurfbain and Dr. Jacque Neufeld of Safari Press, for taking a chance on an incorrigible old wood rat like me.

Last but far from least, my family, Barbara and Crystal, for putting up with my grumpiness, late hours, and generally bad overall disposition. You deserve a medal.

There are many others whom space, regretfully, does not permit me to list. You know who you are. Thanks a million.

DEDICATION

To the victims. . .

COUGARS

Dangle, Wilson, Kennedy, Fehlhaber, Taylor, Wells, Nolan, Samuel, Bergman, Gardipe, Dunton, Schoener, Kenna, Lancaster—the list goes on, but these will do for now. Chances are these names mean little to you. You probably do not know that Scott Lancaster enjoyed playing the blues on his harmonica and biking in the mountains, that Iris Kenna was a school counselor, or that Jake Gardipe liked to ride his tricycle in his front yard. Unless you knew her, Barbara Schoener's love for her two children is an abstraction without substance. These people, plus an unknown number of others whose names will never be known, share a common distinction: They are all dead, their final appointments with Kismet presided over by mountain lions.

American Man-Killers

The mountain lion as a man-killer has for decades been a subject of more than casual debate. One side calls him rare, shy, reclusive, misunderstood, beautiful, and endangered. The other side prefers terms like vermin, overpopulated, bloodthirsty, killer, cruel, and savage, plus several more not suitable for print. In most debates, the truth is like a boll weevil, wandering the desolate middle-ground wastes just lookin' for a home, and it is no different here. Both sides are guilty of felony axe-grinding, although one seems more disposed to fib than the other.

From a purely statistical standpoint, the lion's homicidal record is less than impressive. According to a 1991 study by Paul Beier, then a wildlife ecologist with the Department of Forestry and Resource Management, University of California at Berkeley, fifty-seven people had unsociable encounters with cougars in North America between 1890 and 1990, ten of them fatal. This study is the "bible" of reference most often cited by wildlife officials and media when lion-attack questions arise. Considering the number of people exposed to potential attack over this one hundred-year timespan, the odds of a nasty encounter seem pretty slim. On the other hand, considerable evidence suggests that Beier's data was more than a little flawed, and that he may have been something less than objective in his approach. Whatever the reason, Beier's Epistle to the Cougarites ain't exactly inerrant gospel.

Before going any further, I want to make clear that this is no hog-fattening contest, and I hold no personal grudge of any kind against mountain lions. In fact, I like lions. My life would be somehow diminished without the terror-thrill of knowing they are "out there" as I huddle closer to my dying campfire, nervous and wondering what may stalk the night. Seeing the big, splayed pug marks of a puma intermingled with the buck's spoor rouses the primeval hunter that sleeps in my brain, bringing to life dormant instincts I cannot explain or fully understand. To pit those instincts against the lion's, to hunt the hunter in a rite of passage born of ancestral, saber-toothed memo-

4

ries, is to see life reflected in death and to be thankful. Yes, I like lions. I like them "out there" where any contact is strictly at my initiation. Otherwise, I like my lions very, very dead. That way, you see, they are less prone to bite. . . .

On 2 August 1984, eight-year-old David Vaught, his four-year-old brother Justin, and their mother and stepfather, Kim and Christopher Brown, were on vacation, hiking the rugged trails of Texas's Big Bend National Park. While Kim and Chris stopped in the trail to ward off a fire-ant attack, Justin wandered ahead around a sharp bend, with David a few steps behind. When David rounded the bend, he nearly stumbled over his little brother, frozen statue-like in the trail. Looking over Justin's shoulder, David saw why. A few scant feet away, crouched in the shadow of a rocky overhang, was a cougar, its eyes locked like a heat-seeking missile on the smaller boy. David sized up the situation instantly and threw himself between the cougar and his brother. Shoving Justin back up the trail, he shouted a warning to his family and started running. He had been playing " The Boy Who Cried Wolf" all day with his mother, shouting "Snake!" to watch her jump, and she thought he was at it again with "Mountain lion!" All thought of jokes dissolved when she saw her son's terror-stricken face overshadowed by the extended claws and fanged horror-mask of the airborne cat descending on the boy's head. Faster than you can say "intensive care," the carnivore wrapped him in a clawed death-grip and bit sharply into his skull. Borne down by the predator's weight, he fell prostrate in the trail and lay still.

In an American version of tiger-by-the-tail, Chris rushed in and grabbed the puma by the neck with both hands, causing it to quit its victim and turn all attention fully to him. He rolled to one side, dragging the cat with him. Laying on his back, Chris looked up at the screaming, spitting animal that would probably kill him. All he could think of was holding on so it could not get at David or the rest of his family. The enraged cougar clawed at the man's arms, squirming for freedom. About to lose his grip, Chris decided to try and disable the animal. Drawing up his right leg, he kicked the lion's chest as hard as he could, propelling the cat high in the air to land unhurt several feet away in characteristic feline fashion. The man scrambled up and jumped between the furious lion and his family. It became a battle of screams, the cat venting its rage at the man while Chris screeched back in primal epithets. After what seemed like a couple of weeks, the cat finally dashed off into the brush.

David, lying facedown in a growing halo of blood, had not moved since the initial attack. But by some miracle he was still alive, in spite of having been literally scalped from his hairline clear to the back of his skull. The family started back toward their rented cabin, terrified to see the predator shadowing and feinting in the brush alongside the trail. Continuous shouting and rock barrages kept the animal at bay during the mile-long walk. At the hospital, David underwent the first of what would finally total thirteen surgeries to repair damage the cougar inflicted in just a few seconds. It could have been a lot worse; had the cougar been a full-sized adult instead of a fifty-pound juvenile lacking the jaw size for one-bite skull-crushing—well, use your imagination. To this day, David and his family recall with macabre humor the park ranger who told them the night before the attack, "If you're real lucky, somewhere off in the distance you might get a brief glimpse of a mountain lion."

This incident, though one of the happier ones, embodies a theme that has become all too familiar in recent times. Since 1980 or thereabouts, cougar attacks in the U.S. have been increasing at an unprecedented rate. Most victims have been women and small children, but hairy-chested types have by no means been ignored.

During a March 1989 camping trip in Caspers Wilderness Park, Orange County, California, a cougar grabbed five-year-old Laura Small by the head and started dragging her into the brush. A hiker attracted by the screams assisted the girl's mother in a successful rescue by clubbing the lion with a tree limb. Laura's injuries included the loss of one eye, facial disfigurement, a crushed skull, and permanent partial paralysis.

In September 1989, two (some reports say three) cougars stalked, killed, and ate five-year-old Jake Gardipe while he rode his tricycle thirty yards from the front door of his Missoula, Montana, home.

In January 1991, eighteen-year-old Scott Lancaster, a senior at Clear Creek County High School near Idaho Springs, Colorado, left campus around noon on his daily jog and never returned. His partially eaten body was found two days later, presided over by a 120-pound adult male lion. Killed by game officials, its stomach contained grisly evidence proving an undeniable case of man-eating. From studying the spoor, authorities surmised the youth was chased some distance before being killed from behind with a single bite to the neck. After satiating its hunger, the cat dragged the body into brush and covered it with leaves and dirt in the standard cougar procedure for storing leftovers.

A similar fate nearly befell thirty-nine-year-old Bryan Burdo in January 1996. Just after passing a cedar bush while jogging alone in a wooded area of King County, Washington, Burdo looked behind him for the source of a slight noise. A cougar came boiling out from behind the cedar, stopping its charge at six feet when the man yelled at it. After several minutes of mutual insults, Burdo's punctuated with rocks, the man was finally able to back off enough to get a head start in establishing a new record for the mile.

An attack almost identical to the Vaught incident occurred in March 1992 against nine-year-old Darron Arroyo. Hiking with his family in California's Gaviota State Park, Darron and his two brothers were about 100 yards ahead of their parents on the trail when a lion ambushed the boy from cover. With jaws clamped firmly around Darron's head, the predator dragged him toward some brush. The father, Steven, ran up and smacked the cat between the eyes with a rock, causing it to drop his son and retreat. The emergency-room bill came to $5,150, approximately $10 per stitch.

Another eerily similar case occurred on the shores of Canyon Lake just outside Phoenix, Arizona, when a puma nabbed five-year-old Joshua Walsh and started dragging him off toward sure death. Geological providence again supplied relief when the boy's father, Tim Walsh, managed to drive the cat off with a rock. The boy survived, but came out of the encounter missing an ear and major portions of his scalp. The ear was later found and successfully reattached.

Iris M. Kenna, a fifty-eight-year-old high-school career guidance counselor, was killed and mostly eaten in December 1994 while jogging in Cuyamaca Rancho State Park in southern California. State game officials killed the lion when it returned to feed on what was left of the body, which they had removed.

The death of Barbara Schoener is probably the most widely publicized case of animal predation in U.S. history. On the morning of 24 April 1994, Schoener had gone to Auburn Lake Trails about forty-five miles northeast of Sacramento, California, to practice for an upcoming marathon race. When she didn't return home on schedule, her husband went looking for her. After finding her car parked in the usual place but no sign of Barbara, he became worried and notified authorities. The El Dorado County Sheriff Department's Search and Rescue team began combing the area at 2:30 that afternoon. Hampered by treacherous weather and reduced visibility, the search was called off a little past midnight.

When the search resumed the following morning, a series of coincidences too incredible for a grade-B movie plot ultimately led searchers to Schoener's body. Around 7:30 A.M., a jogger running on the same trail Schoener was believed to have been following met up with one of the search teams, and they began talking. The jogger, who knew Schoener, happened to look down the steep slope beside the trail and recognized the missing woman's sun visor lying some fifty feet below. *The jogger and search team had met at the exact spot where Schoener was attacked!* The probability calculations would short-circuit IBM's finest. From there it was just a matter of following the bloody spoor to the body. With no witnesses, the precise events are anybody's guess, but the evidence suggests something like this:

Schoener was running north along the trail, flanked on one side by a seven-foot rise and on the other by a long, near-vertical slope. The cougar, which had probably been shadowing the woman for some time, waited atop the rise and attacked from behind in a deferred ambush. The predator boarded the woman's back, clamping her neck in a fanged vise, then rode her down the embankment as the unbelievable impact propelled her forcefully from the trail. At the bottom of the slope, she somehow wrenched free of the murderous grip, but the lion was on her again before she could do anything but bleed, the arteries in her neck geysering blood several feet from deep, carotid gashes. The *coup de grâce* came when the predator pierced her brain with its fangs. When the last quiver quit, the lion ate its fill, then dragged the bloody corpse some 100 yards to a thick stand of manzanita-choked trees and buried it for later use.

I could go on ad nauseam, but you should have the idea by now. The state of man-cougar relations in the U.S. has clearly deteriorated, although I have a hunch the lions do not see it that way. Afforded unprecedented legal protection over much of its range, the mountain lion (a.k.a. cougar, puma, panther, catamount, painter, American lion, or any of a dozen or so locally favored sobriquets) has taken up the sport of people-pounding with heretofore unknown enthusiasm.

In spite of what protectionist lion-huggers may say on the matter, most people with sense recognize that cougars today represent a danger to human life wherever they are found. Trouble is, no one is sure exactly of the quantity or rate at which unrefusable invitations to become lunch are being issued, which brings us back to the numbers game.

Discounting for the moment whatever historical attacks Beier might have missed, the number occurring since 1990 alone is downright spooky. Adding the fatal incidents recorded since 1990 to Beier's numbers yields a total of fourteen deaths officially attributed to lion predation in North America. Four of those occurred north

American Man-Killers

of the border, making the score Canada—four, U.S.—ten. At least one other recent U.S. fatality is a near-certainty, but as of this writing, authorities had so far refused to give the devil his due. It happened in California.

Lucy Gomez Dunton, age fifty-one, was reported missing in early November 1988 in a rugged area of Butte County. On 20 November her remains were found in what the autopsy report described as "a state of extreme post-mortem mutilation." The cause of death was listed as undetermined until May 1994, when Butte County Sheriff's Department and coroner officials attributed the woman's demise to a lion attack. Four medical doctors, in addition to the coroner, made the determination after independent examinations of the remains. Nevertheless, as of June 1995, the California Department of Fish and Game still had not included Dunton in its records as a lion fatality.

Contemporary official jitterbugging aside, even the historical numbers do not add up. The data used in Beier's study were derived primarily from old newspaper and magazine reports, plus whatever scientific literature he could find. He must have found the same thing I did (mostly nothing) in the files of the various state game departments, for he states in his introduction, "Only incomplete historical records of cougar attacks are presently available." He further notes that maulings by captive cougars or wild ones deliberately approached or otherwise provoked were specifically excluded, compounding the incompleteness of his work.

The point is not to criticize Beier, even if justified, but to point out that the numbers bandied about by officialdom are both historically and currently wrong. In any event, using the Beier study as a springboard, I perused many of the same records, plus quite a few more that escaped his notice or were beyond the time venue of his study, to ultimately document twenty-five additional U.S. attacks (eight fatal) plus one Canadian incident not mentioned by him, effectively doubling the fatality figure in just over three months of research. Lest my sources' credibility be questioned, I proudly attribute six of the "new" incidents, including four

10

fatalities, to a no less credible source than U.S. President Theodore Roosevelt.

In his book *Outdoor Pastimes of an American Hunter* (1905), Roosevelt records having personal knowledge of at least three fatal cougar encounters. In the first instance, he reports knowing of an Indian killed in 1887 when he bent over a cougar that came to after being knocked down. No particulars are given as to how the cat was "knocked down," but provocation seems evident. Still, dead is dead, provoked or not. Details of the other cases are sketchier still, with Teddy saying only that he knew of "two undoubted cases," one in Mississippi and the other in Florida, where gentlemen of color were killed "while alone in a swamp at night."

The fourth fatal episode was related to Roosevelt by Dr. Hart Merriam, friend and hunting companion to the President, a well-known wildlife biologist of the time who helped found the National Geographic Society and the U.S. Biological Survey, now known as the Fish and Wildlife Service, and whose name was given to the Merriam's elk subspecies. Merriam was even more tight-lipped than the President, saying only that he "knew of one genuine instance of a cougar killing a man whose tracks he had dogged," a reference to the cougar's habit of following humans along woodland tracks, which I can tell you from experience is nerve-wracking as hell.

Roosevelt relates two nonfatal feline *tête-à-têtes*, one being that of a cowboy badly mauled when he and a cougar surprised one another in close quarters near the President's ranch in the Dakota Territories. The other was recorded in a letter written to Merriam in May 1893 by one W. H. Brewer of Yale (presumably the university), wherein he relates a daylight attack against a three-year-old boy playing in his front yard near Mount Shasta. What Brewer described as a "two-thirds grown panther" rushed in, seized the boy by the throat, and started dragging him off. Hearing his screams, the mother administered a few hundred foot-pounds of high-velocity broom, with an "old man at the house" delivering the insurance shot with more conventional armament. The boy survived, but bore scars on the side of his jaw and throat the rest of his life.

American Man-Killers

What is surely the oldest documented fatality is recorded on a tombstone in Pennsylvania. The likeness of a cougar is etched above the name Phillip Tanner and dated 1751; this is probably the same incident mentioned in a 1986 study by Lee Fitzhugh and Paul Gorenzel at UC Davis, documenting sixty-six attacks dating back to 1750.

Sometime around 1850, a Texas woman named McNeill was attacked in her own bedroom when she went to investigate the frantic squawking of a hen brooding a clutch of eggs under her bed. Kneeling and lifting the bedspread, she came eyeball to whiskers with a large puma. It nailed her from behind when she tried to run, biting her severely in the neck. Two men in the next room heard her screams and were able to shoot the cat before it could kill her. Another bedroom encounter took place around 1908 when yet another Texas lion entered a house and attacked a woman in her bed as she recovered from a farm accident. Around 1870, a southern Texas school teacher, a Miss Armstrong, was jumped late one evening by a cougar as she was leaving after dining with a local family named White. Two ranch hands alerted by the screams found her bleeding out by the barn with her dress ripped mostly off, and the cougar embattled with the family dog. The school teacher survived, but the dog later died of its injuries.

A U.S. Cavalry officer named John G. Bourke recorded during the Arizona Apache wars an incident where a wounded man, presumably a soldier, was tracked from a water hole, slain, and eaten. J. Frank Dobie, a talented amateur naturalist and prolific writer of some renown earlier this century, recorded the killing and eating of a five-year-old Mexican girl in the Sierra Madres. The lion was a monster that weighed nearly two hundred pounds field-dressed after it was killed by a man named A. M. Tenney of El Paso, Texas. Buttons found in the cat's intestines confirmed it as the child's killer.

These and other historical records prove that cougars have been killing and eating people for a very long time. More than that, they provide support for the belief held by many (including Yours Truly) that, from

12

a historical perspective, the number of people killed in lion or other animal attacks that we *do not* know about probably exceeds those we do know of. Look at it this way: Early settlers faced a daily gauntlet of privation, disease, outlaws, and unfriendly Indians that makes street-gang life seem tame by comparison. An animal attack here or there didn't mean much, and was hardly worth mentioning in letters to family back East, assuming they could read or write in the first place. Most of our forebears were not disposed to jotting down their memoirs between Indian raids and anthrax outbreaks. Consider too the relative isolation of the typical frontier homestead. Deaths or disappearances of individuals and even entire families could, and did, go undiscovered for months, if at all. Burial sites were typically casual affairs involving piled rocks and crude wooden markers, so even headstone documentation of predator-caused deaths are few. Even so, the settlers left a sufficiently sanguinary legacy to support a case for The Unknown Eaten.

Before getting further into the numbers, theoretical or otherwise, we had best clarify what does and does not constitute a bona fide cougar "attack." Beier defined an attack as "an incident in which the cougar bit, clawed, or knocked down a human." For our purposes, two attack categories, "contact" and "non-contact," will be considered without regard to provocation. (If we were so inclined, further distinctions could be made as to whether an attack was predatory or defensive in nature, but when something is busily rearranging your internal organs, underlying motivations hardly seem relevant.) A third division, loosely labeled "observation," will serve as a catchall for incidents not quite measuring up to attack standards.

Contact encounters are clearly distinguished by their crimson hue, leaving little room for confusion. Non-contact episodes include averted attacks as well as any interaction wherein the cougar demonstrated unsociable conduct such as stalking, chasing, hiding in ambush, bad breath, and so on. Observation incidents are defined as situations in which a cougar knowingly placed itself near any person or occupied human dwelling, with or without provocation. God, I'm getting a headache. Anyway, them's the rules, and, as I think you will soon see, the evidence supports their validity.

Tabulating modern contact encounters is fairly easy; anatomical human contributions to a cougar's diet tend to generate talk, if not press, and are practically self-documenting. Adding my historical discoveries to Beier's, along with the more recent bloody episodes, yields ninety-five documented attacks with twenty-two fatalities. The numbers will have changed by the time you read this, of course; new reports are coming in even as I type. I'll venture out onto an arboreal appendage (all saws must be checked at the door) and predict that by 1998 the total number of attacks will break 100, probably with at least one more fatality.

Non-contact encounters are by their very nature difficult to document. Many potentially nasty encounters have gone unreported simply because the erstwhile victim was sufficiently Disneyized to preclude recognition of the danger. By the same token, a few nervous individuals (and who can blame them?) have run screaming "MOUNTAIN LION!" after spotting one on a ridge at half a mile. Even legitimate reported episodes do not get much attention anymore. In California, for instance, the game department became so overwhelmed by daily lion complaints in 1994 that blood had to be drawn almost before an incident was recorded. Even the news-hungry media taste lion every time they burp these days, their appetites satiated by the glut. Snarl-and-snuggle affairs of a more spectacular nature may get a line or two in the local paper, but for the most part, "casual" lion liaisons just aren't news. Whatever the public attention span, reliable figures from just four of the twelve states with large lion populations show 130 recent officially recorded attacks of the less-determined type, with well over two-thirds occurring in 1990 alone. Extrapolating from these figures, a national tally of several hundred to possibly more than a thousand does not seem unreasonable, and even that is probably on the low side by a considerable margin.

1 • Cougars

Statistics are not only cold, they're boring. Before continuing, let's hang some flesh (unbloodied) on the skeleton of our non-contact number, just to liven things up.

In May 1994, a couple from Yuma, Arizona, vacationing with their three-year-old son in California's Cuyamaca Park, narrowly avoided relegation to the contact category when a cougar charged the boy. The lion, an eighty-three-pound female, leaped out of the brush and ran straight for the child. Seeing what was about to happen, the mother rushed forward, grabbed the boy up, and started screaming bloody murder. The lion stopped about three feet away, crouched, and started hissing, obviously upset at this breach of dining-room etiquette. The boy's father meanwhile, his attention definitely gotten, rushed the cat with a tree-limb club while screaming things even the puma probably found embarrassing, whereupon it excused itself to the branches of a nearby tree and placidly watched the family retreat back down the trail.

Back in 1985, the same park hosted a party involving another family being entertained for the better part of an hour by two high-spirited lions. The festivities included stalking, snarling, some rather creative cursing, and "throwing stuff." Game officials said of the incident, "The only way they [the family] kept from being attacked was to huddle and throw stuff at the lions." Things later turned hairy for game warden Bob Turner when he went looking for the offending felines. He found them, all right, or maybe they found him; either way, Turner quickly went from hunter to huntee when he followed the cats into heavy cover.

With visibility akin to what you would expect inside a coffin, Turner kneeled, hoping for a better view beneath the manzanita tangle, and looked squarely into a pair of gray-green eyes mounted on the business end of the larger cougar, crouched flat, tail lashing with the excited interest a tabby shows in a robin on your front lawn. With thoughts of gladiators and coliseums running through his brain, the warden watched, fascinated, as the big puma slithered forward, steel-hard muscles rippling beneath tawny hide stretched over nearly seven feet of fanged determination. At ten yards, just as the meat-hooked rear

15

paws dug in for the final—and I do mean final—rush, Turner centered the front sight of his .308 Ruger on the tensed chest muscles and pulled the trigger.

You would think any cougar familiar with the finer points of man-lion relations would have fled at the rifle's report. Not this pair. While the first cat went through its death throes, Turner saw the other one coming up from behind it like a second-string quarterback when the home-game hero is down for the count. Another dose of high-velocity persuasion settled the matter in the warden's favor.

In 1991 Montana game warden Mike Quinn had a similar experience while investigating a reported attack on a horse. The sixth sense that helps keep game wardens alive told him to look behind. Over his shoulder, Quinn saw a huge lion crouched less than fifty feet away, showing unfeigned interest in his back. When the man turned, the cat began flowing toward him like molten grease, slithering on its belly with ears pricked attentively forward, its eyes locked with Quinn's. Though he held a 12-gauge autoloader stoked with slugs in his left hand, the man for reasons he cannot explain drew his service revolver and fired two "warning" shots between the puma's front feet. He shouldn't have done that. The puma floated up as its front legs swung forward, reaching for Quinn's face with hooked, inward-turned paws framing a set of switchblade fangs exposed when the black-edged lips peeled back in a rasping snarl. Reflexively, the warden dropped the handgun and swung the shotgun's muzzle up toward the hurtling cat and fired. The charge connected a bit low, a raking shot that ripped the predator open from throat to crotch, disemboweling it in midair. Momentum carried the cat splattering bloodily into the warden's chest, knocking him down. Rolling to one knee, he swung the scattergun to cover the prostrate form, but there was no need. Scratch one more man-killer.

Meanwhile, back in Cuyamaca Park, another lion entered into a dispute with some campers over possession of the chicken they were cooking. The big cat marched right up to the fire, hissed like a locomotive venting steam, and refused to leave even under threat of prosecution. The matter was resolved when the chicken proved overdone for the lion's taste. A few days later, what was presumed to be the same lion attempted to procure a cut of New Jersey sirloin (horse meat), to which the rider strenuously objected. The affair was called off after the cat placed second in a quarter-mile race.

In June 1990, two cougars chased twenty-eight-year-old Linda Walters up a tree in Fourmile Canyon, about three miles from Boulder, Colorado. The cats followed her up the tree (big surprise, no?), where one of them grabbed the woman's pant leg with a forepaw in an attempt to dislodge her. Walters kicked the cat with her other leg and knocked it out of the tree. When the backup squad came in, a sharp jab in the eye with a stick sent it packing as well. The cats circled the base of the tree for half-an-hour, considering, I presume, whether it was worth another kick in the head to try again. When the tawny pair retired to a nearby creek for a strategy session over drinks, Walters made good her escape. Though technically a contact incident, we do not stand on formalities here.

In June 1805, Captain Meriwether Lewis, head honcho of the Lewis and Clark expedition, experienced what is probably the first recorded cougar attack of the nineteenth century. Lewis was already having a bad day, barely escaping attack by Indians, a grizzly bear, and a herd of stampeding bison, when what he called a "tyger cat" decided that a bit of white meat might make a nice departure from its customary redskinned fare. (Though he didn't know what to call it, his detailed description is unquestionably that of a cougar.) He fired a snap shot just as the puma crouched to spring. It retreated at the shot, slinking off into a nearby cave. Lewis was unsure whether he had hit the lion fatally, if at all, but wasn't about to crawl into that dark hole to find out. Smart man.

One of the most interesting historical episodes happened just prior to the Civil War to a Kentucky trapper named Slowtrap. Don't look at me—I just report this stuff. Anyway, Slowtrap was taking a siesta beneath a tree when the rustling of leaves nearby woke him. Cracking an eyelid, he discovered that he was being buried under a pile of flying leaves and twigs. He remained still until things got quiet, then turned his head just in time to see a cougar slip silently away. Knowing what was up, Slowtrap exited the kill-bed and replaced his personage therein with a log, then hid nearby to wait. Sure enough, a female puma shortly appeared with two cubs in tow. The she-cat pounced on the log and "struck the claws of both her forefeet into it." While she puzzled over the strange toughness her meal had developed, the trapper sent her to the big sandbox in the sky.

My all-time favorite lion episode is a bit difficult to classify, for although contact was involved, questions remain as to who contacted whom. I'll let you decide. It happened in September 1994 to Dustin Lyon of Shasta Lake, California. The fifteen-year-old lad was riding horseback near his rural home when his mount, a three-year-old mare named Kelsey, became fidgety. Dustin figured the horse had winded the cougar he'd seen crossing the road some ninety yards to the rear a few minutes prior. No amount of coaxing or threats could steady the terrified equine. With eyes rolling white and ears laid flat, the mare started bucking and pitched Dustin headlong into an eight-foot bush standing apart from the thick tangle of mixed manzanita, pine, and scrub oak lining the road. He crashed through the bush and out the far side, surprised by the softness of his landing on the hard-packed ground. The cushioning effect, it turned out, had been provided by none other than the cougar itself. Lyon had flown some ten feet to land elbow-first on top of the ambushing lion, and I ain't lyin'!

Without even thinking, Dustin reflexively grabbed the 150-pound feline by an ear and pulled its head back, exposing the throat for a swipe of razor-edged stainless steel from the Buck knife on his belt. The lion must have gotten its wind knocked out by the impact, for it endured this treatment up to the point that the big folder clicked open. In an explosion of frenzied motion, it squirmed out from under Dustin and exited stage left, leaving a vapor trail in its wake.

Tough lads, these Californians.

This is the sixth case I know of in which someone fought off or killed a lion with a knife. In March 1965, a forty-three-year-old Canadian man named Jim Baker used his pocketknife to fight a cougar off fifteen-year-old John Simpkins. When the puma let go and ran a few yards to crouch, bleeding, behind a log, Baker tried to finish it off with a claw hammer! The cat had other ideas, and quit the scene posthaste. As a side note, twelve years prior, a man named Gerald Walters had killed a lion with a hand axe in the same general area. In one of those odd coincidences common to lion incidents, he too was forty-three years old.

In December 1976, fourteen-year-old Thane Morgan was jumped by a young, one-eyed puma while hiking near Rye, Colorado. Morgan somehow extracted a four-inch hunting knife from his backpack and began practicing a bit of unlicensed veterinary surgery. The cat hollered "Uncle!" but left Morgan short one eye (an eye for an eye?), scalped, and missing most of his right forefinger. In July 1973, at one of those drive-through wildlife parks, Mrs. Peter Underdahl killed a cougar with a butcher knife as it mauled her eighteen-month-old grandson after climbing through an open window of the family's motor home. In August 1994, four campers in Mendocino County, California, were attacked when they tried to rescue their dog from an attacking cougar. In the ensuing melee, the puma bit off fifty-year-old Troy Winslow's thumb and scratched the holy water out of forty-eight-year-old Kathleen Strehl. Hostilities ceased when the cougar was pinned under a genuine, football-style dog pile and deflated with a twelve-inch bread knife. The most recent case involved a "tame" cougar that attacked its owner's two small children near Quinlan, Texas, on Christmas Day 1995. A family friend, Trent Reed, stabbed the would-be child-killer with his pocketknife when it grabbed six-year-old Erin Schwartz by the head. It then jumped on the girl's three-year-old brother, Jacob, tearing his ear nearly off before Reed again intervened. The cat was later killed by game wardens in some nearby woods.

U.S. House Speaker Newt Gingrich was bitten by a cougar cub during a November 1995 news conference in Washington, D.C. The puma (one of several "endangered" animals brought to the capital by a government-sponsored zoo's curator as part of a lobbying effort for additional funding) drew blood when it nipped Mr. Newt on the chin while he held it in his arms. No information was forthcoming as to the puma's political leanings. I wonder if the curator got his money.

For lo these many years, sentiment has held that people observing cougars in the wild were blessed indeed to have enjoyed such a rare opportunity. Not anymore. The actual number of U.S. "observation" incidents for the decade ending in 1995 is impossible to quantify, but a best guess would be thousands. Furthermore, sightings (and attacks, for that matter) are no longer limited to pristine wilderness settings. Cougars have begun showing up in the oddest places—suburban neighborhoods, garages, parking lots, and shopping malls, to name just a few. Most alarmingly, in view of their propensity to prey on children, several have been spotted and some killed lurking near elementary school yards.

In 1993, outside play activities were suspended at Indian Creek School in El Dorado County, California, after a cougar raided the cafeteria dumpster and was later seen hanging around campus. When a playground supervisor at another school heard a kindergartner shout "Stop that!" several times, she went to investigate what she assumed was a quarrel brewing between classmates. What she found was a big male cougar licking the child's face. When she tried to extract the youngster, one of several gathered watching just feet away, the cat turned nasty, taking a swat or two at the woman before wandering off. Children attending Green Valley Elementary near Cameron Park had their study-hall sentences commuted to early release when a cougar was spotted prowling nearby. A five-year-old Vancouver Island boy wasn't quite so lucky; a cougar killed him on his school's playground in 1992.

With elementary book-learning behind them, the cats moved on to the ivy-covered halls of academia. What students at California State University's Sacramento campus originally mistook for a large dog turned out to be an adolescent puma lounging beside a sidewalk garbage can—this, mind you, just eight and one-half miles from the state capitol building. George Smith barely escaped attack while jogging near UC Santa Cruz by jumping a fence and flagging down a passing motorist. Researchers at UC Davis were more than a little chagrined to learn that their captive black-tailed deer herd was declining because a big cougar had taken up campus residence—presumably not in the dorm, but in California you never know.

I am sitting here now looking at a poster. "WARNING!" it says in bold letters. "Mountain lions have been sighted in, and adjacent to, the American River Parkway. Although your chances of encountering an aggressive lion are remote, please proceed with care." Sacramento County Parks and Recreation Department rangers posted this notice at all entrances to River Park, located within capital-city limits.

Montclair, California, police killed a lion when it advanced toward them after being shot with a tranquilizer dart on the loading dock of J. C. Penney's in the town's shopping mall. At another mall, terrified shoppers competed with a cougar for parking space as it prowled the lot. It took refuge under a car after being darted. In January 1995, another urban lion was spotted in the city of Port Arthur on the Texas Gulf coast, and later that same year, another was reported prowling the streets of Tyler in eastern Texas. One of the state's largest cities, Fort Worth, picked up the nickname "Panther City" back in 1876 when Robert E. Cowart, a lawyer visiting from Dallas, observed a cougar stretched out sleeping in the middle of Main Street. To this day, the badges of Fort Worth's finest sport the image of a prowling puma. In 1992, in the nearby suburb of Keller, numerous reported sightings of a cougar prowling the neighborhood prompted police to initiate a "cougar alert" lasting thirty-nine days.

As if water hazards, green fees, and sand traps weren't trouble enough, duffers at Canyon Oaks Golf Club in Chico, California, added several strokes to their handicaps when a cougar took up residence on the fourteenth hole. Golfers who played around the big feline (I'm not kidding) reported it made several attempts to get up a foursome but was rebuffed with Number 3 woods and, in one instance, a nine-iron. Game Department hunters brought in hounds to track the cat but had to take a Mulligan (replay the hole) when a second, smaller puma was treed by mistake. After the second tee-off, the correct lion was taken with one stroke from a Winchester iron to win the skin. According to rumor, the club pro was last seen boarding a flight to Hawaii (which has no cougars) and eating Valium by the handful.

In late August 1995, a cougar prowling around Marshall Hospital (looking for leftovers, maybe?) in Placerville, California, activated the automatic doors of the emergency-room entrance—a very handy arrangement—before wandering off toward the downtown area, possibly hoping to catch a midnight matinee presentation of *The Lion King*.

When a Glendora, California, man went to investigate strange sounds in his backyard, he found a cougar sitting on his Jacuzzi deck eating his pet Doberman. Several residents of a Colorado community suspected pranksters of activating motion-sensing lights in their backyards, until somebody spotted a cougar strolling through, carrying a neighbor's poodle in its mouth. Dogs taken literally off the leash while being walked are a fairly common occurrence. One man killed a lion on his living-room rug after it chased his pet dachshund inside. A dog in Gold Bug, California, was savaged twice in separate incidents over a ten-month period by what was believed to be the same cougar. Its owner had it put to sleep after the second assault.

Wildlife researchers have documented lions giving birth beneath porches of homes within the city limits of Boulder, Colorado. I know two cases of enterprising cougars storing deer carcasses on or under the porches of mountain cabins; in one case, the cat napped between meals beneath a porch swing.

Perhaps you now see the difficulty in trying to put an exact number on man-lion interactions of any sort. Before moving on to other matters, I want to introduce a final macabre aspect to the numbers game that, as far as I know, has never been elsewhere addressed in any depth: missing persons.

Had the remains of Barbara Schoener or Lucy Dunton never been found (and they almost weren't), into what statistical category would they have been placed? When you consider that enough people are annually reported missing in this country to support an entire genre of TV shows dedicated to their recovery, and that many of them disappear in prime lion country, the ramifications are staggering. Four adults missing in just one southern California county are believed to be lion victims. Police investigators are programmed to think in terms of human foul play, so possible animal predation is rarely considered. Remember too that we are talking only about people *reported* missing. What about unreported ones? Consider this:

The states of Texas, New Mexico, Arizona, and California have three things in common—a common border with Mexico, illegal immigrants, and lions. I cannot help but wonder how many Mexican pilgrims seeking a better life in *El Norte* may even now be fertilizing the American Southwest as economy-size litterbox deposits. Think about it. Border crossings typically occur at night in remote areas to avoid detection. Lone individuals killed and eaten in such circumstances would never be missed, except by family remaining south of the border when the promised letters never came. Even a cougar witnessed taking a member of a large party would most likely go unreported; contact with American authorities usually leads to a hot bus ride back to Mexico, so official entanglements are judiciously avoided. In Texas alone, authorities say that an estimated 300 illegal immigrants are known to die each year, usually showing up as "floaters" in the Rio Grande after drowning or being killed by border bandits, and the majority are never identified. With that many known dead, it certainly seems plausible, albeit unprovable, that at least some are never found and could have fallen to cougars.

Children make excellent candidates for this missing-and-presumed-eaten category. Their small size makes them easy to carry away bodily without leaving drag marks or blood, possibly to some hidden den for the delectation of hungry cubs. In just one state, at least six children are missing and believed to be lion victims. One of them, three-year-old Travis Zweig, disappeared near his family's mountain cabin in Riverside County, California. Searchers followed the boy's tracks up a ridge, where they converged with those of a mountain lion. Only the lion's tracks led away, so you tell me what happened. All that was ever found of Laura Bradbury was her skull cap, washed up in a campground by heavy rains two weeks after she disappeared while hiking with her family in the San Bernardino Mountains. A Boy Scout disappeared after falling behind the troop while hiking. Cougar tracks found on the same trail terminated near the point where he was last seen.

I have talked with a number of law officers and other people specializing in child disappearances. Many of them seemed at first surprised, then enlightened at the suggestion that animal predation rather than human abduction might have been responsible in some cases. A few now include man-killing wildlife in their investigative procedures and suspect lists. Though no correlation can be proven, it is at least interesting that the incidence of lion predation and child disappearances started increasing at about the same time, around 1980. For obvious reasons, it is impossible to put an exact number on unsolved child disappearances that could be animal-related, but it is an area meriting further investigation.

The considerable literary sweat thus far expended, fun though it has been, was designed with one primary goal: to everlastingly convince you that mountain lions can, will, and do kill people. With over half of all attacks recorded during this century occurring in the twenty years

1 • Cougars

prior to 1995, it seems clear that people-eating is a growth industry among lions, even if willing investors are hard to come by. The big question is "Why?" or, more to the point, "Why now?" Funny you'd ask. . . .

Frank Dobie, introduced earlier, opined in a December 1943 *Saturday Evening Post* article, "In my mind there is no doubt that the American lion has become much less aggressive since the advent of the pioneer, through whom he learned the deadliness of man." I wholeheartedly agree. Contrary to what you may have read or heard, cougars and other mammals do not "instinctively" fear humans. Behaviors inherent and common to most species—things like breeding, nurturing of young, territorial aggression, migration where applicable, and so on—are instinctive, whereas hunting skills, prey identification, and hazard recognition and avoidance are *learned*, usually under parental tutelage. Hypothetically, then, if cougars can learn through repeated exposure to man-the-predator that he is a threat to life, liberty, and the pursuit of happiness, one can reasonably conclude they would learn through repeated *nonthreatening* associations that bipedal protein is no less delectable for being ugly, and is certainly easier to catch and kill. The timing of recent events under this premise is, in retrospect, not surprising.

Historical evidence indicates that cougar attacks were relatively common from the time the first blue-blooded Anglo wetbacks piled off the *Mayflower* up until about 1920. During this period, American life was predominantly rural and most problems, animal or otherwise, were addressed with a well-aimed bullet. That cougar aggressiveness was thus assuaged is reflected in the fact that no record exists of a human attack in the U.S. between 1924 and 1953, at least none that I can find. Then, starting in the 1960s, all hell broke loose, relatively speaking. Scarcely a year has passed since 1962 that somebody didn't get his hair parted the hard way. What cataclysmic event could account for this serious breach of the heretofore ironclad proverbial? Would you believe World War II?

Accelerated production of war materiel kicked the plodding Industrial Revolution into high gear. All those farm boys returning from Over There found America much changed in the way of economic opportunity. They traded the guns and plowshares of their former way of life for hard hats and time cards and moved to the big city. From then on, America increasingly became a nation of urbanites, their knowledge of the land and its wildlife limited to parks, zoos, and the Discovery Channel. The cougars, meanwhile, relieved from traditional arsenic and cuprouslead controls on their population, resurged in number and began spreading back into former ranges.

With the 1960s came the "peace" movement and with it the beginnings of the ecology movement, the rose-colored world view of one dovetailing nicely with the Bambi mentality of the other. Sound, biologically based thinking regarding wildlife became wreathed in a cannabis-smoke sentimentality fomented by the students of the Dalai Lama and other deep thinkers, like the Beatles. A new term, "animal rights," became part of American culture. The cougar, for some odd reason, became the animal sentimentalists' poster child, complete with successful calls to ban their killing and have them labeled "endangered" in some areas—which, in the U.S. as a whole, has never been true. The human populace grew mentally fat on a steady diet of Disney and PBS (which I always thought stood for Professional Bull Something-you'd-rather-not-step-in) assurances that cougars were noble, majestic creatures with malice toward none save their natural prey. What the Bambi Bunch didn't bother to explain was that "natural" prey to a cougar is anything within its habitat that can be caught and killed with reasonable success, and whether it is upholstered in fur, feathers, or polyester is not a consideration. So, when the environmentally "enlightened" human population began occupying all those nifty new spilt-level ranchettes with the Jacuzzis out back and built smack in the middle of lion country, guess what happened.

In the wake of recent maulings and killings, the lion-huggers reacted in ways no less maddening for being predictable. Protests were staged when the lion that killed Barbara Schoener was shot. "She deserved to die!" one woman said. "She was jogging in the mountain lion's habitat, and she should have known she would be attacked!" One month after Schoener's death, a trust fund established for her children had received $9,000 in donations. At the same time, a similar fund for the lion's "orphaned" cub, named "Willow," and living today in a California zoo, had received over $21,000. (After this situation was publicized on the Rush Limbaugh TV program, the Schoener account jumped to six figures in less than a week.) A woman living near where Schoener was killed said, "The media is making too much of the incident."

An acquaintance of Iris Kenna said she would have been "furious" to know the lion that killed her had been shot. "She understood that when you're in their habitat, you're part of the food chain," was one sentiment expressed, which, appropriate or not, is chillingly correct. Of the increased incidence of human attacks, pro-lion lobbyist Mark Palmer said, "There is no evidence that there is an increase in mountain lions. We have anecdotal evidence that more people are seeing them, more have been killed, more have been hit on highways. But maybe there's just more traffic out there." At a press conference, Palmer held a cougar cub in his arms and observed that Barbara Schoener's death came "at a terrible time for us politically."

Protesters labeled as "an overreacton" the closing of Cuyamaca Park after a lion attacked a three-year-old. The same day the park reopened, a ten-year-old girl was attacked. One park superintendent said he "got beat to death" by public reaction over the killing of a lion involved in an attack. "Ninety-nine percent of the people who called me were kitty lovers," he said. "They did not understand the complexity of the problem, and didn't want to."

These people seem to be everywhere, including powerful positions within the government and at all levels within state game agencies. When a lion was killed after it attacked a child, a female park ranger was photographed crying over her part in the cat's demise. The same woman was present when Iris Kenna's mutilated, disemboweled, faceless body was recovered; the mounted buck on your wall doesn't have drier eyes. A senior California wildlife official said, "They [lions] are not inherently dangerous creatures." A California senator said during debate over a lion-hunting bill, "I know there is a danger to human life, but we have to remember, the lions were here before the Indian or the white man, and we're encroaching in a way as we did with the native Indians here on their territory." Another senator observed, "I feel there's an imbalance in the controversy because we're not looking at the number of people being killed in other ways in the outdoors. There are many more people being killed by bees than mountain lions, but we're not ready to thin the population of bees."

Excuse me while I puke.

Incidentally, that line about there being no evidence of an increase in lion numbers really is a load of PBS. It should be obvious to even a casual idiot that when lions are turning up by the dozens in cities, the woods must be full of them. Nevertheless, people who do not want you to know any better say the lion is "barely holding on" in eleven western states: Arizona, California, Colorado, Idaho, Montana, Nevada, New Mexico, Oregon, Utah, Washington, and Wyoming. Odd, isn't it, how nonexistent lions in the remaining thirty-eight states can so efficiently turn people into hairy goulash. Texas is an excellent example. In just one of the state's parks, Big Bend, thirty-two encounters ranging from stalking incidents to full-blown bite-and-scratch parties have been documented since 1953. Then there are the "endangered" Florida lions to consider.

The so-called Florida panther, a subspecies not all that different from the standard-issue western variety, has enjoyed totally protected status for some years now. The people who consider it the cutest thing since Thumper say it is in imminent peril of extinction, which may or may not be true, but apparently it has had little effect on the cat's penchant for nasty behavior. In October 1995, a Sumter County woman, Candy Branch, reported that something had entered her yard and attacked her dog. A neighbor's pet tiger was initially suspected, but the four-month-old cub was deemed an unlikely candidate for turning a sixty-two-pound dog into hairy confetti. With their prime suspect in the clear, authorities were mystified as to what had done the deed and left the hellaciously big tracks leading off into the woods. Anybody care to make a guess? Though no assignation of guilt was forthcoming, one sheriff's deputy said, "I'd still advise people to be watchful of their small children."

In case you harbor further doubts about the Florida panther's status, I am pleased to inform you of one other urban example of his existence, reported by a source I consider unimpeachable, none other than the late Peter Hathaway Capstick. In his book, *Maneaters*, Capstick reports finding a set of cougar tracks in a golf-course sand trap near his home in Naples. Other similar reports have been pooh-poohed as misidentified bobcat or dog tracks, but anyone doubting Capstick's ability to identify the spoor of a large predator just doesn't know his Capstick.

The same month that Candy Branch's pooch was nearly purloined, Judy Masishin of Castle County, Delaware, where they make great punch, spotted a cougar stalking her horses as she tended them near their stable. Her description, based on several tense minutes of wide-eyed viewing from just twenty-five yards, is unquestionably that of a cougar. The cat opted to call the whole thing off without hostilities, but I doubt the woman's adrenal system will ever be the same. A fluke? Delaware residents reported four separate cougar sightings in different areas of the state in 1995. Other mid-Atlantic-state sightings occurred that same year in Philadelphia, Pennsylvania, and Newark, New Jersey, placing cougars within one hundred miles of New York City.

As far back as 1973, the U.S. Department of the Interior officially acknowledged cougars roaming the region extending from eastern Canada clear down to the Carolinas. Ted Reed, founder of Friends of the Eastern Panther, which sounds suspiciously huggy to me, reported in 1995 that hundreds of sightings have been recorded in eastern Canada, Vermont, New Hampshire,

American Man-Killers

Maine, eastern Massachusetts, and the Adirondacks. If you doubt the authenticity of the reports, in 1990 a New Brunswick man videotaped a cougar from his bathroom window, clear and convincing evidence to all but California juries. Similarly, in 1993 a hunter in Maine, where cougars have been extinct since 1938, photographed one in a woodland clearing. A 1995 sighting in Port Elisabeth, a hobnobby suburb of Portland, Maine, was authenticated by forensic testing of some fur collected by investigating game wardens. A recent Vermont sighting of a female with cubs was verified by laboratory analysis of a stool sample.

In December 1995, sheriff's deputies shot and killed a large cougar in a Georgia neighborhood after trapping and tranquilizing efforts failed. During its reign, it is believed to have killed and eaten at least one neighborhood dog and a goat.

In 1993 a bowhunter named Jim Widowitz spotted and began stalking what he thought was a deer near Elroy, Wisconsin. He had approached within one hundred yards when the "deer" sprang up, sporting about five feet of tail on one end and a very impressive set of dentures on the other. After watching the cat for several minutes, he drove it off with a couple of rounds over its head from a .22-caliber pistol. In the same general area later that year, Don Triebs saw what he thought was a large dog stalking his cattle. He drove over on his tractor to investigate, getting within thirty feet of the puma before it vented its vocal displeasure at the intrusion and streaked off into cover. Since 1988, Elroy-area residents have reported a number of such sightings, all of which were dismissed by wildlife officials as cases of overactive imagination or rumjug fauna. But there was no denying the cat that approached within fifty yards of Scott Santas's pickup in May 1993; the tracks in the freshly tilled field were unmistakable. Cougars have been officially extinct in Wisconsin since 1920.

If you want to include captive animals in the tally, no state remains cougarless. And the "tame" ones' manners are no better than those of their wild counterparts.

1 • Cougars

Back in 1983, at a roadside zoo near North Carolina's Grandfather Mountain, a captive puma scaled the fifteen-foot wall of its enclosure to attack twenty-six-year-old Pam Kiger. Knocked some ten feet in the initial charge, the woman fell face-first onto the ground, where the cat seized her head in its jaws. Amazingly, a zookeeper attracted by the woman's screams was able to literally call the puma off ("Bad kitty, bad!"). Kiger survived, and it cost her only 130 stitches in her scalp—quite a bargain, when you consider the alternative. That same year, a cougar at another zoo near Edmonton, Alberta, nearly tore the arm off four-year-old Corey Harlow when she tried to pet it through a chain-link fence. The puma grabbed the girl's fingers and pulled her arm through the mesh up to the armpit, then started chewing. The mother, Carrie Harlow, battled the cat through the fence for over half-an-hour, trying everything from the flame of a butane cigarette lighter in the cat's face to prodding and prying with a stick, but was no match for the puma's determination. A zoo worker finally enticed it off with a piece of raw meat.

In August 1975, a pet cougar named "Humphrey Bogart" escaped its owner and attacked Warren L. Hobson of Riverside, Arizona. The man sustained severe scalp and stomach lacerations but was otherwise none the worse for wear. Here's lookin' at you, kid. In 1977, police raiding an illegal methamphetamine lab were more than a little surprised to find it guarded by a 200-pound male cougar. The cat was subdued by animal-control officers armed with tranquilizer guns before it could sample the blue-plate special. In Texas, "pet" cougars attacked and badly injured three children in two separate incidents in 1995.

Obviously, the validity of the "only in eleven states" argument is, to put it charitably, highly questionable. The real truth is that those eleven states, plus Texas, host the lion's share of cats nationally, but they are by no means the only states to have cougars. Actually, there are currently far more states with wild cougar populations than without. Even as far back as 1977, only nineteen of the forty-eight contiguous states reported

31

having no lions within their borders, and in some cases no attempt had been made to count them because nobody in officialdom believed they existed. Putting a specific number on lions nationally is even tougher than accounting for their victims, neither of which form ranks and count off on command. Official census figures provided by game agencies are, at best, guesses based on reported sightings, radio-tracking studies, lions killed by hunters, or encounters with high-velocity Fords. Depending on whose figures you believe, the current total could fall anywhere between 40,000 and 100,000 nationally, and I suspect there are far more cougars around than that. If you include Canada, Mexico, and South America in the tally, the figure could be well over a million. Quantitative specificity notwithstanding, most U.S. states today acknowledge a definite increase in current populations over previous years, to the extent that lions are actually overpopulated in some areas, which we will explore in greater depth later.

Lest anyone miss the point, COUGARS ARE NOT AN ENDANGERED SPECIES, and never have been as far as I can tell—contrary to what an amazing variety of presumably well-meaning but ignorant people will tell you. If you have any questions on this point, I suggest spending a couple of nights in California's Cuyamaca Park. Alone.

A favorite argument of the preservationist crowd is that you are forty-three times more likely to be struck by lightning than killed by a cougar. Statistically speaking, that is true. But an astute observation by one veteran of the lion trenches paints the picture a bit differently. Dave Fjelline is a professional lion hunter for the state of California, the one, incidentally, who tracked down and stamped CANCELED on the cougar that killed Barbara Schoener. A paraphrase of his tack on the lightning vs. lion statistic goes something like this: Yes, more people are annually struck by lightning than are killed or injured by cougars, *but only on a per-capita basis.* What the equation does not take into account is that every man, woman, and child in America will at some time in any year be exposed to possible lightning strike, equating potentially 250 million chances. On the other hand, the

1 • Cougars

number of people exposed to possible lion attack is drastically smaller, limited to only those living or recreating where lions are found. This difference alone increases significantly the odds of attack for any member of the at-risk group. It is sort of like comparing the chances between a CPA and an NFL quarterback getting his neck broken on Super Bowl Sunday. When you add in the fact that the lions are *always* there, and lightning comes and goes with the caprice of the weather, the odds tip most uncomfortably in the lions' favor.

That no reliable record exists of a *multiple* man-killing mountain lion probably owes to offenders traditionally receiving near-instant gun-muzzle prosecution—which meant no opportunity to become repeat offenders. But that may be changing. The current U.S. lion situation compares favorably to circumstances under which leopards in Asia and Africa have killed and eaten people for centuries. Leopards and cougars, which bear not the slightest resemblance to apples or oranges, are surprisingly similar in spite of their taxonomic classifications. Both are segregated into several dozen dubiously valid subspecies, regardless of which you may rest assured that leopards is leopards and cougars is cougars, no matter what color their noses are. Their respective body sizes are nearly identical, females rarely getting much over 100 pounds and males averaging 125 pounds, with the occasional Weight Watchers dropout exceeding 200 pounds. The largest puma recorded by weight that I have found is a 227-pound male killed in Colorado in 1901 by Teddy Roosevelt. I say "by weight" because cougar trophy records are based on skull measurements rather than body size. As for leopards, whose Rowland Ward record entries are based on overall length, I remember reading some years ago in a pulp magazine about one reported at 260 pounds, but this is highly suspect.

Sumo wrestlers or not, both possess strength belied by their small size, and routinely kill prey ten times their own weight. Their habitat range, though in different hemispheres, parallels exactly from snow-capped mountain country to deep, subtropical jungle. Both prefer deer-sized prey as their standard fare but will consume rodents, fish, birds, insects, and human garbage without compunction. Their propensity for livestock-killing binges—behavior labeled "surplus killing" by zoologists, wherein little if any meat is eaten—regularly lands them in trouble. One California lion recently killed over fifty penned sheep in a single night, tearing out their throats but eating only a little meat from just one of them. Hundreds of cases exist of leopards doing the same thing. In one instance, a leopard bit the heads off thirteen ducks belonging to Jim Sutherland, the famous African ivory hunter, without eating so much as a drumstick.

Cougars and leopards share a common love of dog flesh, to the extent of invading occupied homes for a taste of *canine al fido.* Despite a shared reputation for shyness, they can be extremely bold, showing up in populated areas with surprising frequency. Remember the earlier example of the puma under the woman's bed? In *Death in the Dark Continent,* Capstick records the case of a woman in Nairobi, Kenya, entering her bedroom and seeing what she thought was a large dog asleep on her bed. She summoned her father, who killed the "dog," which turned out to be a large male leopard. In another case, the brother of a Nyasaland woman killed a leopard in her bedroom after she saw the tip of its tail sticking out from under the bed.

The big tabbies share the alias "panther," which is technically accurate when applied to leopards, *Pantheria pardus.* Cougars fall under the *Felis concolor* classification, the interesting biological difference being that panthers possess a special hyoid bone in their throats enabling them to roar. Cougars must be content with screaming, hissing, purring, and what can only be described as "yowling." In case you are interested, tigers, jaguars, and African lions are also technically panthers.

This is as good a place as any to digress on the subject of black panthers, of which it is my duty to inform you there ain't no such thing, at least not anymore. American black panthers are actually melanistic (the opposite of albino) specimens of the jaguar, which did exist in North America up until the early twentieth century. Melanism and albinism occur in leopards too, and although a few albino cougars have turned up, I can find no record anywhere of a black one. Something to do with genetics, I suppose. The jaguar, being somewhat less adaptable than the puma, has long since retreated south of the border, where he lives in Mexico and South America under the respective aliases *tigre* where Spanish is spoken, and *onca* in Portuguese, the most formidable predator in the hemisphere.

There are still occasional reports of big, black cats seen prowling some areas of the Southwest. I personally received such a report from a member of a hunting party near Del Rio, Texas, in 1993. The cat was sighted on three separate occasions by different individuals—at a distance of less than twenty yards in one instance, as it stalked a flock of Rio Grande turkeys. I am personally acquainted with all of the men, and know them to be experienced, competent woodsmen not disposed to sensationalism, and therefore have no reason to doubt the report. Nevertheless, jaguars are sufficiently rare in modern times within the U.S. to render them inconsequential as man-killers. Which is probably just as well—jaguars are *big*, balancing comfortably against the largest African lions at up to 400 pounds. One of those boys could eat even a heavyweight like me and still have room for dessert. Anyway, back to leopards and lions.

The kinship of spirits between pumas and leopards extends to the bloody end of the spectrum in their relationships with people. Both prefer women and small children for most recipes, but occasionally take a bull *Homo sapiens* for processing into jerky. The most common injuries sustained are to the victim's head and face, attributable to both cats' habit of killing with bites to the skull or neck. It naturally follows that most deaths occur from crushed skulls or neck vertebrae, or severe hemorrhaging from neck wounds. Both attack from ambush, usually in a blinding rush from behind. Attack by either can be, and has been, averted by strenuous resistance from the victim if—and that's a big if—he sees it coming. Carl Akeley, who personally collected most of the specimens in the American Museum of Natural

History's African Hall, once killed a wounded leopard by strangling it with his bare hands.

Once the assault has been joined, both cats are decidedly determined to finish what they start, attacking repeatedly if initially fought off. Both prefer to work their iniquities under cover of darkness, though not to the exclusion of daytime forays as necessity or opportunity dictates. Other than coloration (one comes in a flashy, two-tone paint job and the other is monochrome) and different methods of storing kills, about the only major difference is in their respective records as man-killers.

As a group, leopards still maintain a reputation for people-shredding established by such individual celebrities as India's Panar leopard, whose lifetime record exceeded four hundred victims before Colonel Jim Corbett settled its hash in 1910. Leopards kill roughly three hundred people a year in India alone. That American lions have yet to achieve this level of efficiency may in some measure be attributed to a difference in temperament, but the record doesn't appear to bear this out. Most likely, the fact that lions haven't had the same opportunities for free enterprise as leopards has made the difference. But, as I said, that may be changing. Here's why:

As observed earlier, America's human population over the first hundred or so years of its history existed primarily as well-armed homesteaders scattered willy-nilly across the fruited plain. The peoples of both India and Africa, however, have always lived in communal villages based on tribal associations. For the same reason a leopard finds a herd of penned cattle so appealing (a handy, well-stocked, all-night deli), predation of villagers was, and is, common. Armed as they were with primitive edged weapons, their ability to successfully fight off an attack was practically nil. Usually, only the men were armed, and they rarely ventured into the bush alone, group hunting parties being safer and more efficient. Consequently, most leopard victims have been women and children snatched at water holes or the edges of villages as they collected the wood, water, and other necessities of daily life.

1 • Cougars

Aside from the impracticality of hunting down an offending feline, attempts to do so were rare for fear of provoking the wrath of some witch doctor who opportunistically claimed black-magic responsibility for the killings in schemes of extortion. In 1977, near Dar es Salaam, Tanzania, officials' efforts to kill a lion that had eaten ten people failed, local villagers said, because the felon was actually a woman turned into a "werelion" by the local witch doctor, and the killings would stop only if the demanded ransom were paid. As recently as 1995, authorities in northern Zimbabwe sanctioned the killing of five elephants to appease a local medicine man who claimed that the elephants were responsible for drought, mice, and crop-eating worms beleaguering an area south of the Zambezi River.

Even the advent of firearms did not change things much. For the average villager to own one was tantamount to a New York cab driver holding title to the World Trade Center, both towers. Today, the aboriginal African possessing a firearm of any kind is still a rarity, and the few who do likely scavenged it from who-knows-where after it blew up or otherwise failed its previous owner. Muzzleloading black-powder smoothbores are still rather common, frequently stoked with chunks of the concrete reinforcing rod we know as rebar. In India, authorities long ago recognized the benefits of gun control for ensuring a manageable, obedient populace; private firearm ownership is strictly regulated and mostly prohibited.

As large a role as these elements play, fatalistic attitudes common among rural villagers probably contribute more to a leopard's ability to kill with impunity than any other factor. Tradition and religion, particularly among India's Hindu practitioners, dictate that man is no more or less than another occupant of the biosphere, with no special claims to the land or even to life itself. When a leopard kills someone, it was simply meant to be. Tomorrow it may kill again, or it may not. *Que sera sera.* According to Dr. Walter E. Howard, a wildlife biology professor at the University of California, Davis, who has studied extensively India's man-predator relationship, "It is difficult for an American to comprehend how some people in India are willing to give their lives to protect a wild animal." Even the enlightened consider the potential modern-day consequences of killing an "endangered," government-protected leopard (or tiger) a fate worse than digestion. Under legislation recently proposed in India, killing a tiger gets you life in the slammer.

With only minor changes to species and geographical references, the above applies almost verbatim to the cougar situation as it exists today in some parts of the U.S. By a wide margin, women and children aggregate the majority of lion attack victims; "neighborhood" is just an alternative term for "village"; most people, through fear born of media hype, view guns as evil incarnate (hunters and target shooters excepted), so the villagers are largely unarmed; those who own guns for protection often lack the skills or, in some cases, the will to use them, and even if they are so inclined, the threat of prosecution where lions are totally protected by law substitutes for appeasing the local witch doctor. As for the one-with-nature attitude, let's see, how did those quotes go? "She deserved to die. . . . She was jogging in the mountain lion's habitat and should have known she would be attacked. . . . She understood that when you're in their habitat, you're part of the food chain."

The place names may not be as exotic, but like its leopard cousin, the lion in America today keeps families and, in some cases, entire neighborhoods cowering behind drawn curtains while it literally roams the streets with impunity. A moment's carelessness, and a child or woman is taken, dragged quietly away with their final screams strangled forever silent in their throats. You think I'm making this up, don't you? Come with me, then, to the streets of one California community, not too far from where Barbara Schoener lived before becoming a mountain lion's entree.

Jim and Mary Castle lived with their two children in a quiet, peaceful neighborhood nestled in a picturesque mountain valley. (These are not their real names. People who protest being stalked, killed, or eaten by lions are frequently targets of harassment and even death threats, so, when requested, identities and locations have been kept secret.) It was like living in a Norman Rockwell painting. Children played and rode bicycles along shady, tree-lined streets. Delicious odors curled from backyard barbecues, mingling with the pine scent of surrounding forested hills. The American Dream at its finest, serenity in a bottle, a Paradise to be lost. On 10 May 1994, the dream became the proverbial when a new resident moved into the neighborhood—a cougar, lean, blonde, and muscular, lounging in a tree on Mary Castle's front lawn.

With the death of Barbara Schoener just a month prior still fresh in her mind, Mary was most alarmed and placed a call to the California Department of Fish and Game. A warden came out the next day and looked around. (The lion was gone by then, of course.) Finding several sets of tracks, claw marks on trees, and so forth, the warden announced there were in all likelihood several lions in the area, and that one of them was probably watching from cover right then, which I'm sure, Mary found most comforting. He further allowed that the tree-lounging lion was of particular concern because of its boldness. After advising Mary to keep the children inside and to call the DFG "Lion Hotline" if the cat showed up again, he handed her a pamphlet, *Living With California Mountain Lions,* and left. (You may find it interesting that a man who spent several hours treed by a cougar was unable to reach the hotline on his cellular phone; the nearest receiving station was out of range.)

By the end of the week, Mary's phone line was showing burn marks from repeated calls to the hotline, up to four a day with each sighting. The cat was seen peering into windows, watching Mary wash dishes or the family eating dinner, warming its face in the clothes-dryer exhaust, sleeping on the steps. On 17 May at 9:58 A.M. (she was keeping a diary by now, which accounts for the preciseness of dates and times), Mary was puttering around behind the carport when she saw the puma advancing from behind a small rise—slinking low to the ground, its tail animated in the characteristic way of a stalking predatory cat. Following the pamphlet's advice, she stood as tall as her five-foot, six-inch frame would allow and spoke in a way she hoped sounded intimidating, then started backing slowly toward the door. The puma stopped at about twenty feet, watching intently. When Mary disappeared through her kitchen door, the cat muttered something in four-letter lionese and stalked off into the trees. Several phone calls to the hotline failed to produce the promised return call from a warden. Finally, after the fourth call, Mary heard from a regional supervisor. After calling her a "hysterical female," he said he was sorry, but there was nothing Fish and Game could do. Its hands were tied by the bureaucratic snarl of legal provisions imposed under Proposition 117.

Proposition 117 was a referendum package passed into law by California voters in 1990 in the wake of a media propaganda blitz (ramrodded by the California Mountain Lion Foundation, a fraternity of professional idiots and lion-huggers) that would have made Joseph Goebbels grow the green mold of envy. It afforded lions total protection, including a ban on importing into the state any part of a lion killed legally elsewhere (another parallel with leopards). Under 117, it is illegal for anyone—including DFG—to kill a mountain lion under all but the most extreme circumstances of predation or threat to human life, and then only with a government-issued permit. Already protected by a hunting moratorium since 1972, the lion population had grown to what some estimated at over 10,000 by the time the provision passed. Even so, Proposition 117 mandated spending $30 million annually for the purchase and maintenance of mountain-lion habitat! (As this was being written, another voter referendum, Proposition 197, which would have relaxed some of the protections of Proposition 117, was placed on the ballot. It was voted down 26 March 1996.)

Meanwhile, Mary Castle didn't give a hoot about the other 9,999 lions; the one she had to deal with was quite enough, thank you. Incidentally, the DFG official who told Mary she was effectively on her own suggested that she get a gun, go find the lion, and kill it. Sounds like good advice to me, but Mary, not being your stereotypical

1 • Cougars

Great White Hunter, understandably dismissed the idea as impractical, notwithstanding the potential legal ramifications. Surely, *someone* could do *something* before the lion killed or injured her or one of her children, couldn't they?

Mary placed calls to several DFG insiders whose names she learned through an acquaintance with the U.S. Fish & Wildlife Service. Though sympathetic, they all said nothing could be done unless the lion was killing her livestock, and even then the cat must be caught in the act. While this went on, Mary watched the cougar stalk a neighbor's dog, had to wait in her car on several occasions for the lion to clear the carport, saw it dragging a deer carcass through her front yard, and watched terrified as it stalked one of her children.

On 22 May, Mary's five-year-old daughter was walking toward the barn where her father, Jim, was working. Mary had escorted the child halfway (the children never went out without an adult escort), and was watching her progress over the last 100 yards. Suddenly, over a small rise, the cougar came into view and locked its eyes on the girl, creeping forward in a stalk. Mary didn't know what to do. There was no way to get to her daughter ahead of the lion. Her only option was to try and distract it so the child could escape. The woman shouted for her daughter to run, then pulled out a small handgun she had started carrying for just such emergencies and began firing at the lion. The cougar, unfazed by the lead popping the ground all around it, rushed the girl when she started running. Fortunately, Jim had come out to see what all the commotion was and foiled the charge just in time.

Encounter followed encounter in the succeeding weeks. The little community took on the aura of a ghost town. The barbecue grills grew cold. Other residents, terrified by Mary's experiences as well as episodes of their own, kept dogs and children indoors. Armed hosts escorted nighttime guests to and from their cars. Mostly, though, the lion (or lions) singled out Mary and her family for its reign of terror. In one instance, it stood in the carport pinning Mary in her car for fifteen minutes of premature eternity. Through the window, she dosed it with pepper spray, which made it really mad. The cat snarled, blinking its eyes. Mary wondered idly if her insurance would pay for a new window and torn, bloodied upholstery (the car's, not hers) should the lion come crashing in. Fortunately, she never found out, since the cat, after lingering several more minutes despite the chemical burning its eyes, stalked off. The overall siege finally ended two months later when a DFG lion hunter who had befriended Mary killed the cougar, a 140-pound male, about a mile from her house. She drove to his home when he called; she wanted to see it for herself, touch it, and know for a certainty that it was unquestionably, irrevocably dead. At last, Mary Castle, her family, neighbors, and friends were free. At least for now.

The Mary Castle saga is by no means unique, except that the lion seemed to reserve most of its attentions exclusively for her family. The same scenario has played out time and again, in California and several other states as well. Though most states do not ban killing lions outright, some have the next best thing—a prohibition against using dogs to hunt them. In Oregon, for instance, lion-loving preservationists employed the voter-referendum-on-the-heels-of-a-propaganda-blitz tactic to pass anti-chase laws, thus effectively outlawing hunting by making it impractical.

Without the use of hounds, hunting options are few. The puma's habitat preferences and secretive nature (the better to sneak up on you with, my dear) make spooring and tracking impossible, unless you have tracking snow and are very, very good. Baiting with live, tethered animals can be most effective (works wonders on leopards and jaguars), but the practice is banned in many areas as "inhumane." Sometimes you can lure them with various calling techniques. Predator hunters have successfully brought cougars to the gun with dying-rabbit calls. It doesn't always work, and you usually wind up with more foxes, coyotes, and bobcats than you know what to do with, but it is something to bear in mind, if for no other reason than to remind you to look over your shoulder once in a while. I know of at least two cases, one recent, where deer hunters using antlers to rattle in white-tailed bucks attracted cougars instead. Though I have never tried it, one of those calls that imitate the bleat of a fawn should be highly effective. About the only other way to hunt pumas is to simply stand around in lion country hoping for a chance encounter. This method can produce an undesired result in which the hunter comes out on the wrong end, usually about twelve hours after being ingested, which is probably what the lion-protectionist folks envisioned in the first place.

Since we are on the subject, I suppose I should say that little danger is involved in the actual practice of lion hunting. This probably owes to the cat's disinclination to charge when met with force, even if wounded, and that it is surprisingly easy to kill. It does not take advanced magnum persuasion to deflate a cougar. In fact, seasoned lion hunters find a .22 rimfire applied just behind the ear to be quite adequate. One or two cases exist of hunters being attacked when approaching treed animals, but the state of affairs suggested the men may have just gotten in the way of the lion's attempted escape. In any event, I can find no record of a hunter being seriously injured or killed in actual hunting circumstances.

Back in the Save the Lions offices, the fact that nearly every instance of attack in the twenty years prior to 1995 occurred where lions are in some measure protected deserves further scrutiny. My collection of gore-smeared records indicates that attack incidence is directly proportional to the degree of protection. For the lions, that is. You may have noticed that most of the recent incidents you've read about here—particularly the fatal ones—occurred in California, where lions have been totally protected since the 1970s. A big chunk of the rest is divided between Oregon, Colorado, and Montana, where intervention is less direct, with the remainder occurring in other states where cougars are hunted but their harvest is limited by seasons and bag limits.

All of the traditional lion states have protective measures of one form or another in place, except one—Texas.

American Man-Killers

In the Lone Star State, lions are classified as they have always been, vermin to be shot at will. No closed season. No permits. No limits. Nevertheless, old *Felis* stalks the streets of proper towns (where hunting or discharge of firearms is not allowed), and still finds time between being "endangered" and "relentlessly slaughtered" to kill a few hundred head of livestock each year, and even sample a bite of *Homo sapiens tartare* from time to time. Realize, though, that every recent attack occurred where the cats are totally protected, which in Texas mostly means state and national parks, particularly Big Bend. The point is that hunting lions puts the fear of Winchester, if not God, into them while simultaneously thinning their numbers. And, to paraphrase the old cliche about capital punishment, dead lions never injure or kill anybody.

The huggers—when forced by incontrovertible evidence to admit that, yes, lions do kill a *few* people, and are partially conditioned to do so through lack of negative encounters—remain adamant in their opposition to sport hunting as a reasonable and practical solution. Their contention that without total protection pumas would be hunted to extinction is a crock. On average, in states where lions are classed as game animals and hunted, the annual harvest rarely exceeds 200—a relative drop in the trough. The combined records of the Boone and Crockett and Pope and Young Clubs list just slightly over 1,000 entries dating back to the turn of the century, hardly evidence of "relentless slaughter." Still, in what may be a reflection of their accustomed lifestyles, preservationists insist the best answer lies in chemical deterrents and rubber bullets. We already have a pretty good idea of the deterrent spray's effectiveness (zilch), so let's see about the bouncing bullets.

I have here in my hand a memo dated 24 May 1995, from the U.S. Department of the Interior's National Park Service, addressed to someone with the game department in one of the states we've discussed. It describes a situation wherein a lion invaded an occupied national-park campground and refused to leave. Rangers at the scene had on hand some rubber bullets designed to fire in a 12-gauge shotgun but decided not to try them because, lacking prior experience, the lion's reaction could not be predicted and the campground was full of people. They decided instead to mark the lion for future identification with a paint-ball gun. It trotted off after being splatted with green paint, and a couple of rangers chased it a ways to reinforce the message. While the rangers chatted with some campers, it came back. Based on its reaction to the paint pellet, they decided to give the rubber bullets a try. The lion jumped at the shot, ran about ten feet, and stopped. Looking over its shoulder at the ranger as if to say "I'll remember you, buddy!" it then walked calmly into the forest. The next day, some campers reported the puma had returned less than an hour after the rangers left, killing and eating a raccoon within sight of the campground. The memo wraps up with the observation, "Next time I am faced with a similar situation, I will probably not try using rubber [bullets] to convince a mountain lion to move on."

In case you are interested, vulcanized bullets cost $4.80 each.

Rubber bullets and similar nonsense have been suggested as means of dealing with lion populations established in urban areas, which I guarantee will not work. In fact, there is no realistic way to eliminate or control urban lions, period. Opportunistic sight-shooting with city-safe shotguns by police and animal-control officers may take out a few, but this option becomes increasingly difficult as lions grow wary and learn to stay out of range. Not only is the same true of tranquilizer guns, but a lion can run a considerable distance before the drug takes effect, possibly hiding out and going unlocated until it wears off. High-velocity bullets ricocheting around the downtown area is bad for business, so long-range sniping is out. Trapping lions is akin to stuffing feathers in a thimble while wearing boxing gloves, and all those dogs and cats in the traps don't leave enough room for a lion, anyway. You are not going to find a houndsman willing to risk even one of his very expensive and difficult-to-train dogs in city traffic. The only workable solution is to thin lions from outlying remote areas in hopes that city lions will be drawn out into the vacated territory. Which leads to the question of why lions establish themselves in urban areas in the first place. Glad you asked. . . .

In polite lion society, a class hierarchy exists based on territory. Individual territory size ranges widely under a somewhat complicated relationship between lion and prey-species density, but 100 square miles is about average. Males typically have larger territories encompassing the smaller ones of several females. She-cats are relatively tolerant of overlaps, but not so the males. A trespassing tom is met with aggression by the resident stud and either driven out or killed, with cannibalism resulting in the latter case. Territorial conflicts arise from any number of causes. When prey availability decreases due to environmental or other influences, lions are forced to expand their ranges or starve. Young lions driven off by their mothers at maturity must establish a turf somewhere, and are more likely to be eaten by than to supplant the local bully. So, like it or not, an expanding lion population must inevitably spread into areas of human occupancy.

This territorial expansion is reflected in the fact that young lions account for something on the order of sixty percent of recent human attacks, particularly in areas of high people density. Adult lions present in urban and suburban settings may have simply grown up there, but other factors may be involved. When lions saturate their habitat, prey depletion occurs. Adult lions of either sex kill an average of one deer (their favorite prey) a week. Multiplying the number of lions in a given area by the fifty-two weeks in a year illustrates that hunters have been right all along in claiming that cougars deplete deer populations, which is corroborated in biologist Donald L. Neal's 1987 study of California's declining North Kings deer herd in the central Sierra Nevadas. Consider the potential number of deer California's estimated 10,000 lions eat annually from a herd of approximately 750,000, and you'll see the point. Further, alternative lion prey, such as rodents, birds, and each other, cannot sustain the load any better than the deer. In a bad year for prey reproduction, lions will be particularly hard hit and go seeking alternatives. And as Texas lion expert Billy Pat McKinney puts it, "In some places, humans are the most abundant prey."

With their ability to hide in a petite-size string bikini, cougars may be well established in a human-populated area before their presence is noticed. The first usual sign is the unexplained disappearance of pets and livestock. By the time this starts happening, rest assured that I, thee, and thine are already on the menu.

Since methods of correcting the situation as it now exists are at best slow to produce results, and their implementation is predicated on politicians developing some sense, we, the ignorant, unwashed masses, must for the foreseeable future remain staple items in the cougar's diet. It seems therefore prudent to examine the man-lion relationship from a predator-prey perspective, and formulate appropriate defense strategies.

Defending oneself in an attack presupposes the opportunity to do so—which, if the lion has paid attention in class, may not be forthcoming. Lions attack from ambush, usually in a setup arrangement after he spots you moving quietly along the trail. Kneeling, you study the buck's spoor, so hot it's smoking, and try to envision the antlers that go with the big, splayed hoofprints. You glance ahead, trying to jigsaw the curve of a leg or flash of an antler out of the shadows. You crack open the bolt a snicker for the brassy gleam that assures the 180-grain softpoint is ready for business. Just as you straighten up and start off on the track, you sense something—not sound or movement, but a feeling on the back of your neck like someone is staring at you from across a room. You may peripherally glimpse a tawny blur or feel the first prick as his claws dig deeply into your back, but the lights will go out before you can be sure when he drives those long, canine spikes into your brain. If he's having a bad day, you may feel the wet, steel-vise grip of his jaws on your neck, and get to watch yourself bleed to death from the bone-deep gashes. But it is hard to see much when you are lying facedown in the dirt and leaves with one hundred-plus pounds of hungry puma on your back, so maybe you'll only get to listen to the ragged, blood-gurgling rasp of your lungs trying to restore the breath knocked out when he hit you. You will probably not feel any pain, thanks to shock or the merciful paralysis of a broken neck, so just be patient. It doesn't take very long. Cougars are very efficient assassins.

A cougar's charge is incredibly powerful, impacting with enough force to literally knock victims out of their shoes, like a pedestrian struck by a Lincoln Towne Car. This little-explored aspect of cougar assault may account for why victims not badly injured or killed outright initially, frequently offer no resistance to further attack. Cougars sometimes deliberately forgo initial use of the teeth and claws to first stun their victims into immobility by slamming into them with their chests, a handy stratagem for dealing with large prey that might fight back.

Self-defense is all but impossible unless you see the attack coming, and lions make their livings ensuring that you won't. Despite what you may have seen on TV, a predatory attack is never tipped off with one of those bloodcurdling snarls or screams (no blood found at any scene of attack was ever curdled). Vocalizations made prior to or during an attack (by the cougar, not you) usually indicate some intent other than predation, such as defense of a kill you didn't see, or nearby young.

Of the various nomenclature tagged to mountain lions, "silent hunter" and "ghost of the mountains" are most apt. They pad around silently on feet soundproofed with tufts of hair stained yellow by glandular secretions between the toes. (Some biologists believe the "claw-sharpening" behavior common to felines may actually be territorial scent-marking with these secretions, a belief supported by the fact that declawed cats continue the exercise.) If the cat makes no mistakes, stealth combined with the natural camouflage afforded by its light-to-medium-brown hide makes spotting an ambushing cougar virtually impossible. Mature pumas rarely make mistakes, but young, inexperienced ones often do, a fact that has accounted for more than a few human lives. Of the forty-seven nonfatal attacks in the Beier study, eighteen of thirty-one cases in which the animal's age could be determined involved juvenile lions. Of attacks occurring since 1990, roughly two-thirds involved lions in on-the-job training programs. I know of no instance in which a lone, unarmed person has survived attack from the rear by a healthy adult puma.

Assuming that you see what's coming, case histories indicate you stand an excellent chance of coming out at least alive, if a few pounds lighter. The three basic rules of survival are: Never turn your back, do not run, and fight with everything you've got. Letting a cougar get behind you is equivalent to displaying a neon BITE ME sign on your back, an invitation usually met with immediate compliance. There is some evidence to suggest that plain-sight stalking and tail lashing may be stratagems designed to frighten the victim into flight, hence exposing the back, which explains rule number two. Rule three provides more room for creativity. Fighting off an attack may be accomplished by wrenching free of the teeth and claws through vigorous movements, or offensive measures with whatever is handy, including fists. A British Columbia man put a cougar off its feed by punching it in the nose when it sprang at him. Weapons come in many forms, firearms being the most obvious, but the opportunity to use them isn't as pat as you might think.

In April 1992, California hunter Arthur Eichele nearly answered the bell toll while attempting to call in a bull turkey. A lion showed up, doubtlessly hoping for a turkey dinner with or without all the trimmings, and jumped Eichele from behind in a surprise charge. The impact knocked the man's rifle out of his hands as the puma balled up on his head. Realizing the "turkey" was a bit bigger than expected, the cougar broke off the attack and vamoosed before the hunter could retrieve his rifle. Over a three-day period in August 1994, four California bowhunters were stalked by lions; the animals came close enough that one was shot and another shot at within easy bow range. Three of the incidents happened on the same day, 23 August.

Lacking a firearm, other weapons that have proven reliable include assorted knives, antique swords, axes, hammers, rocks, clubs, and, in one instance, a gas can. The point is, anything applied with sufficient vigor may save your life in a pinch. And by no means should you ever give up. When met with resistance, cougars usually blink first. Do not, however, make the fatal assumption that it has given up if the attack is broken off. Cougars often temporarily retreat, only to regroup and try again if you give them an opening. Always face the puma dead-on (no pun intended, believe it or not) and back away slowly toward any handy refuge. Water makes an excellent bulwark, as do trees in some circumstances. Cats obviously can climb trees unimpeded but are obliged to maintain balance and grip. Any slight off-balance may provide you the needed edge for giving yon pussy a first-class, gravity-assisted limb-thumping after a bit of Vibram-soled discouragement.

Loud vocalizations, known in some quarters as screaming your head off, may prove surprisingly effective at quelling a cougar's murderous bent. Pumas seem especially sensitive to sudden, loud noises, which is why they flee from barking dogs they would eat in other circumstances. One California mountain biker scared off an attacking puma by barking like a dog. By the way, the recommended bear-attack defense of "playing dead" has a way of rapidly deteriorating into the real thing when applied to a cougar. Lying down or rolling up into a ball makes you appear smaller and/or submissive, and serves only to encourage things along. Neither should you stoop or kneel in close areas with limited visibility, otherwise known as good ambush locations. The bigger you appear, the less appealing you are, especially to young pumas.

An ounce of prevention may be worth a couple of pints of blood. Since only personal-injury lawyers believe life should be risk-free, you probably appreciate that eliminating all risk of attack is impossible if you live or recreate in lion country (unless, that is, you are willing to remain indefinitely indoors behind boarded windows). But there are measures for cutting the odds. The best advice, though pathetically cliche, is *be careful*. Keep your eyes open and remain aware of your surroundings, even when puttering around the yard or out in the barn. Spotting the reflexive, nervous twitch of an excited cougar's tail has helped many a would-be victim avoid the meat grinder. Such was the case for eleven-year-old Susan Turner, who spotted a nervous-tailed cougar crouching just outside the barn door as she was gathering eggs. She shouted for her father, Jack, who relieved the erstwhile child-killer of its mortal coil with a single .30-30 bullet through the brain.

If you are the athletic type, I suggest finding some-place other than lion country to jog, hike, or go bicycling. These and similar activities stimulate a chase response in cougars, substantiating my long-held belief that exercise is bad for your health. Strange as it may sound, many experts believe that wearing a rearward-facing effigial face or mask during such activities may prevent attack. It doesn't have to be elaborate—a smiley-face painted on a cloth worn Foreign Legion-style on the back of your cap does nicely. It seems to me a face-painted helmet of some kind might be a better choice, affording protection to the head and neck in case you encounter an above-average lion.

Stories about cougars following people for consider-able distances without apparent aggression are staples of lion lore. It has been suggested by some that this habit indicates benevolence on the cougar's part, that it may be acting as some sort of protective escort through danger-ous areas. This belief has led to cougars being re-ferred to in some parts of South America as "the friend of Christians," which, if true, would certainly make it worthwhile for atheists to rethink their position. Current trends, however, indicate that such following behavior is most likely reconnaissance to determine whether yon biped will fit in the meat drawer of the refrigerator. The only assumption you should ever make about a cougar's intentions is that his interest in you is strictly culinary.

Where children are involved, no chance should ever be taken. I recommend that any child (or adult, for that matter) under five feet tall should stay out of lion country, period, especially if a cat has been recently sighted. The risk is too great, and an attack can happen faster than you can believe. The presence of an adult is no guarantee of prevention either. Most of the child attacks you have read here occurred with adults present. Five-year-old Andrew Braun of Kitsap County, Washington, was snatched while standing just three feet from his father.

If you live in prime lion country, think twice about letting your children play outdoors without armed adult supervision. Hold that thought, the one about "paranoid nut," while I tell you about California's Caspers Park. In 1987 authorities there deemed one area of the park so potentially dangerous that no one under age eighteen was allowed in, making it the first X-rated public area in the nation. Since then, red-lettered signs warning "MOUNTAIN LION COUNTRY . . . No Minors Allowed" have been cropping up in parks all over the state almost as frequently as "No Littering" signs. Failing to heed the latter will get you fined, but ignoring the former may result in penalties considerably more severe. I know how ridiculous all of this sounds, but I would hate to think some innocent kid got brutally killed or maimed because I didn't tell it like it is. I may not be very popular, but at least I'm cute.

Personally, I adhere to the old caveat that the best defense is a good offense, paraphrased as shoot first and ask questions later, also known as the triple-S principle of shoot, shovel, and shutup. If a lion starts hanging around your home, kill the damned thing and bury it. Chances are your neighbors will be delighted, with no finkery ensuing. If you are inclined to total honesty, notify authorities only after calling the local news media. Official viewpoints tend to be more charitable under the harsh glare of TV lights. Besides, it may be your only chance for fifteen minutes of fame.

The incidents you have read here represent just a small portion of what has occurred in recent years— recounting them all would easily fill a book this size. The purpose here is not to unduly frighten or incite anyone to mass lioncide. As I said in the beginning, I like lions. I value them as magnificent examples of nature's handi-work, predators of the finest ilk, and superb game animals. But I place a greater value on the sanctity of life, the inalienable right to which is endowed by the Creator to man alone. Under no circumstance should that right be willingly forfeited to a soulless animal. If you do not share this viewpoint, that's okay. There are more than a few cuddly felines out there who will most happily accommodate you. Personally, I have no intention of purchasing a ticket in the mountain-lion lottery. It would be just my luck to win.

BEARS

Balanced in the dirt in an upright kneeling position, half-hidden behind the gnarled, upended roots of a deadfall pine, the man looked like a bloody, penitent scarecrow fallen from its perch. Hundreds of flies buzzed around him in an iridescent green cloud, planting their eggs in the dark, clotted glaze that covered the nearly naked body, the clothes torn into tatters. The head lolled grotesquely to one side, nearly severed at the neck. The lower jaw swung by a thin sliver of muscle, twisting slowly in the breeze with a thick skein of congealed blood dangling from the chin. The right hand gripped a knife slickened from point to pommel with gore, the left entwined in the neck fur of a mammoth grizzly, dead of wounds inflicted by the blade, its forelegs wrapping the torn man in a lethal embrace.

American Man-Killers

The two ranch hands who stumbled upon the awful scene in the Mogollon Mountains of southwestern New Mexico that day in 1883 figured the best available treatment for such injuries was a gravedigger's shovel. But they were amazed to discover the man was alive when one of them glimpsed his heart beating through a ragged hole in his chest. Rigging a travois from poles and saddle blankets, they carted him half-dead to Magdalena, where he was literally patched back together and, amazingly, later recovered. Perhaps "recovered" is too strong a word, for though fully ambulatory, he was never again quite whole. His jaw had been so destroyed that he could not chew like a normal man. A gaping hole in his cheek made repulsive sucking sounds whenever he ate. He grew what beard he could and let his hair grow long to hide as much as possible the oozing, keloid mask that remained of his face. The rest he covered with a filthy rag on the rare occasions that brought him into other men's company, and that only at night. He became a recluse, hidden away in the mountains from the stares of men and the horrified gasps of women. Though rarely seen, the prospector from Missouri became well known around New Mexico's Silver City, Turkey Creek, and Gila River region as "Bear" Moore, the Grizzly Hater.

To say that James A. Moore hated grizzly bears is akin to saying Stalin didn't like capitalists very much. From the time he recovered from his overdose of bear until his death in 1924, Moore dedicated himself to exacting severe retribution on the bruin tribe. Not content to simply kill every grizzly he could find, borrow, or steal, he tortured them to death in the most brutal ways imaginable. One method, as surreptitiously witnessed and reported by a ranch hand, involved capturing the bear alive in a box trap made of logs and baited with a deer carcass, then punching iron rods heated white-hot in a nearby fire deep into the animal's body. As the bear's tortured cries mingled with the oily, stink-laden smoke of scorched flesh and fur, Moore evidenced his delight by giggling and dancing about like the madman he was, the final *pièce de résistance* before death to burn out the creature's eyes.

56

2 • Bears

It seems only fitting that a chapter addressing some of the *Ursus* clan's less-endearing qualities should begin with a nice, bloody grizzly story. The griz is, after all, the largest living land carnivore in the world, and has a name to live up to: *Ursus arctos horribilis*, as it is rendered in formal Latin, the "horrible bear" in the King's English, the suitability of which is more than clearly demonstrated in the creature's past and present behavior toward mankind. Not that we ourselves have been all that charitable toward Old Ephraim, which is not to imply he didn't deserve it—I just want to be as fair and objective as possible, which ain't always easy when it comes to grizzlies. There is just something about them that affects some people in a very negative way, and I doubt it stems from any association with Pooh, Paddington, or Yogi.

As man-killers go, the grizzly is top bear among North America's terrible triumvirate of heavyweight predators, which includes the polar and black bears. Not that the two others don't kill people—it's just that grizzlies do it so well. In case you haven't heard, bears in general and grizzlies in particular can be singularly unpleasant creatures. The more-or-less modern history of their relationship with man in America is marked by such notable events as decapitations, limb removal, disembowelment, and consuming living young from the womb. And that's just what they did to the livestock. Wait till you hear what they've done to some people!

For many of the same reasons cited elsewhere regarding other felonious fauna, we cannot be sure just how many people have been introduced to The Maker by grizzlies. Among the best available figures are those compiled by Dr. Stephen Herrero, an animal-behavior specialist with the University of Calgary, Alberta, who began compiling attack data in 1967 shortly after graduating with a Ph.D. from the University of California, Berkeley. The vast majority of incidents he has examined came from U.S. and Canadian national-park files, which he accurately cites as the only major source of reliable records, dating back to 1872 when Yellowstone was founded. In 1985 Herrero compiled his findings, along with quite a few slaughterhouse-type anecdotal references he had collected, into the book *Bear Attacks: Their Causes and Avoidance* an excellent reference that I highly recommend.

Like the Beier cougar study discussed elsewhere, Herrero's work has quite a few holes numbers-wise, but not because of any negligence on his part. Necessarily concerned about scientific validity, he purposely excluded a number of incidents deemed insufficiently documented to ensure accuracy. Collectively, he analyzed 279 less-than-friendly grizzly encounters, of which 246 occurred in national parks between 1872 and 1980, with thirty-three more recorded elsewhere between 1960 and 1980, resulting in 165 injuries including nineteen deaths. Remember, this is just what Herrero was able to document under rather strict self-imposed criteria, voluntarily admitting that the actual number is probably at least doubled, and his time venue encompassed only the years 1900 to 1980.

That Herrero's figures are severely on the low side is illustrated by one turn-of-the-century report citing "several gentlemen in California who had been horribly mutilated by these ferocious animals," and further alluding to "various cases in which men had been otherwise crippled for life or killed on the spot." Of course, the great bear exists in California today only in effigy form on the state's flag. Nevertheless, the fact that one man knew of "several" and "various" cases of attack or death in just one of the states inhabited by grizzlies suggests that the bears' overall contribution to the local graveyard is far greater than we will ever know.

A couple of other interesting grizzly-crimes references are *Alaska Bear Tales* and the sequel, *More Alaska Bear Tales*, by Larry Kaniut. As the titles indicate, Kaniut's works deal strictly with Alaska incidents, comprising 152 bona-fide grizzly maulings, forty-four fatal, between 1900 and 1989, overlapping with Herrero in only a few instances. The combined numbers yield 317 attacks resulting in injury, with sixty-three deaths. These figures are extremely limited in scope, restricted to deeds done within national parks in the one case and those occurring within a single state in the other, although the Alaska grizzly's contributions can hardly be considered something to sneeze at.

On the subject of Alaska, I deliberated for some time over whether to include the Last Frontier in this chapter. The state is sufficiently remote from the rest of the U.S. to seem almost a country unto itself, which it practically was until granted statehood in 1959. At over half a million square miles and with a human population roughly one-third that of Rhode Island's, it seems to be a place most people would rather visit than live, and of which few ever think when contemplating "America." But, considering that of an estimated 44,000 grizzlies in the U.S., 43,000 live in Alaska (twice the number in all of Canada) and account for more recorded unfriendly incidents than any other geographical area in the world, one could hardly write a book about American man-killers without including the state.

This circumstance should not be construed as indicating that one must travel to the Great North to get spindled, folded, or mutilated by a grizzly. The relative few in the lower forty-eight hold up their end of the coffin quite well, thank you, annually giving quite a few campers, hikers, and hunters the chop in Montana and Wyoming, with Washington and Idaho thrown in as wild cards.

Lest confusion reign in this ode to the lifestyle of the big and scary, we had best clear up a few things relating to taxonomy. "Grizzly" is the common name most often applied to members of the *Arctos* genera of the subfamily *Ursinae* in the *Carnivora* order. With my repertoire of Latin thus nearly exhausted, suffice it to say that if it is big and brown (or silver, or blond, or jet black, or a plethora of other color variations) and it bites, most people call it a grizzly. Two other common labels are "coastal brown" and "Kodiak," the latter being that giant among giants hailing from the Alaskan island for which it is named, and the former applying to bears that live, well, on the coast. All of which seems rather silly since they are the same bear, relative size being the only significant distinguishing factor. (Coast-dwelling bears, including Kodiaks, grow bigger because of the abundance of food, at least according to one theory.) If so inclined, you can adopt the position that all are brown bears and be totally correct. Furthermore, you can march right up to the tsar, or whoever is in charge of Russia these days, and announce that you have killed the largest post-Bering-land-bridge grizzly in his Eurasian bailiwick, with none to gainsay you save the KGB, assuming it is still in business. If you have ever yearned to see pandemonium at its finest, just plop an oversized interior grizzly or undersized coastal brown on the head table at a zoologists' convention and ask that it be identified.

Since we are muddying the waters anyway, I might as well tell you the Boone and Crockett Club's official take on all this for trophy record-keeping purposes, which is the only practical reason for knowing the difference anyway. According to the club's *Records of North American Big Game*:

> A line of separation between the larger growing coastal brown bear and the smaller interior grizzly has been developed such that west and south of this line (to and including Unimak Island) bear trophies are recorded as Alaska brown bear. North and east of this line, bear trophies are recorded as grizzly bear. The boundary line is as follows: Starting at Pearse Canal and following the Canadian-Alaskan boundary north-westerly to Mt. St. Elias on the 141 degree meridian; thence north along the Canadian-Alaskan boundary to Mt. Natazhat; thence west along the divide of the Wrangell Range to Mt. Jarvis at the western end of the Wrangell Range; thence north along the divide of the Mentasta Range to Mentasta Pass; thence in a general westerly direction along the divide of the Alaska Range to Houston Pass; thence westerly following the 62nd parallel of latitude to the Bering Sea.

Got all that? Good. There will be a quiz at the end of the chapter. Aren't you glad I am not going to discuss by geographical breakdown the other eighty-six grizzly sub-species that were once recognized in North America? The whole point of this rather dull literary oration on bear-wheres is to clarify that for our purposes a grizzly is a grizzly regardless of which side of the mountain it comes from. So, if I herein make reference to a grizzly violently rearranging someone's anatomical nether regions in a geographical location considered strictly the habitat of brownies, please do not write me any letters.

With our taxonomy and geography firmly established, a few words are in order concerning how incidents of grizzly malfeasance get officially pigeonholed. It can be convincingly argued that grizzly attacks come in only one flavor, bad, but there is sufficient variation in method, motivation, and outcome to justify a class system based on criteria considerably more sanguine than race, color, or creed. Most professionals recognize four basic attack classes: *provoked, surprised, defensive,* and *"other"* for situations that don't seem to fit any particular mold.

Provoked attacks are those wherein the victim did something the bear found displeasing, such as just being there. It doesn't take a whole lot to incite a grizzly to mayhem. They are born with chips on their shoulders, and you never know what will set them off. For that matter, I doubt even the bears know. Grizzlies have been reliably reported as running up to two-hundred yards for the privilege of examining a human from the inside. On the other hand, some run away like the scalded proverbial from hand-clapping, arm-waving, shouting, police whistles, air-powered marine signaling horns, or some combination thereof. I am trying hard to avoid the overworked "unpredictable" description, but it is the only thing that fits. In truth, bears and other animals are wholly predictable if we could just learn to recognize and interpret the subtleties of vocalization, scent, and body language that make up their communication systems. Barring that, the best generalization is that *all* grizzlies will attack—it is simply a question of when and under what circumstances.

Bears have little patience with people who put off-center holes in them, and it is axiomatic that attacks by bears wounded in hunting situations are both provoked and defensive. So are cases of deliberate approach by would-be nature photographers or low-IQ tourists. The first fatal attack recorded in a national park took place around 1900 when a Yellowstone tourist chased a grizzly cub up a tree, to which its mother demonstrated her displeasure by ripping out the man's breastbone and one lung. Sows with cubs are especially hair-triggered and do not ordinarily require such extreme provocation. So it is with mating bears, who take a dim view of voyeuristic ogling by woodland Peeping Toms. Approaching the cached carcass of an animal killed or otherwise procured by a bear will get you violently subdivided into several bloody chunks in no time, as many a hunter returning to pack out that last load of moose meat has learned. So will letting Fido run loose in grizzly country; several attacks have occurred after dogs led bears into their owners' laps when chased.

Sudden encounter attacks occur when man and bear surprise one another in close quarters. Grizzlies are extremely sensitive to violations of their "personal space," which varies in size among individuals but may be 100 yards or more, and offenders are frequently dealt with in the severest extreme. A typical scenario would be a backpacker rounding a blind corner in the trail from downwind and, SURPRISE! Instant human *paté*. Ditto for the bear too preoccupied with digging a marmot out of its hole to hear the bells on yon hiker's toes, which are intended to herald human approach and let the bear avoid the encounter without losing face. In this situation it is usually the hiker who loses face, or arm, or head.

The "other" category is for cases in which no reasonable explanation can be found for the attack. No provocation is evident, terrain precludes a surprise encounter, no dogs, food, firearms, or Yankees whistling Dixie are involved—it just happened. Frankly, I am of the opinion that this category was created by and for people who do not want to face up to the cold, hard facts. A grizzly doesn't *need* a reason to do its food-processor impersonation with active audience participation, but some bear professionals will not admit this. In their way of thinking, when a grizzly attacks a person, it is always somehow the person's fault. This view is somewhat reflected in other catego-

2 • Bears

ries—the word "provoked" is a good example and implies the attackee deliberately did something to irritate the bear. It may be true in some cases, but often as not, the victim didn't know there was a bear within a hundred miles. Of course, not all persons bearing such sentiments have axes in need of grinding. After talking rather extensively with some of the country's top bear men, I have come to understand how this attitude might develop. One national park's chief ranger once told me:

> When you have been observing the same bear for what may be years, sometimes watching it grow up from a cub, you can't help but develop feelings like you know the animal in some personal way. They become almost like children. When one of them is involved in a bad encounter, the temptation is to be defensive in their behalf. Most professionals try to avoid anthropomorphism [assigning human characteristics to animals], but when you see behavior and even what appear to be attitudes in them that are similar to those common in our own species, it's pretty easy to get sucked in.

Partly for reasons cited and partly because I believe the usual classification system is too vague, this analysis of the ursine fertilizer production process and its effects on the environment will be categorized under the headings *predatory, competitive, defensive, unprovoked,* and *weird.* Yeah, I know. But trust me, that last category is both justifiable and necessary, as you will later see.

In predatory attacks, a bear unstitches a human for no other apparent purpose than to eat him—skeptics, stand by to be convinced. Competitive attacks occur when the bear commits strong-arm robbery to procure food or other items of interest from an unwilling person. Defensive attacks occur when the victim commits or attempts to commit blatant trespass, robbery, assault, or kidnap against the person or property of the bear. In unprovoked attacks, the victim did not do or say anything to offend the bear, or did so inadvertently with no reasonable expectation that he would know of the bear's presence. Weird attacks are, well, weird. Like the bear that ate a family's Christmas dinner after chasing them out of their cabin, then fell asleep on the floor. Since some situations involve elements from more than one category, overlaps are inevitable. In some cases, what starts out as one attack type may evolve into another—competitive becoming predatory when the bear decides to eat the victim, and such. Whatever the underlying motivations may be, one factor common to all bear attacks remains absolute: They are extremely unpleasant.

Sometime around 1910, a trapper named King Thurmond was found dead in his cabin near the base of Alaska's Kenai Peninsula. The corpse looked like somebody had gone over it from shoulder to ankle with a dull chain saw. Big chunks of flesh had been ripped from the arms and legs, the ribs separated from the spine, and the right arm and hand chewed into something not recognizable as human. Though the exact circumstances will never be known, the man left a legacy for whoever would eventually find him, a macabre diary painfully written over what was probably several days on the back of an old mining-claim document. "Have ben tore up by a brown bear," it said. "No show to get out. Good by [sic]." Most of the rest was illegible, owing in no small part to the pain, I am sure, and a ruined right hand necessitating a left-handed scrawl, but enough was decipherable to leave little doubt of how his final, tortured hours must have gone. "I'm sane but suffering," read one legible entry. Sometime after making the final entry, "the [two words illegible] of death," Thurmond found merciful relief in putting a pistol bullet through his own brain.

This is not the only example of a grizzly victim providing postmortem documentation of his or her fate. At least two other grizzly casualties gave up-to-the-minute reports of their deaths, dictated "as it happened," a far better choice of words than "live" considering the circumstances. They occurred on the same night, 13 August 1967. One of them involved a group of friends and coworkers, seasonal employees of Glacier Park Inc., a contract concessionaire, who were camped at Trout Lake in Montana's Glacier National Park. Around 2 A.M. they were awakened by something sniffing around their

2 • Bears

sleeping bags, a monster grizzly resembling a Brahman bull in a fur coat looking for a late-night snack. The bear took a tentative bite out of Paul Dunn's bedroll, tearing the back off his sweatshirt in the process. Dunn had been trying to follow procedure and play dead, but this was too much. He exploded out of the nylon shroud and was up a tree in seconds, followed in short order by the rest of the campers scattering into the blackness and up trees. All but one of them.

Whether nineteen-year-old Michele Koons was too frightened to get out of her sleeping bag or unable because of a stuck zipper remains a point of disagreement to this day. One report says Dunn yelled for her to unzip the bag, and she answered back that the bear had the zipper in its mouth. Whether this was the cause or an effect of her inability to escape is rather academic. In a scene right out of a cheap horror flick, the bear lifted the woman clear of the ground in its jaws and carried her screaming into the dark woods, the flickering orange illumination of the campfire lending a surreal stop-motion effect to the proceedings. Then it started eating her. Alive. Dunn and the others listened, terrified, as Michele screamed out the details of her own death, punctuated by the soggy sounds of cracking bones and ripping flesh as the grizzly literally tore her apart. Most of the agonized wails were unintelligible, but "My arm is gone!" was one utterance all agreed on. Everyone was relieved when the woman's suffering at last ended, her final sobbed words, "Oh, God, I'm dead," echoing faintly off the granite bluffs.

To paraphrase *Star Trek's* Klingons, it must have been a good night to die. Two hours earlier and twenty miles away, another pair of campers—also Glacier Park Inc. employees—had attracted nocturnal ursine attention. Roy Ducat and Julie Helgeson (not "Helgerson," as reported in other tomes) were asleep in a campground near Granite Park Chalet, having pitched their sleeping bags in the open when the lodge ran out of accommodations. Around 12:45 A.M., Ducat was more than a little perplexed when awakened by Helgeson's stage-whispered instructions to play dead. The reason

65

became all too apparent seconds later when both were knocked violently out of their bags by some force invisible in the inky blackness.

The grizzly, a smallish 265-pound sow, pounced on Ducat and started gnawing his shoulder. Lying facedown, he pushed his mouth against the ground to help stifle the scream of pain that welled up in his throat, willing himself to silence as huge teeth grated against bone and ripped flesh with a wet, slobbering sound. After what couldn't have been more than a couple of weeks of this treatment, the predator quit Ducat and turned its attentions on the woman lying a few feet away. Julie made no sound at first, despite the obvious pain as her upper legs and buttocks were chewed into sausage stuffing. The bear switched back and forth between them several times, alternately biting one and then the other as if trying to decide which had the better flavor. Ducat later recalled hearing Julie piteously whimper "It hurts" a couple of times when the bear was on her. When her endurance gave way and she started to scream, that, for whatever reason, was the deciding factor in who was to die. She screamed for help, for relief from the pain, and for her "Mommy!" as the grizzly carried her away into the forest, her agonized pleas becoming fainter and fainter until they stopped altogether.

A rescue team of volunteers from the chalet found her just at daylight, a measured 342 feet from the campground. There was no doubt the bear had partially eaten the girl; only bone remained between the hand and elbow of her right arm, and big chunks of meat had been torn from her upper legs and buttocks. Adding to the horror was the fact that she was still alive, weakly croaking "It hurts" over and over like some kind of macabre mantra. One of the rescuers, a doctor named Lindan, noted with grim certainty that she couldn't last much longer. Even if he could immediately replace the ninety percent of her blood volume that had seeped into the ground, death by suffocation from collapsed lungs, evidenced by pink foam oozing from sucking gashes in her chest, was inescapable. Right he was. Julie Helgeson died on a makeshift operating table in the chalet's dining room at 4:12 A.M. She too was nineteen years old.

It is unlikely that age or vocation figured in the deaths of Jane Ammerman and Kim Eberlee, both nineteen years old and Glacier Park concession employees, but a spooky coincidence nonetheless. Their partially eaten bodies were discovered the afternoon of 24 July 1980 by a fisherman on one of the park's trout streams. There were no witnesses, but circumstantial evidence indicated a scenario something like this: The previous night, the two had camped just outside a developed campground, pitching their small tent in a wooded area near St. Mary Resort. Sometime in the early morning hours, a grizzly had torn through the flimsy tent, killed them, and dragged their bodies a short distance before feeding.

If there is anything park authorities dread more than people inconsiderately getting themselves eaten, it is obliging bears who do so in violation of the established rules for such activities. Good bears kill people only when so prompted by food or garbage left carelessly around campsites, in defense of cubs or food sources, or when repelling intruders. None of these factors was evident in the Koons, Helgeson, Ammerman, or Eberlee deaths, so the experts went to work to explain what had happened. One possible explanation, a variation on the ever-popular "blame the victim" theme, suggested that the smell of cosmetics or menstruation may have been an attractant. But there was that one male morsel to contend with, wasn't there? In that case, the theory was modified to include the sounds or smells associated with the couple doing what young people of the opposite sex are prone to do when alone in a tent at night—an interesting theory, not to mention a sterling testimonial to the benefits of abstinence. Another theory, which I like to call the Blood and Thunder Hypothesis, suggested the bears were just in a bad mood from the irritation of lightning storms or sonic booms from low-flying aircraft. No, I am not kidding. In view of the outcomes, it would appear that the most obvious explanation got overlooked. Maybe the investigators suffered from forest-for-the-trees myopia, or were perhaps distracted in contemplation of all the "good time" the perpetrators had amassed over the years. Whatever the case, not one of the records or speculative observations I have examined suggested the possibility that the bears were simply hungry.

That most people find it morally repugnant for an animal to deliberately stalk and kill a human for the express purpose of eating him does little to obviate the fact that it does happen. Bears are predators, though not exclusively so, and care not one whit in Who's image man is made. Not burdened with ideas concerning the morality of whence dietary protein needs are met, a nice, tender maiden is most delectable, once you get past the nylon upholstery. Those annoying zippers can be hell on the bridgework, though.

The subject of conditioning as it relates to human predation by bears has received no small amount of attention in scientific circles. Though some professionals reject the idea of human predation as "unnatural," others view the matter more objectively. Jim Rearden, a former U.S. Fish & Wildlife Service agent who has studied and written about bears for years, flatly states in his book *Tales of Alaska's Big Bears*, "Bears attack humans because they are hungry." Likewise, Herrero observes that "Bears may prey on campers during the night," with the qualification that most offenders have been conditioned to associate people with food through garbage and midnight cooler raids, a circumstance labeled "habituation."

Habituation occurs when bears (or any other animal) learn through repeated exposure to accept a given circumstance and its consequences as normal in their environment. In the old days, it was "normal" for bears to flee from the sight or smell of people, since contact almost invariably led to a very painful hole in the hide courtesy of Messrs. Winchester, Remington, *et al*. These days, it is frequently just the opposite.

Due to their mostly protected status in the lower forty-eight states, bears and people intermingle with unparalleled regularity, especially in the parks. They have learned that humans usually present no immediate threat, and are often sources of tasty goodies. Most people living in bear country are acquainted with "dump bears" to the extent that a Saturday-night date may include a stint of bear-watching at the local landfill. In tourist areas, some bears make their livings as part-time muggers, having learned that hikers throw backpacks containing food when approached or *woofed* at. Since the most common injuries sustained in unprovoked, non-predatory attacks are to the back, buttocks, and rear of the head, I have often wondered whether the bears thought they were opening a backpack. In less commercial settings, people graciously provide handy meals in the form of easily caught livestock, or game animals conveniently killed and dressed by hunters. In the latter case, bears have been observed actually running *toward* the sound of gunfire, associating the report with a free lunch. One of the most recent examples of this behavior occurred 9 October 1995 when two British Columbia hunters, Shane Fumerton and William Caspell, were killed by a bear that coveted their elk meat. Though both men carried heavy rifles, at least one of which had a round chambered and ready to fire, neither had time to get off a shot, so quick and furious was the attack. According to B.C. wildlife authorities, as of October 1995 such competitive attacks had resulted in an average of four maulings per year, including six deaths in the preceding ten years. To alleviate the problem, the B.C. Ministry of Environment declared that as of the fall 1996 hunting season, all open grizzly-bear areas would be closed. And you thought America's claim to the World's Dumbest Bureaucrats title was exclusive.

In whatever form food habituation may exist, all experts agree it is a dangerous circumstance if for no other reason than it attracts bears into proximity with people. The greatest danger, though, lies in the fact that the leap from associating humans *with* food to viewing them *as* food is not a big one. To convince the Doubting Disneys, I again point to that great laboratory for man-predator experiments, Africa.

In contemplating behavioral similarities between Africa's and America's great predators, a number of interesting parallels emerge. In the chapter on cougars, we discussed their similarity to leopards. Likewise, our grizzly bear shares many traits with the Dark Continent's lion. Both are the largest predators in each of their respective bailiwicks, although a big grizzly outclasses the largest lion three to one, a disadvantage compensated for by the fact that lions operate in groups. Each will rob other predators of kills by brute force, and consume carrion with genuine zeal. Both lack a sense of humor and tend to nuke first and ask questions later if caught by surprise or in compromising positions related to mating. Corralled livestock is a temptation neither can resist, which brings them into unwanted human company on a regular basis. Lions too have learned to associate gunfire with easy pickings, swarming in to contest with hunters or cropping officers over possession of kills. Both are active predators, their respective prey being of similar size and conformation, which includes me, you, and cousin Earl. And, most importantly, they probably learn the vagaries of people-eating in similar ways.

In the days of yore, common wisdom held that man-eating lions were driven to the practice when age or other incapacitation rendered them incapable of killing "normal" prey, or that they were simply insane and therefore "rogues" bent on homicidal conduct regardless of which political party was in office. That many emaciated, tooth-worn lions of retirement age have chosen man-eating as preferable to starvation is beyond question, but by no means is it always the case. Actually, most lions that have gained fame if not fortune for their people-eating talents have proven abnormal only in that they were above average health-wise, owing in all probability to their steady, high-protein diets. A bit of digging turned up that *simba,* in a curious form of habituation peculiar to Third World societies, was developing "the taste" through free samples provided by the aboriginal practice of leaving human bodies to bush scavengers in lieu of the more labor-intensive European burial custom. It actually went a bit further than that, with the sick and old often abandoned to whatever not-so-gentle fate lurked in the African night, giving enterprising lions the chance to try their paws at the real thing. By way of illustration, you may recall the legendary Tsavo man-eaters, a frolicsome pair who took the hint after dining on abandoned bodies of Indian coolies imported to build Africa's Mombasa-Victoria-Uganda Railway. After a few courses of corpus delicti, they moved on to the fresh stuff to the tune of 100 victims before Lt. Col. John Henry Patterson revoked their licenses at the turn of the twentieth century. A quick perusal of today's headlines reveals how similar situations can still develop, the sheer force of numbers precluding immediate burial of all those who die from the witch's brew of disease, famine, and armed conflict common to modern Africa.

Fine for Africa, you say, but this is America, land of the free, home of the brave and the $5,000 funeral. We don't leave our dead lying around in the bush with last rites administered by scavengers. We are civilized. Okay, that's fair. But what of the dead we don't get the chance to bury? Will a bear avail himself of the opportunity, or pledge to preserve the sanctity of the dearly departed? Well, here are a couple of possible answers:

From the *Denver Post:*

BEAR PARTLY EATS APPARENT SUICIDE VICTIM

Kittredge (Colorado), 30 July 1993—The body of an apparent suicide victim was discovered just over the hill from Troublesome Gulch—and there were signs it had been partially eaten by a black bear. . . .

From the *Record Courier:*

BEAR DIGS UP A BODY

Gardnerville (Nevada), 18 August 1977—The Alpine County Sheriff's Office is investigating the murder of an unidentified man whose body was found in a shallow grave near Monitor Pass. No identification has been made on the body, which was found wrapped in a sleeping bag and shot through the head. According to Sheriff Stuart Merril, a bear dug up the grave and uncovered the body. . . .

71

American Man-Killers

Though black bears were involved in both instances, I think the point should nevertheless be clear. In case you are inclined to nitpicking, I doubt anyone will disagree that Cape Kumlik, located on the bleak, rugged coast of Alaska's namesake peninsula, is grizzly country. That's where the white, red-trimmed Piper Super Cub piloted by Darrell Pennington and carrying as a passenger famed handgun hunter Al Goerg was found 28 July 1966, ten months after it disappeared. All that was found of the men were some tattered bits of clothing and a few scattered bone fragments. All those grizzly droppings and tracks among the wreckage were just a coincidence, I am sure.

In October 1980, Glacier Park employees found thirty-three-year-old Lawrence Gordon's partially eaten body near his campsite at Elizabeth Lake. A board of inquiry found evidence to suggest the man had died of natural causes or was killed by a different bear than the one who ate him.

Another possible in this category is the tragic case of seven-year-old David Michael Borer, listed as missing since 25 April 1989, when he disappeared while hiking with his family near Wasilla, Alaska. You may have seen his picture on a milk carton or potato-chip package. At one point it was suspected he had been killed by a grizzly, but this was ruled out after extensive investigation. Alaska State Police investigators told me they believe the boy most likely drowned after falling through spongy, spring-melt river ice and was swept away. His body has never been found.

If these examples of bears feeding on human dead they did not personally kill fail to shoot down any doubts volplaning through your mind's savannas, I don't know what will. If you read the newspaper, you already know the frequency with which BODY FOUND IN WOODED AREA-type headlines appear. Extrapolating from this, the probable number of murder victims or people who die of natural or unnatural causes in remote areas and are never found—except possibly by bears—is quite sobering.

2 • Bears

Though a bit off the subject, you may find it interesting, as I did, that in September 1995 the body of a man, one of my fellow Texans named Howard Ellis Deal, was found in the mountains of Jefferson County, Colorado, where he disappeared while bowhunting in—ready for this?—1965! The coroner decided no foul play was involved, and speculated that the man had become lost and died of hypothermia. It seems odd to me that anything would be left of a body after thirty years among scavengers, let alone sufficiently intact to determine the cause of death. Even dry bones are usually consumed by mice, porcupines, and other rodents, which is why we are not hip-deep in animal skeletons and shed antlers. I suppose the body's location may have prevented scavenging, perhaps in a tree or other inaccessible spot; the reports didn't say, but in my mind this one will always be a mystery.

Anyway, where was I? Oh, yes: How to become a man-eating lion or bear in one or two easy lessons. The other way in which African lions learn to prey on people can be termed "accidental," inasmuch as the lion didn't really mean to eat anybody, it just sort of worked out that way. It may start with a curious bite of that dead villager over there, who paid the price for rudely interrupting *simba's* afternoon siesta. He decides it is not so bad with a little steak sauce, and doesn't have the "kick" of zebra. Later, while sizing up a new shipment of gazelle cutlets, another of those oddly hairless apes comes along and old *silwane* decides to give it another try. No muss, no fuss, and the kids just love the leftovers. Another man-eater gets his diploma.

In July 1976, Barbara Chapman and Andrew Stepniewski were hiking along an old logging road in Cougar Valley of British Columbia's Glacier Park (yes, they have one too). In a classic unprovoked, sudden-encounter scenario, the pair walked unexpectedly into a sow grizzly with three cubs at a bend in the trail. The mother bear ran huffing up to Stepniewski, who was slightly ahead, and started counseling him in the finer points of trail etiquette. The man wisely played dead, lying facedown with his hands protecting the back of his neck and head, and the attack ended after just a few seconds. Things didn't work out quite so well when the grizzly turned its attentions on the woman. Chapman, a park naturalist who should have known better, fought back, kicking at the bear several times in the early stages. The assault persisted for as long as she struggled, about thirty seconds, and when it was over, Barbara Chapman lay dead. After the bear left, Stepniewski, badly injured with wounds to his neck, face, and body, hobbled out to the Trans-Canada Highway and summoned help. When rescuers arrived a few hours later, they discovered the bear had returned and fed on the woman after dragging her 200 feet into heavy cover.

It is highly unlikely that the attack started out predatory. That the bear left after "neutralizing the threat" (cute phrase, what?), had cubs in tow, and had been surprised in close quarters all point to defense as the primary motivation. It is impossible to know whether the grizzly's previous experiences may have included episodes of man-bashing, killing, or eating, but it is certainly conceivable. Many of the perpetrators you have read about here were never identified or killed, so it could even have been one of them. In fact, five years prior, a sow grizzly had badly injured three people in two separate incidents just three miles from where Chapman was killed. Most likely, though, it was a simple case of "since I've already killed it anyway." I am sure Barbara Chapman would be greatly comforted knowing the bear ate her as an afterthought.

There is a place in the gory annals of bear-related happenstance for the Missing and Presumed Eaten. The official Glacier Park incident report on twenty-nine-year-old Gary J. Goeden initially listed him as "missing" after he disappeared 24 July 1987 while hiking in the Elk Mountain area. Two months later, in a brushy section of Appekunny Cirque, park rangers found what was left of him: one torn plaid flannel shirt stained with body fluids; one boot, complete with foot; ribs, sternum, some cervical vertebrae, and a few skull fragments containing teeth. The report noted, "Bear diggings and scat of the year numerous and widely dispersed throughout the area." Evidence suggested Goeden had attempted escape by climbing a tree, but, and I quote, "It appears that the victim did not make it up the tree." Whether Goeden was killed by one bear and eaten by another remains open to speculation. By the way, guess who was Goeden's employer. Glacier Park Inc.

Bear predation has been suspected but never proven in quite a number of unsolved disappearances, such as that of Alaska hunting guide Ralph Reischl, who went into the woods on Admiralty Island one day and never returned. Some vanishings may be accountable to natural deaths, accidents, or even murder, but some curious items found in bear droppings over the years probably explain a lot more. Shirt buttons, clothing fragments, pieces of ink pens, and, if memory serves, a wristwatch have been found deposited in locations too remote to blame on garbage scavenging. I suppose campsite plundering is a possibility, but why a grizzly would be interested in a wristwatch is beyond me. Maybe it was late for an appointment.

A few disappearances, though ultimately solved, remain mysteries in terms of circumstantial details. A U.S. deputy marshal dispatched to investigate reports of bootlegging on Admiralty Island never reported back in. Later, sundry pieces of his body were found, with his revolver lying nearby, all chambers fired, and a bloody bear trail leading off into the alders. A few chewed-on bones and bits of clothing belonging to Lawrence Swenson were found about forty miles south of Fairbanks, two months after he was last seen. His age of eighty years led some to speculate that his body may have been scavenged after death by natural causes, but evidence one way or the other was hard to come by.

Before we switch off the Bears in Africa channel, if your mind works with any similarity to my own (may God pity you), you may be wondering how a bear would fare one-on-one against a lion. According to an account by Horace Bell in *On The Old West Coast*, in Monterey, Mexico, sometime in the 1920s, a grizzly was pitted against an African lion named Parnell, a purported man-eater of some renown. The big furry guy dethroned the King of Beasts with the greatest of ease, killing him "so quickly that the big audience hardly knew how it was done." This event was a variation on the practice known as "bear-baiting," a definitely un-dull pastime with roots in the Roman Coliseum in which bears were pitted against various opponents ranging from mastiffs to fighting bulls in arenas called "bear gardens." According to all accounts, the bear won invariably. These and similar shenanigans were all the rage in many parts of Europe as well as North America before they were universally outlawed in the early part of this century.

A couple of final points of African commonality deserve mentioning, if only because they are interesting. They involve comparisons of grizzlies with, of all things, elephants. We know elephants never eat people, except in that one case reported by Peter Hathaway Capstick of a zoo elephant eating a secretary named Bertha Walt—certainly an anomalous event without precedent or succeeding example; it is, nevertheless, a superb illustration of the axiom "never say never." Beyond that, the two species demonstrate a certain like-mindedness in their respective habits of going around burying people. For reasons known only to them, elephants have been frequently observed covering human bodies with twigs and other forest debris, even ones in whose undoing they had no personal, uh, trunk. In one instance, elephants buried an African woman unharmed after she fell asleep beneath a tree. Grizzlies do the same thing, the fundamental difference between them is that the grizzlies intend to return later for a snack. Several attack victims who survived by playing dead or becoming unconscious reported that they too were prematurely entombed.

Another curious commonality between Dumbo and Not-So-Gentle Ben is that the odds are about even for seeing either of them at the local bar—not as a result of your own imbibing but theirs. Bears and elephants dearly love their liquor. No cracks, now. I can prove this. Aside from the numerous accounts of elephants running amuck in a state of inebriation after eating fruit overripened to the point of fermentation, duly reported in more than a few African and Asian tomes, I offer the following

2 • Bears

Associated Press wire report, carried in newspapers across the country on 13 December 1995:

ELEPHANTS KILL MAN TO GET LIQUOR

New Delhi, India—Attracted by the smell of freshly brewed liquor, five thirsty elephants raided a remote tribal village in northeastern India, smashing huts and fatally crushing one man. The incident occurred Sunday night at Simbulbari, 430 miles north of Calcutta. The elephants tried to get to the vats of the warm brew, but villagers beat drums and ran after the animals with flaming torches, said Keshay Pradhan, a reporter in *Siligurr.*

My wife, yes. My dog, maybe. My beer, never!

A bar fight featuring tanked-up pachyderms is an imposing thought, but I would hate to have lived around Essex, Montana, in August 1985 when a train derailment there spilled 1,700 tons of corn along the track. Most of it was cleaned up, but 400 unsalvageable tons between the ties began to ferment when wetted by rains. Within a day, the area was besieged by dozens of drunk, unruly bears that showed up for Happy Hour. Observers reported that black bears seemed to make happy drunks, entertaining locals with their clownish antics, whereas grizzlies were mean drunks and chased quite a few sightseers and shutterbugs up trees, even if a bit unsteady on their pins. Though no people were hurt, several boozed-up bruins were killed by passing trains when they didn't, or couldn't, clear the tracks in time. Citing the situation as "a powder keg," authorities considered forcing the railroad to tear up the tracks and remove the contaminated soil, but acidized-lime treatments successfully rendered the mash unpalatable. The episode resulted in corn and other fermentable spills being classed as "toxic" and hence presumably eligible for EPA Superfund cleanup financing. Nowhere but America.

There are quite a few stories about moonshiners who would have preferred dealing with revenuers rather than the bears that routinely busted up their stills. Several people with "pet" bears reportedly kept them manageable with a daily ration of 100-proof stump-blower. In 1969 a bruin twosome stumbled into the town of Florida, Massachusetts, motherless drunk on fermented apples. What all this indicates I cannot be sure, but I always carry a hip flask whenever I am in bear country, just in case.

Back in the Hungry Bears and Lonely Hearts department, I guess we had best give poor old Glacier Park a rest. Quite a few good man-eater stories still lurk in there, but it would be a shame to ride a good horse to death when fresh mounts are stabled right next door, relatively speaking, in Yellowstone.

For the simple reason that "Come vacation among our scenic vistas and killer wildlife" doesn't make the best ad copy for attracting tourists, Yellowstone is better known for its geysers (in which a surprising number of people have been boiled to death) than as a charnel house featuring man-eating bears. As noted earlier, this park logged the first fatal grizzly attack recorded in the national-park system, which may or may not be coincidental with its being the first one established. Despite such auspicious beginnings, park records indicate that only five people have gotten fatally into bruin's way. Even without the grizzly's contributions, Yellowstone is still a pretty lively place. While preparing this book, I requested a listing of all human deaths or serious injuries caused by animal attacks (bison, elk, and so forth, as well as bears) within the park since 1980—a span of only fifteen years at the time. I got back a one-page letter from chief ranger Dan Sholly that said, in part, "What you have asked is monumental. To fulfill your request would require hundreds of hours of research and reading time plus copying." He signed off with a gracious offer to open the park's files for my perusal, which I unfortunately did not have time to do just then. I guess all those nifty anecdotes will have to wait for my next book. But take heart, I am not about to leave you with fantasies unfulfilled; Yellowstone's grizzlies are most accommodating.

2 • Bears

It was 2:30 on the morning of 24 June 1983, dandy camping weather with nary a cloud to obscure the coin of moon cascading silver light over the Big Sky country. Ted Moore and Roger May were camped at Rainbow Point in Galatin National Forest, adjacent to Yellowstone, when they were awakened by the sound of rattling tent poles and convulsing canvas, even though the wind wasn't blowing. Moore spoke to the other man, making reference to somebody pulling a Boy Scout-type prank, and was answered by a terrified shriek as May was pulled violently through a ragged hole that suddenly materialized in the tent's roof. Moore exited through the same hole, and in the moonlight saw his friend pinned beneath a raging thunderstorm dressed in a bear suit. Upon seeing Moore, the bear grabbed May by an ankle and ran off about thirty feet, dragging the man with him. Moore, who had a lot more guts than brains, started screeching like a drunken banshee and charged the grizzly—the very large, man-eating grizzly—with a tent pole! It worked too, believe it or not. The bear, probably as surprised as Moore, actually backed off a few feet but didn't leave. "Are you all right?" Moore asked his stricken friend. May, understandably confused, replied, "I'm okay—but I'm not doing so good," which would shortly qualify as the understatement of the year. When Moore went back to the tent for his glasses and a flashlight, he heard the other man scream one last time. When he looked back, the bear was gone. And so was Roger May.

About an hour later, a search party followed the blood trail to May and the grizzly, forcing the predator to again flee with its meal hanging limp and bloody in its jaws. Pressed by the pursuing rescue team, the bear finally dropped the corpse and disappeared into the night. In just under an hour, the grizzly had consumed more than seventy pounds of May's body.

Whoever initially found the campsite of Brigitta Fredenhagen, a vacationing Swiss camped alone near Yellowstone's White Lake, 1 August 1984, must have gotten quite a shock. As bear-country campsites go, it was textbook in its cleanliness and well-ordered appearance, right down to the food cached far away and high off the ground between a couple of trees. Yes sir, everything was in its place, except for one or two items: One upper lip and a piece of scalp containing human hair cast carelessly on the ground beside an empty, rumpled sleeping bag lying about six feet from the tent's torn front flap. Understandably concerned about this discovery, park authorities launched a search, which turned up what was left of the woman's body in a thicket about 250 feet from the campsite. Investigators concluded the woman had been killed sometime after 10:30 P.M. the night of 29 July, possibly after the bear had climbed (climbed!), twelve feet up the tree where Fredenhagen's food was stored, eating everything except one granola bar. What this indicates about bear tastes and health food in general I'll leave up to you. In this case too, stormy weather was suggested as a possible trigger for the attack, a highly dramatic backdrop for the proceedings no matter how unlikely. The bear, incidentally, judged from the evidence to have been a subadult male grizzly, was never found.

Lest you develop the idea that only food-conditioned park bears are inclined to bad table manners, I offer for your contemplation the case of one Harvey Cardinal. A member of the Doig River Indian Band, Cardinal was hunting near Fort St. John north of British Columbia's Peace River, as wild and remote a piece of real estate as you'd care to visit, trailing through the deep snows of a mid-January Canadian winter on the track of a huge grizzly. Now, there's an odd bit of circumstance. Grizzlies, as you may well know, spend the food-scarce winter months sleeping off a spring and summer's worth of gluttony in hibernation dens—or at least they are supposed to. That this one wasn't may indicate some extraordinary factor to account for its behavior, but I doubt it. Whatever the reason, Cardinal was about to become one of the statistical aberrations that disprove the popular rule concerning food conditioning and man-eating grizzlies.

The man's excitement grew with the freshness of the track as it meandered among the ice-crusted muskeg swamps and patchy alder scrub above the river. A winter-prime grizzly pelt—not to mention the meat, claws, and skull—was worth a lot of hard money in 1970, and Cardinal was intent on cashing in. This distraction may have accounted for the experienced woodsman's failure to see the trap he was walking into. The bear, having seen or sensed the man dogging its tracks, had fishhooked back to lie waiting in ambush on its own spoor behind a mossy, head-high hummock. Cardinal probably never saw or heard the thing that killed him. His rifle lay exactly where it had fallen from his mittened hands, safety on and unfired, when wildlife officers found it days later. The man's grisly remains lay stiff and frozen nearby, devoured from crotch to clavicle.

When the grizzly was later killed (a monumental effort involving a helicopter and every man and boy in the region who could squeeze a trigger), its three inches of body fat allayed any ideas about starvation as a motivating factor. Except for a few broken teeth and a weltering scar on its nose, attributed to having battled with another bear, the grizzly was a 575-pound example of health. We can only assume that the sale of its hide, claws, and skull helped defray the funeral expenses.

Just to be fair, we might as well toss a bone to the starving-bear crowd. The way I figure, the outcome is the same anyway, so whether a bear eats you because it is starving or just bulking up for a Hard Bodies competition doesn't make a whole lot of difference. Twenty-five-year-old Alan Precup may not have seen it that way, but his opinion doesn't carry much "weight" these days.

A tourist from Illinois aboard the tour vessel *Thunder Bay*, one of those excursion boats offering "Pacific Coast adventures," Precup had gone ashore 9 September 1976 for a few days of camping and backpacking in Glacier Bay National Monument on Alaska's southwestern coast. Eight days later, searchers found Precup's body, eaten right down to the bones with only the booted feet and one hand still intact, about 150 feet from his destroyed camp. They concluded he had probably been killed by a grizzly. Their suspicions were confirmed after the film in Precup's camera was developed. There were two photographs of what experts judged to be a three-year-old grizzly, of which it was agreed that "Its appearance and behavior indicate the bear was undernourished." Investigators noted no sign of struggle, suggesting the bear most likely snatched the man while he was asleep, probably having a nightmare.

On the other extreme, the bloody clothes, belt, sheath knife, and a few ribs aggregating the mortal remains of Jay B. L. Reeves were found beside a stream literally swimming with spring salmon, a favorite grizzly food, which fact must have escaped the bear's notice.

You may have noted from earlier examples that people involved in predatory attacks tend to do a lot of screaming. Never having personally been killed by a bear, I can't say for sure why this is, but I suspect it is probably because it hurts like hell. Grizzlies, being poorly versed in human anatomy, are a bit clumsy in their techniques of killing (another trait shared with African lions), and it sometimes takes a while to let out your stuffing. Being omnivores, bears are predators on only a part-time basis and have not developed the assassin-quick efficiency of the big cats. Oh, they do pretty well with moose, elk, livestock, and the like but seem uncertain of what to do with a human once they catch up with one. Usually they just start biting, randomly pulping arms, legs, or whatever else is handy until they luck onto something vital or the victim stops struggling. This isn't always the case; sometimes they just start eating. Either way, it can take a very, very long time to die, which victims of predatory attacks do almost invariably; survival after passing through a predator's digestive tract is practically unheard of.

Another possible reason for enthusiastic vocalizations by bear-attack victims is simple terror. It has been said that it is instinctive for humans to fear bears. If true, it may trace to some of our earliest experiences with the giant short-faced or "bulldog" bear, *Arctodus simus*, a predatory Pleistocene monstrosity that could, and probably did, eat giant vegetarian cave bears (*Ursus spelaeus*) to cleanse its palate between mastodons. The first This Happened To Yours Truly stories, recorded in cave paintings by Cro-Magnon outdoor writers, featured hunts for deer and other herd animals on the well-lit frontal walls. But the deep, dark, dank recesses were reserved for bear tales, which may have been stored in like manner deep within our minds. Carl Jung, the Swiss psychiatrist who narrowly lost the Founder of Modern Psychoanalysis title to Freud (who probably had a better press agent), observed that mankind's collective unconscious contains the image of a bear with glowing eyes. Be that as it may, it seems to me only natural to fear something of such size and power that it can bite your head off with the ease of a kid decapitating chocolate Easter bunnies, and that screaming would be quite normal and even expected of the process.

We can assume at this juncture to have answered with reasonable satisfaction the question of why predatory attacks occur (hunger), but inquiring minds will still yearn to know why one person would be chosen over another as tonight's entree. It's a good question, actually, the answer to which could prove more than casually interesting when planning your next vacation. Unfortunately, there isn't one, at least not one likely to be proven by the empirical method. The most common explanation is the presence of food, garbage, or associated smells on or near the person's person, but that dog don't always hunt. In each of the cases thus far examined, such olfactory provocateurs were officially ruled out after intense scrutiny by official boards of inquiry. And even if it were always true, why would a bear step over one or more humans ringed quaking in their sleeping bags around a campfire, sniffing each one, to single out one individual who smells no more or less strongly of toasted marshmallows than the others? Well, for what it is worth, I have a theory.

To fully understand Zaidle's Theory of Human-based Ursine Gastronomic Gratification, or THUGG, we must go back to 1967 or thereabouts, on a journey that leads from the labyrinthine hallways and cipher-locked doors of a U.S. defense contractor to the steamy jungles of Southeast Asia (better known as Vietnam), where we will examine the inner workings of a top-secret defense project. Code name: Batboy.

American Man-Killers

Pardon the hype. I've always wanted to write a best-selling techno-thriller but just don't seem to have the knack. Anyway, Project Batboy, which really was its code name, was not a nuclear thingamajig or CIA torture device but an electronic nose that could smell people. No kidding. Batboy consisted of a gas chromatograph paired with a radiotelemetry unit that could essentially tell the difference between meat-eaters and herbivores by scent. It operated on the theory that American troops, whose diets included a lot of red meat, would have different scent signatures from the mostly fish- and vegetable-eating VC and NVA regulars. The units were dropped into the DMZ via parachute, where they sniffed out nearby herbivores and then sent a radio signal to an artillery fire-control base or Navy ship, resulting in a high-explosive shell barrage that would obliterate any life form within half a mile. A lot of enemy troops were killed that way, as were quite a few peasants, water buffalo, and other non-carnivorous miscellany, which is why the project was abandoned and rarely spoken of except in very select circles.

Rest assured the foregoing revelation in no way compromises national security, Batboy having been long ago declassified. In fact, an August 1984 article, "Scent of the Carnivore," by Langbourne Rust in *Sports Afield* magazine, centerpieced Batboy in a theory concerning human scent and bowhunting. It raised this question: If predators smelled differently because of their diets, would a vegetarian hunter smell less threatening to sharp-nosed deer and other game? Rust had conducted a few field experiments, which were mostly inconclusive, but he opined that overall, going meatless for a couple of weeks prior to hunting seemed to make a difference.

It is noteworthy that many of the world's aboriginal people, including American Indians, have for centuries observed pre-hunt rituals involving fasting, sweat baths, consumption of pungent herbs, or some combination thereof. The famous Yana Indian, Ishi, friend and confidant to Saxton Pope of Pope and Young fame, would hunt only after several days of fasting and sweat-lodge internment. These practices, though religious in purpose, would undoubtedly reduce chemical-induced body scents associated with eating meat. In a similar vein, a predator experiencing a slump in his batting average may find it increasingly easy to approach prey unbetrayed by wind shifts, its tip-off carnivorous scent diminishing with each meatless day.

The question arises as to whether animals catalog scents into specific categories, *deer, cat, man, acorn, wolf, cougar,* etc., or do they generalize—*food, water, predator, non-predator,* and so on. Circumstantial evidence suggests the latter. Your average American white-tailed deer, which in its life has never seen or smelled a leopard, tiger, or African lion, will turn inside-out in its haste to flee a garden full of fresh, luscious veggies seeded with manure from these predators obtained at the local zoo. Likewise, hunting dogs trained on bobwhite quail adapt readily to grouse, chukar, and pheasant, the last two being foreign species imported into this country from overseas. Jersey cows are not deer, elk, or antelope, yet bears, cougars, and wolves recognize them as prey. Assuming this premise as true, and that Batboy proved rather conclusively that all herbivores smell more or less alike, even if bipedal, wouldn't it make sense that a vegetarian human lying next to a meat-eater would smell more like "natural" food to a bear or other predator, and therefore more likely to be chosen as prey?

I posed my THUGG hypothesis to several top bear gurus, including Dr. Herrero. Some of the responses were difficult to decipher through all the raucous laughter, but a few said it seemed at least plausible. Herrero, to my gratification, seemed intrigued. He said the question of vegetarianism has never been considered for statistical inclusion when profiling bear attacks, and indicated he might do just that in the future. If so, I hope he remembers who gave him the idea should a Nobel prize or other monetary remuneration be in the offing.

The dietary habits of the victims thus far examined are unknown. I do find it interesting, however, that Brigitta Fredenhagen's larder included granola bars, a staple among vegetarians, and that at least one source specifically mentions that another victim, Mary Pat Mahoney, carried no meat into the park. What this indicates is purely speculative, but it certainly provides food for thought.

One final aspect of THUGG deserves inclusion, though it sure won't win me any friends among the animal-rights activists, the Ingrid "Just Call Me Pig" Newkirk crowd. Did you ever stop to think that practically every member of any animal-rights organization you care to name *is a vegetarian?*

I think we have maligned the grizzly's character enough to establish that he is a talented man-killer and man-eater with a flamboyant style all his own. Predatory attacks are certainly the most spectacular form of grizzly misbehavior, but they are, thankfully, also the rarest. It therefore seems only fair to examine the other side of the corpse, from whence issue the putrid oozings of that other great classic of animal behavior: defense. A true case of self-defense is both understandable and justifiable from the bear's perspective, and is best illustrated by sanguine example.

In September 1907, Dr. Charles B. Penrose, the brother of Senator Bois Penrose of Philadelphia, shot and killed a nearly full-grown grizzly cub while hunting in the area today known as the Bob Marshall Wilderness, Montana. After dispatching the bear with three shots from his Mauser rifle, a magazine model imported from the Krupp gun works at Essen, Germany, the good doctor laid the gun on a rock while he went to examine the fallen bruin. Being largely unfamiliar with grizzlies, Penrose did not know he had shot a cub, albeit a big one, until informed of such fact by none other than the bear's extremely upset mother. While bent over examining the carcass, Penrose heard behind him a crashing of brush punctuated by the kind of bellowed scream only an enraged grizzly can make. He turned and looked full into a toothy maw big enough to accommodate a watermelon, backed by a quarter-ton of impending death rushing toward him from less than thirty yards. Houston, we have a problem.

Snatching up his rifle, Penrose fired two quick shots, emptying the magazine. The bullets went true, at least one piercing the heart, but the bear never broke stride.

2 • Bears

With speed borne of adrenaline-fueled panic, Penrose extracted a third cartridge—his last—from a pocket, chambered it, and fired just as the beast was on him. Now it was bruin's turn. As a warm-up exercise, she swatted the doctor a blow that sent him flying eight feet into a nearby shallow ditch. She then got down to the serious business of killing him, grabbing the stunned man in her jaws by the thorax to shake and worry him like a terrier with a rat before slamming him hard onto the rocks, adding a few more broken ribs to those already crushed in the steel-vise jaws. Not satisfied with her work, the sow jerked him clear of the ground again, this time by the head, ripping scalp, cheek, and throat tissue free of their moorings. Another body slam (a favorite grizzly technique) knocked out what little breath remained to Penrose, fuzzying his perception of what he was sure would be his final sensations as the bear grabbed him again. Fortunately, the doctor's good shooting had finally taken effect. The bear weakened and dropped him, then staggered off a few steps before falling dead.

The erstwhile bear hunter lay broken and bleeding, gasping cold air that chilled teeth exposed from wisdoms to bicuspids where a tusk had torn away his cheek. His right thigh looked like a badly carved roast, hand-sized pieces of shredded meat flapping and slipping aside each time he moved. His left wrist was twisted and broken, the bones protruding from the quivering flesh. The good news was that the inches-long tear in his neck evidenced no signs of arterial damage, so he wasn't going to bleed to death, at least not right away. In a few moments, however, Penrose would almost wish that he had.

After catching his breath and regaining some of his senses, the man sat up to take stock of his injuries and try to decide what to do. Wounded to the point of death, miles from companions who didn't know where he was, and two days travel over rugged terrain from anywhere even remotely resembling civilization, Penrose was not having a good day. Just when it looked as if things couldn't get any worse, thcy did. Suddenly, a crashing of brush signaled the rapid approach of another heavy animal. Sure enough, a third bear, probably the sow's other cub, came boiling out of the trees headed straight for Penrose. So much for optimism. The grizzly ran up to the gore-covered man, stopping short just feet away. It sniffed and growled around him for several minutes, trying to decide what to do. It examined with its nose the bodies of its dead mother and sibling, then gave the man one more sidelong look before dashing off into the forest with a cry of mixed rage and fright.

I won't go into the nightmarish details of Penrose's ultimate rescue and recovery, except to say that once back in camp, he personally directed his own first-aid treatment by firelight, including the surgical removal of the shattered bones protruding from his wrist—without benefit of anesthetic—and survived to hunt another day. One other note: The February 1908 *National Geographic* magazine article in which this story first appeared did not mention what caliber rifle Penrose was using, but I believe it can be assumed with reasonable certainty to have been 6.5mm, a popular chambering among European gunmakers of the time and the bore of choice for many of that continent's armies. The fact that the bullets he used were described as "steel jacketed" reinforces a probable military connection. If correct, temptation's spiny rowels afflict me sore to chastise Penrose for deliberately taking on a grizzly with such puny armament. Rifles with bores only slightly smaller than train tunnels are all the rage among seasoned bear hunters. Even in the hyper-velocity Wide World of Weatherby, slugs under .33 caliber are considered worse than marginal; for close-in bear work, they are downright suicidal. If you have ever marveled at tales of African Cape buffalo doing the cha-cha on some poor bwana while carrying a couple of dozen extra pounds of high-velocity cuprous lead, allow me to illustrate by further gory example the grizzly's bullet-absorption talents.

In 1988, British Columbia hunting guide Roy Pattison was guiding a German woman on her first bear hunt. Late in the day, she killed a black bear with one shot from her 9.3mm Mauser, roughly equating .35 caliber and potent bear medicine. The late hour prompted Pattison to put off the skinning until the next day; he knew there were grizzlies about and didn't relish the idea of fooling around in the dark with a bloody carcass. The following morning, Pattison and his client wisely approached the kill site with caution. Lo and behold, a boar grizzly had taken possession of the black's carcass during the night, a huge specimen in the thousand-pound class. Maneuvering the client quietly into position, Pattison whispered instructions for her to shoot for bone in the shoulder to immobilize the big boy lest he get ideas. Well, Murphy, of Murphy's Law fame, was working overtime that day. The lady's scope was cranked up to nine power, and at the intervening distance of only twenty-five yards, all she could see was bear hair. Why she did not crank it down a notch or two I'll never know. Anyway, she didn't, choosing instead to make an uneducated guess as to where the cross hairs were and pull the trigger. She hit it, all right, but instead of falling down dead like a good bear, it threw a ground-zero-class temper tantrum, biting at the wound and roaring like an avalanche before flickering off into the willows without giving Pattison a chance to put in a finisher.

If you think only paid African bwanas have to root wounded, dangerous game out of the thick stuff, you don't know anything about bear hunting. In the finest tradition of the profession, Pattison put his client out of harm's way, checked the loads in his .30-06 bolt rifle—more than a bit light—and entered the thicket where half a ton of wounded, angry bear lay waiting. It didn't take long to find it; he spotted it almost immediately, lying half-hidden behind a log. He thought it must be mortally wounded to have gone to ground so quickly, and therefore not hyped to hostilities. He didn't know then that the client had shot the bear in the hump, a mass of muscle tissue grizzlies carry on their shoulders that has zero value in terms of shot placement. The fact that it laid up quickly after so slight a wound makes me suspect skullduggery in the form of an ambush. In any event, Pattison saw an easy chance to end a potentially messy situation. He lined up the open sights, aiming for the heart, and fired off a high-velocity greeting card. Instantly, the big grizzly was on its feet in a bear-line charge from less than sixty feet away.

Grizzlies charge with incredible speed, especially one nursing an industrial-strength grudge against somebody it holds personally responsible for all of life's little problems, and can easily cover sixty feet in the time it takes to say it. Once the introductions have been made, only a few seconds more are required for tearing the intended along the dotted lines unless dissuaded with rapid, accurate firepower. Pattison was doing his best to convince the hirsute widow-maker that it was all a big mistake, issuing 180-grain appeals for truce as fast as he could work the bolt. His second shot connected behind an ear, putting the bear down, but it was back up and coming again within seconds, madder than a snake and giving Pattison a look that spoke volumes about his immediate future.

The man slammed home one more bullet that caught the lower jaw just before the grizzly bulled into him. He went sprawling about ten feet from where he had been standing, his rifle smashed, flying who-knows-where from his hands. In a performance that would be envied by NFL nose tackles, the grizzly had hit Pattison with only its shoulder, initially forgoing the use of its teeth or claws. Though basically unhurt, the guide did not know where his gun had landed, which seemed awfully important at the time, so you can understand his being somewhat nervous at seeing the big grizzly haul up and swap directions, bellowing like a runaway locomotive as it came for him again. Greatly motivated, Pattison scrambled to his feet and lit out for the nearest climbable tree some fifty feet away.

He didn't make it.

When the talk around bear hunters' campfires turns to getting caught up with by a grizzly, the consequences are commonly described as getting a certain part of your anatomy bitten off. I digress with this bit of trivia to point out that I am not being deliberately crude or indelicate in relating what next happened to Pattison, for in his case it was quite literally true. *The bear knocked his ass off with a single pawstroke!* Or half of it anyway, ripping loose the large *gluteus maximus* muscle on his left hip when it caught up with him. The tremendous blow sent the guide flying once again to land bleeding in a crumpled heap about ten yards away. The enraged boar was on him in a heartbeat, lifting the man clear of the ground by an ankle to shake him with bone-jarring ferocity. The guide knew he was in serious trouble with no apparent way out. Already badly wounded, his gun lost, and help from the client unlikely since he had sent her back to the truck parked a mile away, Pattison figured this was going to be the big IT. Salvation appeared in an unexpected form, however, when Pattison's German shepherd came on the scene. The dog, named Radar, had demonstrated effective bear-handling talents on more than one previous occasion, and this would prove his best performance yet. Frantically barking and nipping at the bear, Radar distracted it from Pattison sufficiently that it loosed its hold and dropped the man from its jaws. It looked around at the intruding canine for a few seconds, seeming confused, then swaggered off into the forest, grumbling in four-letter Bruinese.

Pattison was delighted with this turn of events and on the spot promised Radar a little something extra with his kibbles that night. But what of the bear? Was it truly gone, perhaps lying dead nearby? Or was it watching from behind that jumble of deadfall over there, taking stock before launching another big spring sale? Not knowing which, Pattison figured his chances of getting out of there alive would be much improved if he could find his gun. He searched for quite a while, glancing nervously over his shoulder every microsecond or two, but could not locate it. He finally gave up and started hobbling back up the trail leading out to the road. He later told me that, given the difficulty of walking with a shattered ankle and dislocated backside and the very real possibility that the bear might be waiting behind the next tree, it was the longest mile of his life.

Later that day, Pattison drove himself to the hospital, where he spent three weeks recovering from injuries he initially thought not too serious. The bear, by the way, was in far better shape than him; it returned that night to feed on the black-bear carcass, despite having absorbed an aggregate 7,200 foot-pounds in the kisser at point-blank range.

The story doesn't end there. The following year, Pattison was guiding the same lady client when she wounded *another* grizzly. While searching for it with assistance from the woman's husband, who was also a client, Pattison spotted another bear closely matching in size the one that had nailed him. Without going into the blow-by-blow details, this bear charged and in the process absorbed a total of fifteen rounds from the combined firepower of two .30-06s fired by Pattison and another guide, plus the client's .303, before taking leave of its mortal coil. While skinning it out, the guide found two old bullet wounds, one in the jaw, the other behind an ear. He cut out the bullets, flattened to the size of silver dollars against the bear's skull but intact enough to be later miked at .308 inches and weighed at 180 grains. They were Pattison's bullets, the ones he had fired into this same bear when it charged him the previous year. Oh, by the way, he did follow up the lady's most recent contribution to his ever-increasing blood pressure—with a borrowed .458 Winchester Magnum—and settled its hash without further incident. Pattison now uses a .338 Winchester Magnum exclusively.

I didn't really intend for this to develop into a dissertation on terminal ballistics, but since we are in the neighborhood anyway, and seeing as how many cases of bear-bite develop under hunting circumstances, we might as well go the full treatment. The Penrose and Pattison cases, both classic examples of provoked, defensive attack, illustrate clearly the importance of ballistics where grizzlies are concerned. Several cases exist of hard-hit bears covering more than one hundred yards with nothing more than bloody applesauce where their hearts used to be, and still having enough moxie to kill the man or men who shot them. In one case, a grizzly killed two men of a three-man party and badly injured the third after being shot a total of seven times in the chest, twice in the heart. Even head shots do not guarantee a passing grade on your survival test, especially when inadequate calibers are used. For illustration, let's examine the saga of Old Groaner.

The story begins in 1923 on the upper reaches of Alaska's Unuk River, where a trapper named Jess Sethington, a Canadian from British Columbia, was spending the winter collecting furs. The day he set out from Ketchikan, armed with a .33-caliber rifle and a .38 pistol, was the last anyone ever saw of him; he simply vanished without a trace. Ten years later, the Johnstone brothers, Jack and Bruce, were seeking gold up the Unuk and had camped along Cripple Creek in the same area Sethington had operated. In the night they heard strange sounds in the alders around camp, an eerie, groaning wail neither of the experienced woodsmen could identify. The haunted cry continued nightly for some time, the men speculating—vividly, I imagine—about its source. Over time they traced the spooky sounds to a very large and most unfriendly bear they appropriately dubbed "Old Groaner."

The Johnstones had quite a few encounters with the bear in their annual trips up the Unuk, including several instances of it stalking them as they worked around camp. They had been lucky always to see it in time to drive it off with shots over its head before it could close in for a charge, but it was getting smarter, and bolder. Bruce finally killed it when it ambushed him from cover at just ten feet, shooting from the hip with the rifle's muzzle almost touching the bear's neck. Now able to examine the grizzly up close, the Johnstones solved the mystery of its curious groaning. Its head was horribly deformed, big hunks of skull having been shot away in some previous encounter. In healing, the tissues had contracted and twisted the muzzle into a grotesque horror-mask with protruding, misshapen teeth. The shattered right jaw hinge had healed in a way rendering normal operation impossible, partially accounting for the eerie quality of the bear's pained wails. The Johnstones dug five bullets out of the skull, two from a .33-caliber rifle and three .38 pistol slugs, the same combination carried by Jess Sethington. The bullets' positions showed they had been fired upward into the skull through the lower jaw. It doesn't take a lot of imagination to figure out what position a man would have to be in to shoot from that angle. The mystery of the vanished trapper had been solved as well.

Though Sethington's .33 rifle sounds like a real stomper, it was probably the now obsolete .33 Winchester chambered in an 1886 lever model, a nothing cartridge by modern standards at something less than 2,000 foot-pounds of muzzle energy with a standard 200-grain bullet. Compare this against the 2,700 fps and 2,400 foot-pounds of a modern 180-grain .30-06 factory load—which turned fink on Roy Pattison—and I think you will see my point.

Obviously, choosing firearms for hunting or defense against bears requires greater attention to caliber, velocity, and bullet-construction details than does selecting a white-tailed deer gun. As a general rule, bigger is better, the weight of a large slug having the momentum to ensure adequate penetration, but not to the point of overgunning with resultant recoil-induced flinching, which may cause discomfort or death when an incensed bear is involved. Velocity is important only to the extent necessary to aid penetration, or bone-breaking when called for, but should not be excessive lest instability or "cratering" develop. Most of the over-.30-caliber magnums are adequate, with the newly "discovered" .338 Winchester, which has been around since 1958, being quite popular. The venerable .375 H&H Magnum has proven safe and effective in clinical trials on both Alaska's and Africa's biting machines. Some bear-hunting guides carry .458s for backing up clients, which is not a bad idea, and if you already have one, there is no need to look for something else. I wouldn't recommend it as a first purchase, though, for reasons of recoil previously cited.

Bullet performance, or more properly a lack of it, can in some instances eclipse the presumed advantages of a lot of *whumph.* All bullets are not created equal, and many designs that do well on deer and other thin-skinned game have a depressing tendency to come apart on striking a bear's thick hide and hair, die with a strangled whimper in the hawser-thick muscles, or flatten against massive bones before reaching anything the bear considers vital. Premium loads specifically designed for dangerous game are the hands-down best choice, although handloads properly constructed with something good and tough in the business end, like Barnes or Nosler Partition bullets, cannot be discounted. On the solids vs. softpoints question, I do not have the personal experience to make suggestions one way or the other, having never fired a solid bullet at game in a lifetime of hunting. I can tell you, based on what I have learned from others, that stacking the magazine with alternating solids and softpoints is probably a good strategy. If you ventilate your bear from a nice, safe distance, which usually means having time to place your shots precisely, that first softpoint out the spout will usually demolish bruin's boiler room with no resulting hostilities. If, on the other hand, things turn nasty and yon carnivore decides to get up close and personal to discuss your ill manners, the solids will assure bone breakage or penetration lengthwise from adenoids to anus when necessary, with ensuing disruption of all vital organs in between.

Now we come to the part you've been waiting for, the defense guns. All those marvelous foot-pounds of high-velocity how-de-doo waiting snug in their chambers to lash out with the violence and lethality of a constipated cobra. You know what I am talking about, the Big Daddy of hand-held mayhem, the poor man's artillery piece, the stomping, slicing, dicing, unleashed fury of the mighty .44 Magnum, "The Most Powerful Handgun in the World!" Well, I've got sad news for you, friend. It ain't. As far as man-bear peacekeeping is concerned, the .44 is a wimp.

Hold on, now. Before you run screaming "Heresy!" and making supplication at the tomb of Elmer Keith, wipe the foam off your lips (most unbecoming) and pay attention while I explain. Yeah and verily, the .44 is a good cartridge as handgun cartridges go. At the time of its introduction back in 1953, it was indeed the most powerful *production* handgun in the world. These days it ranks way down on the totem pole beneath such wildcats-turned-legitimate-fire-breathers as the .454 Casull and .30 Herrett, and even the .45-70 U.S. Government cartridge, for which some masochistic soul designed a single-action, five-shot revolver weighing six pounds and having a six-inch barrel, the muzzle blast alone of which could at least deafen if not defoliate a bear at ten yards.

Of course, in a life-or-death dispute, handguns beat rocks or fists all hollow, but they simply do not measure up as first-line defensive weapons against a determined grizzly; they just don't have the *chutzpah.* The .44 Mag, for instance, packs a maximum of only 1,200 foot-pounds or so right at the end of that impressive-looking muzzle, and if you have a murder-bent grizzly that handy, all the foot-pounds in China probably won't make much difference. You may get lucky, of course, as did Jerry Austin of Saint Michael, Alaska, one day back in the 1960s, when he had to cool a charging grizzly at close range with his .44 Magnum. The 180-grain Nosler bullet deflected off the monster's skull and lucked into its neck, dropping the bear in its tracks. *Ah-ha! A testament to the .44's efficacy as a bear-stopper!* Did I mention that "close" range in this instance entailed the revolver's barrel being literally in the bear's mouth?

You can't get a much closer shot than from literally inside a bear, yet it was by purest chance that the underpowered slug deflected into something important enough to send Ephraim mortally packing. Anybody willing to let a bear get that close and depend on ballistic happenstance to make everything turn out all right is dumber than the luck to which he entrusts his life. What you want is something that will put out the critter's lights before its lack of dental hygiene becomes apparent, something relatively lightweight, compact, and quick-handling but with enough ballistic hair on its chest to do the job both here and yonder. I am pleased to inform you not only that such a weapon exists but also that you probably have one sitting in your gun cabinet. It is none other than the old, reliable 12-gauge scattergun.

Back in 1976, while vacationing in Glacier National Park, the wife of an editorial staff member of one of the Big Three outdoor magazines was perplexed at finding a couple of empty shotgun hulls. Knowing hunting was not allowed in the park, she showed them to her husband and asked for an explanation. His eyes popped at the words *Express Magnum 12 ga. Rifled Slug* imprinted on the green plastic casing. "These are what the rangers use on bears," he said, his voice trailing off as the full implications dawned on him. The night of 23 September that same year, twenty-two-year-old Mary Pat Mahoney had been dragged from her tent and eaten by a grizzly. Within hours, park rangers killed it and a sibling as they shared Mary Pat's body. The writer and his wife were standing on the very spot where the tragedy occurred. Somehow, the rest of their vacation seemed less enjoyable.

As to the shotgun's suitability for defense against things that go a lot more than just "bump" in the night, you couldn't find a better endorsement than that it is the weapon of choice among professionals whose jobs include sorting out known man-killers under less-than-ideal conditions. Slug-stoked scatterguns are standard-issue equipment for game wardens, biologists, park rangers, and foresters working in bear areas. Africa's professional hunting fraternity remains largely free of leopard scars thanks to the utility of buckshot. Little this side of an M79 grenade launcher can rival a shotgun in terms of short-range lethality. When things turn hairy, even a load of birdshot will turn skulls into bone-slivered oatmeal when applied at halitosis range. The best defense loads are, naturally, slugs and buckshot, preferably administered from the muzzle of a pump-action 12-gauge with the magazine plug removed. Bearing in mind the last-in, first-out nature of magazine loading, you want the first two or three out the chute to be slugs, followed by however many buckshot loads you can crowd in. The idea is that if you can't adjust a bad actor's attitude with a couple of solid, one-ounce persuaders at twenty yards or so, the buckshot takes over as the critter closes in, allowing a bit of room for stress-induced marksmanship errors.

The subject of buckshot has been addressed in great detail in other books written by people with eminently superior qualifications, and I see no reason to attempt a half-soling effort here. My best advice is that if you can find some Magnum Number 1 buck loads, cherish them as the life-preserving treasures they are.

American Man-Killers

Even with adequate armament, self-defense in a grizzly attack is a mighty dicey proposition. If you think buck fever is bad, imagine if you can the systemic jitterbugging produced when something the size of a Simmental bull is closing in on you with incredible speed from a distance about equal to the width of your living room, roaring like a *Tyrannosaurus* in need of Rolaids. The head, surrounded by a bristling corona of erect guard hairs, is about half-again as big around as the trash cans on your sidewalk. From it, two oddly small black orbs of eyes burn into yours with a fury best described as pure hatred. The tusks that will crush and tear you into something suitable for a hamburger grill a few seconds from now are yellow, and about the same size as your thumb. Three-inch claws, which can rip through a car door as if it were cardboard, rattle like ten tiny sabers each time the massive forefeet hit the ground. It is coming. And if you do not place a shot very precisely into the brain inside that bobbing, weaving head sometime within the next 100 milliseconds, your remains will later be delivered to your widow in a plastic bucket, or maybe two if you are a big fellow.

All of the foregoing presumes your horizons are about to get expanded in a location where firearms may be carried. If you're in a national park, forget it. The powers that be consider park visitors possessing firearms to be a greater threat to other patrons than are the bears, and in view of some of the Loony-Tunes they get, they may be right. Even among experienced guides and hunters, situations have developed in which the human victim got accidentally plugged by the individual doing the shooting.

In 1996, Ralph Borders underwent surgery to remove a .30-06 slug from his leg. Oddly, the bullet had been lodged in Borders' calf muscle since 1992, when his partner accidentally shot him during an attack by a sow grizzly while the two were on a goat hunt near Fairbanks, Alaska. The bullet had gone unnoticed by the doctors who originally patched the man up; they suspected the bullet wound was just another fang hole. The shallow penetration was credited to the slug's having slowed considerably after passing through the bear. Border had it framed as a memento.

With the guns safely stowed in the locker, what is a rational person armed only with his trusty Nikon supposed to do when faced with an impending bear? A few strategies that have worked include running, climbing a tree, playing dead, fighting back, and screaming a lot. A few that have *not* worked include running, climbing a tree, playing dead, fighting back, and screaming a lot. Nothing is ever pat where grizzlies are concerned, and what works in one situation may not in another. Discerning the nature and circumstances of an attack is critical if your future plans extend beyond the next couple of minutes. Since most bears do not respond well to questioning under even the best of circumstances, it is up to the individual to ascertain the facts beforehand through observation, preferably before the necessary sensory organs are removed or rendered inoperable.

Grizzlies will bluff-charge at times, usually with a lot of huffing, grunting, and teeth-popping after they see you from a distance and want to scare you off, lest you consume major portions of their recently acquired dead moose. Short-range bluffs are rare, but they do happen. The difficulty is in deciding just when a bluff turns into the real thing. There are several clues which, when properly interpreted, are fairly reliable indicators of a bear's intentions beyond the obvious of maiming or death. One of them is the ears.

If you have spent much time around dogs or horses, you are probably familiar with ear dynamics as indicators of less-than-benevolent intentions. Erect bear-ears in most cases signal curiosity, which the bear circling you or standing erect—the better to see and smell you by, my dear—will confirm. Once bruin gets a snoot full of your scent, he may *woof*, growl, or pop his teeth, indicating he is upset and would prefer that you vacate the premises. He may run away, approach slowly, or come for you at a dead run. Either way, backing away gently toward any handy, climbable tree is advisable. If at any time the ears swivel back to lay flat against the neck, you had best prepare to repel boarders because *Ursus horribilis* is about to demonstrate why he is so named. At this point, your options are to run, climb, or play dead, hoping the charge will not deteriorate into the real thing.

Running is always a dicey thing, since it tends to provoke chasing, and is usually employed as a means of reaching a tree, vehicle, or other refuge ahead of the bear. You absolutely cannot outrun a grizzly, whose speed is estimated at up to forty miles an hour in a short sprint. On the other hand, as the old joke goes, you don't have to outrun a grizzly if you can outrun whoever happens to be with you. By the way, that old bit about bears not being able to run fast downhill is a load of bull cookies. Don't try it.

Climbing a tree usually will put you out of harm's way, but there are no guarantees. Roy Pattison told me about a 900-pound boar with both shoulders broken that climbed twenty feet up a pine. Botanist Napier Shelton found out the hard way that "The bear who never climbs" does, a bit of information learned at the cost of five days in the hospital. A grizzly sow severely mauled Patricia Janz after climbing ten feet and dragging her to the ground. When playing dead didn't work, she finally got the bear off her by tweaking its nose! It is not common for mature grizzlies to climb trees, although young ones regularly do, but it happens often enough that experts recommend climbing at least thirty-three feet (the highest point a grizzly has been known to achieve) to ensure reasonable safety.

Playing dead is a second-to-last resort in situations where attack is unavoidable, typical of sudden encounter or defensive situations that leave no time for other options. Playing possum will not necessarily prevent attack but may shorten its duration. Some bears run up and start biting or cuffing the victim with their paws, often attempting to turn the person over to get at the face and soft underbelly, before deeming the threat neutralized and wandering off. Others may sniff and go *woof* for a while without ever making physical contact. Then there are those that just don't give a damn and will kill you anyway. When that happens, your best, last resort is to fight.

2 • Bears

An attack that persists longer than an eternity—or thirty seconds, whichever is greater—against a person not screaming or actively resisting indicates one of two possibilities: The bear is dead set on outright annihilation, or it intends to eat you. Either way, playing dead will get you that way for real, and the only other option is to fight back as if your life depends on it, because it does. Right now, you have a piece of knowledge that could have meant the difference between literal life or death for quite a few people over the years. In the extremely rare event of someone beating the odds and surviving a predatory attack, fierce resistance or aggressive third-party intervention is invariably credited. Strangely, some grizzlies seem tentative almost to the point of timidity in their approach to people-purloining, rarely given to growling or other vocal volcanics in what may be exaggerated caution under conditions they find uncomfortable. Even slight resistance may be all that is needed to convince bruin that maybe this wasn't such a good idea. Persistence is all-important, as illustrated earlier by Ted Moore's backing a grizzly off its victim with a tent pole. Had Moore pressed his "attack," the chances are about even that Roger May would be alive today. Of course, it could have gone the other way too, with the bear getting two meals for the price of one. As I said, nothing is ever pat where grizzlies are concerned, but the odds favor survival when victims enthusiastically resist being eaten.

Coming out alive after grappling with a half-ton bear is sort of like a six-year-old prevailing against an NFL linebacker armed with a double fistful of switchblades and an industrial food processor for a mouth, but it has been done in a surprising number of cases. In several instances, attacks were broken off when the victim hit, kicked, twisted, or otherwise assaulted a grizzly's nose, the closest thing to a soft spot there is on the critter. Eye-gouging with fingers or foreign objects has worked in a couple of cases. I can find no record of anyone attempting to attack a boar grizzly's testicles, possibly because they are out of reach six or more feet away as the bear stands over you, and it may not be effective anyway. If

101

you have any practical experience in this area, please let me know, assuming you can still hold a pen to write.

Any kind of weapon will tilt the odds in your favor. A number of people have driven off or killed grizzlies with knives, such as James Moore, cited at the beginning of this chapter, and the great general Stonewall Jackson. Wade Hampton, the famous frontier bear hunter, killed between thirty and forty bears with a knife—on purpose, no less—and was injured only once! Alexie Pitka, an Athabaskan Indian, knifed a bear to death as it stood over him during a discussion of the finer points of nonlethal marksmanship. More recently, in October 1995, Bob Nichols killed a 300-pound grizzly with a hunting knife after it attacked him unprovoked while he soaked his feet in a stream near Fort St. James, British Columbia. He blamed the attack on the bear being attracted by his smelly feet. Other weapons that have proven effective include axes, swords, hot water, hats, ropes, thermos bottles, and, in one extraordinary case, the broken half of an aluminum hunting arrow. The arrow incident was unusual in many respects, particularly as it relates to timing and location, and fits well in the "weird" category.

Much conjecture, correct or otherwise, has been written about hunting guide Ed Wiseman killing a 500-pound sow grizzly with a hand-held arrow as it mauled him in an unprovoked attack in the San Juan Mountains of Colorado in 1979. Wiseman, tagged as "the man who killed the last Colorado grizzly," was accused of lying about the incident and investigated by the U.S. Fish & Wildlife Service with an eye toward prosecution under the Endangered Species Act. He was ultimately exonerated, but only after enduring six months of seemingly endless questioning, lie-detector tests (which he passed), and bureaucratic entanglement that included being advised of his rights as he lay recovering in a hospital bed. Not trusting the official or published versions of the event, I contacted Ed directly at his Colorado home, where he still operates a successful guide and outfitting business. Here is his story:

It was a glorious Colorado afternoon. Even John Denver would have overdosed on the symphony of colors and scents pervading the mountains in a teasing prelude to autumn in the high country. From the top of a small spruce, a red-tailed hawk keened a blade-edge cry that quivered and hung against the bluffs at the far end of the canyon. Below, a small stream marking the headwaters of the Navajo River chuckled among aspens glinting gold around the edges in sunlight pure and unfiltered in the thin mountain air. A fine day to go elk hunting, and that's just what Ed Wiseman and his bowhunting client, Mike Nederee, a Kansas farmer, were doing.

Nestled between mountain peaks, the shallow canyon formed a natural funnel that emptied against a sheer, 300-foot bluff at the far end—a perfect setup for a drive. With Nederee stationed against the bluff, Wiseman worked his way down a game trail contouring along a little shelf on one side of the canyon. Any bulls lounging in the shaded timber would push down ahead of him right into the client's lap. From the acute angle of the sunshafts, Wiseman knew this would be the last drive of the day. He also knew the outlook was bright for his client to arrow a good bull, so he took his time, careful not to press too hard and spook the elk into wild flight, instead gently nudging them down the canyon. As he moved, he caught a flicker of movement about thirty yards ahead and slightly to his right: A grizzly was boiling straight down the trail toward him.

Wiseman doesn't remember just what happened between the time he first saw the bear and when he was laying flat on his back with it on top of him, a period of one second or less. He does recall clearly the sound of the grizzly's teeth crunching down on his right leg, and the odd feeling of intense pressure suddenly releasing with a meat-cleaver *snick* as the flesh tore away. His mind worked clearly in spite of the impossible circumstances—attacked by a grizzly where there were no grizzlies—and he remembered he was supposed to play dead. Turning on his side and drawing up his knees to protect his stomach and chest, clasped hands protecting the back of his neck and head, he lay perfectly still. The bear continued savaging his lower leg, occasionally lifting him completely clear of the ground to shake him until his teeth rattled. Suddenly, the shaking stopped and he thought it was over, but the bear was just shifting its grip. With renewed vigor, it then grabbed him by the right shoulder. Tiring of this, it switched back to his leg again.

Wiseman doesn't know how long he lay there with the bear chewing his leg and shoulder into chili meat, but he recalls thinking, "This thing isn't going to stop until I'm dead." It was about then that he felt something cool and smooth beneath his left hand, the aluminum shaft of one of his hunting arrows fallen from its bow-mounted quiver, the broadhead-tipped business end pointing toward the bear. He picked it up and in one fluid motion rolled onto his back and thrust at the bear's neck. The broadhead razored in, the shaft snapping in two when the tip jammed against the third cervical vertebra in the neck. The grizzly didn't like that very much, which it demonstrated by dropping the man's leg and performing its Cuisinart impersonation on his right hand and forearm. Wiseman drew out the broken shaft and punched it hard against the bear's chest as it straddled him. He felt it slide slickly all the way in up to his fist, entering the chest cavity through what amounted to the bear's right armpit between the second and third ribs, ranging upward to sever the aortic artery above the heart. That did it. The bear quit the broken man, moved off a little way, and lay still; it was dead within three minutes from massive internal hemorrhaging.

Wiseman does not recall whether he or the bear made any vocalizations during the attack, but one of them must have said something—probably unprintable—for Nederee heard the battle and came running. The guide sent the client for the horses and, with his help, mounted up and started riding back toward camp. But the shock wore off before they had gone two miles, and Wiseman, sick and in terrible pain, could not continue. It was getting dark by then, the trail ahead treacherous even in daylight, so the men stayed the night in a small mountain meadow, the client leaving at daylight to summon help. Wiseman lay bleeding on the mountain for fifteen hours before a helicopter arrived to carry him out.

The ensuing investigation by U.S. wildlife authorities was right out of a Keystone Cops episode, a comedy of errors that included the crashing of two helicopters, parts of the bear being lost or discarded, and its carcass decomposing on the mountain for nearly a week before recovery. Federal investigators never visited the scene of the mauling, yet concluded skullduggery was involved and sought evidence with which to prosecute Wiseman. They didn't find it, and the case was stamped "CLOSED" after six months. Closed for them, maybe, but not for Wiseman. For nine months, the man battled secondary infections and abscesses that resulted from pathogens on the carrion-eating bear's teeth, muzzle, and claws, enduring four surgeries, skin grafts, and the removal of splintered bone fragments floating around in his body.

Of all the questions raised over this incident, one that has never been satisfactorily answered is where on earth that bear came from. Grizzlies had long since been labeled extinct in Colorado. It seems highly unlikely that one could have escaped for long the notice of one of the hikers, nature photographers, trout fishermen, game wardens, and biologists (not to mention an annual phalanx of hunters) that regularly invade southwestern Colorado in great numbers. You'd think somebody would have at the very least seen and recognized a track sometime during the bear's life. Neither is it conceivable that it had recently migrated into the area over the vast distances from Montana, Wyoming, or Canada. The most likely answer would seem to be that someone released it there, but authorities ruled out that possibility based on the fact that the bear's teeth did not display the characteristic chipping of captive animals that bite the heavy wire of their enclosures. There is one theory that may answer many aspects of the equation:

PBS still occasionally airs a documentary, made some years ago, about a female grizzly bear raised and subsequently released into the wild by the film's producer (guess where) at a time compatible with the date of Wiseman's mauling. That the producer's philosophy regarding wildlife is openly anthropomorphic suggests he might have taken extraordinary precautions against the bear's injuring itself or damaging its teeth while caged. In fact, as I remember it, he kept it in the house most of the time.

This would certainly account for the lack of clues to indicate prior captivity in the bear that tagged Wiseman, if it was in fact the same bear. At this stage in the game, it is all rather academic anyway. As a side note, knowledgeable people have long held that many of the "wild" scenes depicted in this same producer's videos were obviously staged. Turns out they were right. In a 9 February 1996 *Denver Post* article, several former employees accused him of "staging fights between predators and filming supposedly wild scenes in cages." Is there any wonder why so many have so little respect for PBS wildlife programs?

A few other cases falling under the weird classification do so not because of extraordinary circumstances, but because of their outcomes. Old Groaner certainly qualifies, but since we used him elsewhere, let's take a look at what I like to call the Marie Antoinette bear.

A guide, his assistant, and their client were traveling by boat along a river in southeastern Alaska. The assistant had gone ashore in a skiff to pick blueberries when a big sow grizzly decided to evict him from what she considered her personal berry patch. The young guide, who apparently wasn't very bright, threw his pail at her and started running back to the beach. The other men watched helplessly from the anchored cruiser as the big sow caught up with the fleeing lad and, with a single pawstroke, knocked his head quite literally off. They later reported that the decapitated body continued running "about ten or fifteen more steps" before falling over at the water's edge. The bear, meanwhile, amused itself with batting the head around like a bloody, hirsute soccer ball.

Another riverine encounter, recorded by Charles J. Keim in *Alaska Game Trails with a Master Guide* also involved a guide and his assistant anchoring in a large cruiser just inside the mouth of a river, across from Excursion Inlet. A second cruiser was anchored nearby, its skiff missing, which they assumed meant the captain had gone ashore to hunt or conduct other business. They were just preparing to launch their own skiff for an upstream reconnoiter when the empty skiff from the other boat came drifting downriver and out into the open bay, from whence it would eventually drift out to sea. Figuring it had gotten away from the owner somehow, the two guides decided to tow it along and maybe save somebody a long walk back. When they drew alongside, they found the boat wasn't empty after all. A man lay unconscious on the floorboards, awash in a syrupy pool of his own blood. They concluded right away that a bear had hold of him; one leg was broken and chewed into bloody coleslaw, the back deeply lacerated, and the scalp torn loose to hang limp and wet over one ear and along the neck. The man, who was still alive, explained later that a grizzly had nailed him when he went to retrieve a black-tailed deer shot for camp provisions, not knowing the bear had claimed prior finders-keepers rights. After working him over, it picked up the deer carcass and left. The man then crawled and reboarded the boat, hoping to drift back down to his cruiser when the tide refloated the skiff. He hadn't counted on passing out from blood loss. But for some uncannily good luck, he would have drifted out to sea to join the ranks of the Missing But Not Necessarily Eaten.

As proof of the invalidity of the claim "the only good bear is a dead one," a man was nearly killed when the paw of a "dead" grizzly connected with his head as he and two companions rolled the bear over for skinning. He too was scalped, and lost one eye. Scalping, by the way, is among the most common injuries sustained by mauling victims.

We have barely scratched the surface of all that pertains to the tenuous state of man-grizzly relations. Chronicling all those dead and maimed in the name of good, clean grizzly fun would, and does, fill several books this size. One would think the polar bear (*Ursus maritimus*), being the grizzly's equal in size and reportedly of similar poor humor, would be the next closest rival, but it ain't so. The ice bear has undeniably killed and eaten a lot of Eskimos and even some whites over the years, adding some spice to the lives of quite a few explorers, hunters, weather-station staffers, and others who ventured into its frozen haunts. The thing is, old *Nanuk* just doesn't get that many opportunities to pop a human's mortal top, and even if he is pretty good at it when he gets the chance, I say we leave the poor guy alone. He has enough problems already. Besides, as nasty as he and Ephraim can be, both may actually be second-rate man-killers when compared to their smaller, less bellicose relative, the bear with the all-American moniker of *Ursus americanus*, better known as the black bear.

Few would argue that the black bear is of notably better overall disposition than the grizzly. Animal behaviorists credit this fact to the divergent paths of their respective evolutions: Black bears, living for the most part in forests, where escaping danger was a simple matter of shinnying up the nearest tree, evolved as pacifists of a sort, learning that peace, and hence survival, lay in avoiding confrontations. Grizzlies, on the other hand, up to and including the twentieth century, were predominantly dwellers of treeless plains and tundra, where survival depended on flat-out, no-kidding annihilation of threats to self, kith, or kin, there being nowhere to run to and nowhere to hide.

With the average black weighing about the same as your overweight mother-in-law, and of considerably better temperament, *americanus* seems a most unlikely candidate for toppling the grizzly from its throne as the King of Terror. The black's roly-poly appearance, augmented by sometimes hilarious antics, give him the deceptive qualities of a rather shy clown in a bear suit. But there was nothing shy or funny, except maybe in a gallows-humor sense, about the black bear that killed Collin McClelland.

In the summer of 1993, twenty-four-year-old McClelland was camped on a parcel of U.S. Bureau of Land Management property near Cotopaxi, Colorado, just north of the Arkansas River, where he worked as a freelance woodcutter. He had told friends about having problems with a black bear invading his camp but was not taken seriously. Several days later, they found his body, or what was left of it, in the forest just outside his camp. Since there were no witnesses, no one can say with certainty what happened. But based on the evidence, it went something like this:

The night of 10 August, McClelland was awakened by the bear, a 240-pound male, trying to break through his camper-trailer door. He fired through the door with a .30-06 rifle, grazing the predator nonfatally along the ribs. The enraged bruin then tore the door off its hinges and entered the trailer to settle accounts with McClelland. The trailer's inside looked like ground zero at a nuclear whiz-kid contest, indicating the woodcutter put up a pretty good fight. At some point the predator prevailed, dragged McClelland outside, and ate him. Two days later, Colorado Division of Wildlife officers trapped the bear in the same area; pieces of McClelland found in its digestive tract proved the officers had found the right bear.

It is tragedies like this that have prompted several knowledgeable wildlife professionals and experienced amateurs to opine, "Although the grizzly is by far more ill-tempered and formidable, the black bear has mangled and killed many more people than its larger relative," as expressed by Edward R. Ricciuti in his book, *Killer Animals*. Not everyone agrees with this view, but there are several possible reasons why it could be true. The black's seemingly innocuous nature and smaller size make people less cautious, even contemptuous of him, and hence more vulnerable. That his modern range is about equal to that of the cougar, occupying forty-two U.S. states and twelve Canadian provinces and territories in numbers approaching one million, vastly increases the likelihood of an encounter. Herrero reports that over five hundred people were injured by black bears between 1960 and 1980. Most of those events were relatively minor, occurring during episodes of bear-petting or feeding in parks. As far as I am concerned, anybody idiot enough to pet or hand-feed a wild bear deserves what he gets, and doesn't merit elevation to attack or victim status—unless children are involved, in which case they are actually victims of their own parents' stupidity.

There are plenty of legitimate episodes to work with though, some suggesting other factors to explain the black's underestimated lethality, but it is not worth the literary sweat to reproduce them, since I already have a pretty good suspicion about the real reason. Though a black bear is more likely to take its business elsewhere than to cloud up and rain all over you if it finds you poaching huckleberries in its favorite patch, and a sow with cubs is more prone to follow Junior up a tree than to hammer you for surprising her on the trail, when a black bear does decide to try you on for size, chances are it is with one overriding purpose in mind: It wants to eat you.

You do not have to tell me about your Uncle Ethan fighting off that murderous black in the Poconos last year, after wounding it with a .22. Blacks will unquestionably fight back if you wound or corner them, and viciously at that. So will a grapefruit, squirting you in the eye for all it is worth when attacked with a spoon. But when it comes to attacking unprovoked in the dead of night (or, as Herrero says is more likely, the dead of day) to collect the main ingredient in a very ancient recipe, the little camp robber shines as a most accomplished felon. Of the black-bear-inflicted deaths analyzed by Herrero, of which he had only a handpicked twenty or so to work with, ninety percent were predatory attacks and most occurred during daylight hours. Why daylight attacks would more often prove fatal is anybody's guess, but it may have something to do with the boldness and determination required in risking a daytime assault. And make no mistake, blacks so inclined are of a most determined nature.

In May 1978, four teenage boys—Richard Rhindress, his brother Billy, and their friends George and Mark Halfkenny—were fishing for trout in Algonquin Park, Ontario. They split up late in the day, George going off by himself to add a few more speckled trout to the five he had already, with Mark and Billy teaming up for an assault of their own. Richard, the oldest at eighteen and the driver, was tired and decided to catch a few winks in the back seat of the car before the long drive home. He was a bit surprised but not overly concerned when he woke up around 6:30 P.M. and found the others had not yet returned. He yelled, blew the car's horn, and searched for quite a while before deciding something was amiss. He drove home to report what had happened, and a search party was soon organized. It didn't take long to find the bodies.

From the sign, George had been the first to die when a 276-pound male black bear stalked him from thick cover bordering the creek, killing him from behind while he fished. Later, when the other two came looking for George, the bear either killed them as they approached the cached body or intercepted and ambushed them along the trail, breaking their necks in instant death. The bear stored their bodies alongside George's, and was lying up guarding its windfall when discovered by the search team. Tissue from two of the bodies was found in its stomach. At no time had the victims been more than four hundred feet from their car.

North American grizzlies have been reported as killing or mauling as many as three men in a single defensive encounter. And according to a biblical account recorded in 2 Kings, a pair of Asian brown bears killed forty-two street punks in one fell swoop after they taunted the prophet Elisha about his male-pattern baldness. But only blacks seem to go on killing binges for purely culinary purposes, saving up the bodies for a rainy day. This may indicate that black bears are prone to frenzy or "surplus" killing of human prey, which grizzlies seem to do only where cattle are involved. In another case, after killing and partially eating forty-two-year-old geologist Leeson Morris, a black added the body of twenty-four-year-old Carol Marshall to its larder when she and a companion, Martin Ellis, went looking for Morris. It pulled the woman out of the tree she and Ellis had climbed, shook her by the neck until it broke, then cached her beside Morris. Ellis narrowly escaped the same fate and only because a man named Bud Whiting showed up and shot the bear to death.

Even though the victims in many of these cases attempted to fight off the attack, the fact that it didn't work should not be construed as indicating it is a bad idea. A vastly larger number of people in near-identical situations survived because they fought the son-of-a-biscuit-eater like there was no tomorrow, which there wouldn't have been if they hadn't. Cynthia Dusel-Bacon was everlastingly convinced of this truism in 1977 when a rather small black bear attacked and, while she played dead, ate most of the flesh from both her arms while dragging her around the forest for over an hour. Thanks to having a two-way radio, she was ultimately rescued and later fitted with prosthetic limbs.

Daylight attacks such as these seem to be relatively rare. It is beyond question that black bears will also prey on sleeping campers in the night, or at least attempt to, of which more than a few bloody examples exist. Almost all cases of nighttime attack I have examined occurred in campgrounds or other developed areas, suggesting habituation as a factor. Curiously, Herrero is of the opinion that habituated blacks are actually less prone to attack and even less likely to kill than are wild ones having little prior human association. He bases his idea on the fact that, of known black-bear fatalities, all but a couple occurred under circumstances that fairly ruled out habituation behavior. He also cites the thousands of annual interactions between people and black bears in various parks around the country that result in not so much as a hangnail. He may be right, but I am not so sure.

Though it's true that nearly every known case of black-bear-inflicted death took place in a remote setting and was a clear case of predation, at least eleven cases of attempted nighttime predation have been recorded in Glacier Park alone, equaling nearly half the number of known deaths. That the attacks were not successful does not obviate that they *could* have turned out the other way, and that park bears intimately acquainted with people were involved. My files contain dozens of similar cases:

In 1992, near Strawberry Reservoir, Utah, a black bear dragged nine-year-old Krystal Gadd out of a pickup camper in the middle of the night after breaking through a window. The girl's grandfather chased the bear down and smacked it with a flashlight, causing it to drop her and run off. In May 1986, seven-year-old Alene Sompas was asleep in the grassy center of a circular driveway surrounded by buildings near Durango, Colorado, when a black started dragging her off in her sleeping bag. She screamed and the bear left, only to return moments later and grab her eleven-year-old sister, Emily. Apparently confused or frightened by the chorus of shrieks that erupted from the four other campers, the bear dropped the second girl as well and vamoosed for good, leaving Emily with a crescent-shaped scar on her head that probably made her an instant celebrity at slumber parties. In another Colorado incident, a black bear yanked four-year-old Jeffrey Shawcroft out of his sleeping bag and started off with him, but called it quits after the boy's eighteen-year-old brother, Robert, pelted it with rocks.

We could fill a book with such incidents, but I think the point is clear. Black bears habituated to people *do* attack, and will obviously do so at night, particularly against children. How do you suppose the above incidents would have turned out had third-party assistance not been immediately forthcoming? I have a pretty good hunch. . . .

On the afternoon of 7 July 1948, three-year-old Carol Ann Pomranky was playing in her back yard near Sault Ste. Marie, Michigan, when from inside the house her mother heard her crying in obvious alarm. The woman ran to the back door and saw her daughter on hands and knees on the porch, one hand touching the screen, and a black bear lumbering up the back steps toward her. The bear growled once, showed its teeth, then grabbed the little girl by an arm and carried her screaming toward some nearby trees. The frantic woman ran for her husband's .32-20 revolver, but with her shaking hands could not load it. When she ran back to the door, the bear and little Carol Ann were gone.

A short time later, a rescue team assisted by tracking dogs found the child's pitiful remains, reclining as if asleep with her head resting against the base of an oak. Her shirt was rolled up beneath her arms; her pants were pulled down, untorn, around her ankles. The entire abdomen was gone, as were the fronts of both legs down to the knees, the bones plainly visible. An eight-foot length of intestine lay draped on some nearby bushes. The face was untouched. A healthy, 125-pound bear was killed shortly thereafter, in whose stomach portions of Carol Ann's body were found.

The same reasons cited elsewhere of poor record-keeping, witnessed incidents never reported, and the Great Unknown probably account for the relatively small number of recorded fatal attacks by black bears. I personally believe that a good number of deaths and maulings attributed to grizzlies may have involved black bears. In spite of the name, not all black bears are black. They come in a wide variety of color schemes ranging from almost pure white to blue, prompting a confusion of names such as cinnamon bear, Kermode or "ghost" bear, glacier bear, and Mexican bear, all of which are localized color variations of the same species. The brown, silver, and blond ones can look an awful lot like grizzlies, especially when viewed from distances great enough to make recognition of subtle, distinguishing features impossible. Quite a few national-park incident reports carry descriptions of "a big, brown bear" given by people who had arm's-length unfriendly encounters but could not say positively whether it was a black or grizzly. This is certainly understandable, since few people think to whip out their Field Guide to North American Fauna while a bear is actively giving them the once-over. That the grizzly's reputation as a bad actor is so well known makes him an instant suspect whenever blood is spilled, so Old Slewfoot probably gets away with it more often than not, snickering up his sleeve while Griz takes the fall.

In recent years, black bears have begun encroaching into human population areas to the extent that urban sightings are now rather common. Space does not permit a detailed treatment, but consider the following excerpts from newspapers around the country, a small sampling from my files:

Triangle Review, Ft. Collins, CO, 24 Aug. 1994: Rancher Kills Bear in Defense of Family and Pets— A ranching family in Kim, Colo. was terrorized in

2 • Bears

the night of July 28 by a female bear and a single cub. The rancher was forced to kill the bear as it attempted to get into the house to attack his wife. . . .

Rocky Mountain News, Trinidad, CO, 17 Aug. 1994: State Kills 33 Pest Bears—The Colorado Division of Wildlife's new 'tough love' policy for nuisance bears has resulted in the destruction of 33 bruins this year. By comparison, 20 bears were killed by wildlife officers in 1993. . . .

Sullivan Review, Dushore, PA, 9 Nov. 1995: Bear Sighted—Bill Rouse of North Turnpike area, Dushore, saw a 400-pound bear on his farm Tuesday around noon. It was headed toward Dushore downtown. . . .

Sunday Times, Scranton, PA, 19 Nov. 1995: State's Bear Population Tripled in Last 10 Years—Black bears wandering into urban areas of Northeastern Pennsylvania used to cause quite a stir but in recent years it has become somewhat commonplace . . . the state's bear population [is] . . . triple what it was in the mid-1980s. . . .

New York Times, New York, NY, 17 Dec. 1995: When Bears Get Too Close for Comfort—Bears have become a problem in the most densely populated state in the country . . . the main reason is simple: more bears.

Press & Sun Bulletin, Binghamton, NY, 8 Nov. 1995: Bear Visits, Dines at Candor Home—When Debbie Collier heard a noise about 9 P.M. Tuesday behind her West Candor Road home, she opened the door expecting to see a raccoon or woodchuck. She had to raise her eyes six or seven feet. "It was a huge bear," said Collier, a librarian at Candor Elementary School. . . .

Paradise Post, Paradise, CA, 21 Oct. 1995: The Three Bears Stop By for Grub—Kathy Rosetta has had a bear of a time getting rid of her uninvited breakfast guests. Two cub bears, she said, climb four flights of decks to partake of cat food left there periodically over the past few weeks. . . .

American Man-Killers

A few other black-bear headlines contemporary with the above include: "Wardens Kill Bear After It Bites Girl"; "Father: State Responsible for Son's Killing by Bear;" "Bear Killed After Attack." I do not see much to suggest the situation will improve anytime soon, rather just the opposite. There are a lot of huggers out there resisting wildlife managers' efforts to control bear populations, particularly in urban areas. A Maryland man, in a letter to the *Washington Post* regarding the state game department's suggesting that a black-bear hunting season was the best answer to ever-increasing bear problems said, in part, "I believe the bears do not have to be killed. I would suggest the Maryland Department of Natural Resources should trap the bears and ship them to Northwestern states." In Michigan, Citizens United for Bears, or CUB, as the local loonies call themselves, launched a petition drive to force a ballot referendum banning the use of hounds or bait in hunting bears. Similar efforts have succeeded elsewhere—California, Colorado, and Oregon among them. When a Colorado man killed a black bear that was trying to break into a neighbor lady's house, the outcry from bear-loving locals resulted in his prosecution, the DA promising to "take a hard line." If this man is convicted and jailed, do you think they will parole a child molester or a murderer to make room for him?

I, for one, do not wish to live in a bearless world, a sentiment shared by most people. Since bears will always be bears, however, this poses the interesting moral dilemma of accepting the fact that as long as bears and people share the same real estate, part of the price for their presence will be paid in human lives. We just have to decide if it is worth it.

ALLIGATORS

It came from the water, ten and one-half feet of dark malignancy exploding onto the beach in a depth charge of flying mud and debris. The great jaws slammed shut, and the reptile slithered backward into the lake, dragging its helpless victim in the grip of huge, spiked teeth. A few feet out from shore, as the jaws shifted for a better grip, the prey miraculously wriggled free and in panicked terror scrambled ashore. Seeing its meal escaping up the beach, the predator launched completely out of the water in pursuit, charging the last few feet on powerful legs to snatch its victim again, held better by the midriff. The monster boiled back into the lake and submerged, a small patch of bloody foam marking the spot as it powered toward deeper water.

American Man-Killers

As the last fading ripples lapped quietly against the bank, life along the lakeshore resumed as if nothing had happened. A pair of mockingbirds swooped and chandelled above the mangroves, wings flashing gold at the edges in the backlight of a sun snagged between two palm trees to the west. Dragonflies hovered like tiny helicopters over the surface, their fuselages flickering from electric blue to gunmetal gray as they dived into the shaded lairs of insect prey. A great blue heron stalked the shallows on spindle shanks, probing for small aquatic life flushed from hiding by the disturbance. And somewhere out beneath the still, cool waters, a four-year-old girl struggled out the final seconds of her life, forced at last to breathe, in dark, watery death, anchored to the bottom in the jaws of a saurian nightmare.

It was around midnight on 4 June 1988 when wildlife officers killed the alligator after spotting it cruising southwest Florida's Hidden Lake, the whitewashed corpse stark against the black hulk as it powered away from the lights. In deference to reader sensitivities, the published reports didn't come right out and say whether any flesh was eaten, but why would it matter anyway? Erin Glover would still be dead.

It should come as no surprise that any creature as thoroughly evil-looking and so marvelously equipped to do something about it as is the American alligator (*Alligator mississippiensis*) would be a man-killer. What else would you expect from something that slithers around in primordial swamps, viewing the world through vertically slit, silver-gray eyes that reflect blood-red in the night; attacks its prey from ambush, swallowing it whole or in big, bloody chunks twisted off the way a Frenchman tears off a piece of bread; and is more cold-blooded than your mother-in-law. Yet, based on official representations of his accomplishments, the alligator would appear to be an underachiever.

In a textbook example of statistics manipulated to mean whatever their compilers want, the gator's official human tally is routinely reported at "only seven since 1948." What they don't tell you is that all of them were

3 • Alligators

killed in Florida, and the first one was in 1973! Now, I find that more than just a little bit curious. Why on earth would a predator possessing such obvious capabilities decide to start eating people only just now, in the waning years of the twentieth century, and do so in only one of the ten states it inhabits? The truth is, Br'er Gator didn't just recently start eating people, but he did start eating them with greater enthusiasm after his previously canceled Diner's Club card was reinstated.

Official representations that no fatal alligator attacks predating 1973 have been documented is, to put it charitably, an obfuscation of the facts. The "only seven deaths" bit traces directly to the Florida Game and Fresh Water Fish Commission, the only agency with attack records, some of them gleaned from old newspaper reports dating back to 1948. Gratifying though it is to see them at least making the effort, I am frankly a bit surprised they have any records at all—not that there is any lack of scaly encounters to record but rather because of the way they pick and choose like a housewife squeezing tomatoes at a produce market.

If you think getting approved for a Platinum Master Card is tough, just try getting your name enshrined on Florida's official gator-victim list. With sworn testimony from the pope or another credible witness and verifiable physical evidence such as your half-eaten remains, preferably undigested prior to authentication by coroner and wildlife officials, you just might be accepted. Lest you think this assessment unfair, let's take a look at that infamous "first" fatality, sixteen-year-old Sharon Holmes, killed and partially eaten on 16 August 1973 by an eleven-foot, three-inch bull alligator.

The girl was swimming with her father, Bert, in a small lake in Oscar Scherer State Park in Sarasota County. She was standing a little way off in waist-deep water when Bert heard her scream "Daddy!" just once. When he turned to look, Sharon was nowhere in sight. Scanning the water, he saw a hand flash briefly above the surface, then disappear. With guidance from his wife standing on shore, Bert swam to the spot and started searching. He spotted the tip of a finger and dived after it, coming up with a handful of Sharon's hip-length blonde hair. He grabbed it with both hands and started pulling but was no match for the determined reptile. It yanked the girl away and swam off with her to some hidden hole. Several hours later, rescue divers recovered the body after violently contesting with the gator for possession. In its stomach, they found one of Sharon's hands and an elbow.

Given two eyewitnesses and the fact that the gator was found in possession of the body with sundry pieces thereof in its stomach, this seems to be a pretty clear-cut case to me, but apparently not to the state of Florida. It was nearly a week before officials grudgingly admitted that, yes, it appeared one of their highly prized and mostly misunderstood charges had actually gone and killed someone. Tourists need to understand that when an alligator demonstrates this kind of antisocial conduct, mitigating factors are usually involved—the gator's mistreatment in childhood, perhaps, or low self-esteem stemming from substandard socioeconomic influences. Great care must be taken before we apply stigmatizing labels like "man-killer." Why, the entire alligator community could be demoralized.

Surely, these or similar considerations account for the no fewer than six cases rejected from inclusion on Florida's fatality list. After all, the only evidence was the alligators' gastronomic possession of the bodies. One of them, a nine-year-old boy found mauled in 1957 in Brevard County, was ruled ineligible on the basis that he had drowned before the gators got him. Nearly the same thing happened again near Daytona Beach in 1959. If this was ever substantiated by an autopsy, my sources do not mention it. There's probably a good reason for that. Alligators kill terrestrial prey by drowning them; death from secondary causes, such as blood loss or a broken neck, is purely coincidental.

Postmortem evidence that a body was dead a considerable time before consumption doesn't mean much either. Fresh bodies too large to be swallowed whole cannot be effectively subdivided with a gator's rounded, picket-fence dentition, so kills are sometimes stored beneath underwater rocks or logs until decomposition softens them up enough for manageable chunks to be shaken or twisted off. Charming. That tooth-torn bodies may float out of the meat drawer and up to the surface probably accounts for the curious category of "accidental" gator-caused deaths, the body presumably abandoned when the dragon realized its error.

The 10 September 1978 case involving fourteen-year-old Phillip Rastrelli was initially entered on the "kill" list, then later reclassified as unconfirmed, the evidence deemed "inconclusive as to whether the victim's death occurred before or after the alligator attacked him." Far be it from me to dwell on semantics, but "attacked" hardly seems an appropriate term in the context of a person already dead. I seem to remember reading somewhere something about a "Freudian slip." Since I cannot recall whether the source was a psychology textbook or a Victoria's Secret catalog, I guess we'll have to skip it. Pity.

The point is not so much to beat up on Florida, even if the wildlife officials there deserve it, as to provide a basis for examining alligator misbehavior from a historical perspective, when even the modern numbers do not tell the whole story. I suppose it all comes down to what one does and does not accept as "documented" evidence.

It is completely understandable that the word of a living, half-drunk individual swearing his great Uncle Gus was killed and eaten by an alligator and still has the scars to prove it would be rejected as unreliable. Likewise, the writings of historical literary types noted for sensationalism should be viewed with skepticism. But personal notes, diaries, and journals of individuals other than politicians are routinely accepted by courts, historians, and physical scientists as accurate documentation of witnessed events. To do otherwise would mean rejecting the Lewis and Clark journals, the Anne Frank diaries, the Bible, and the works of Aldo Leopold, Alex Haley, and Theodore Roosevelt, to name a few. Ergo (a Latin term meaning "therefore" that I hoped would impart some class to my writing),

American Man-Killers

I see no reason, other than bias, for rejecting historical records of human deaths caused by alligators, or any other bestial nasties, as accurate documentation.

With this concept firmly in mind, we direct the court's attention to United States Department of Agriculture Technical Bulletin No. 147, *The Habits and Economic Importance of Alligators*, December 1929, by Dr. Remington Kellog, Assistant Curator of Mammals, United States National Museum. Suitably impressed? Good. Among other interesting observations, Kellog offers as authentic the reported death and presumed consumption of a man named King (no relation to the famed Texas ranching family) by an alligator in the Trinity River above Anahuac, Texas, sometime in 1836.

King and his family were part of a large crowd queued up to cross the river, fleeing toward Louisiana before the advancing Mexican Army. When the King family's turn came to board the one operational ferry boat, it became stuck in the mud under the weight of their belongings, and King was obliged to push off. Wading up to his waist and levering with a timber, he suddenly screamed and disappeared in a flurry of bloody foam, never to be seen again. Though no one actually saw an alligator take him in the muddy waters, something sure as hell did, and several of the large, toothy reptiles visible above and below the ferry crossing left little room for speculation. Now you know why your mother always told you to travel light and wear clean underwear.

Later, when the same group was camped on an island in the Sabine River near Nibletts Bluff, an alligator crawled up to a tent in the night, grabbed a fourteen-year-old black servant sleeping outside, and started dragging him by a foot toward the river. The servant, a "waiting boy" named Jack, vocalized his anxiety with sufficient vigor to rouse the occupant of the tent, one Dr. James Kerr, who would later become a central figure in the war with the Mexicans as an army officer, and the namesake of Kerr County, Texas. The white man bolted outside and, upon assaying the situation, snatched a brand from the fire and thrust it at the gator's eyes, causing it to release the boy and skedaddle back to the river.

The alligators must have had a mutual-aid pact with the Mexicans, for it was just a short time later that another young man from the same group was seized in the Brazos River near St. Filipe. As the gator swam off with him toward deep water, one of the other bathers, a young man named Ben McCulloch, proceeded to demonstrate the pluck that would later win him an army generalship and a Texas county named in his honor by leaping astride the big saurian and pummeling it about the head with his fists. Finding this ineffective, he switched to eye-gouging with his fingers, providing sufficient distraction that the gator released its victim and power-dived off in search of easier pickings.

I don't know, maybe I'm gullible, but when a highly qualified and respected researcher relates in that kind of detail events involving well-known historical figures, with no question of authenticity expressed or implied, that, my dear, skeptical friend, is what I call *documented*. In total, Kellog mentions no fewer than twelve attacks, seven fatal, and alludes to additional reports appearing "in the press from time to time of attacks on persons by alligators."

Despite obvious diligence, Kellog was by no means privy to all the alligator deaths on record at the turn of the century. I bet you can see the feathers in my whiskers already: In the moldering records ensconced deep in the courthouse of Natchitoches, Louisiana, a death certificate dated 10 August 1734 details the death and subsequent burial of one Jacques du Bois, a blacksmith found dead in the Red River with alligator wounds on his head and neck. The clerk from nearby Fort St. Jean-Baptiste, who filed the document, held that the man had been attacked while bathing in the river, since the body was nude when found.

Between what we already know as fact and what can be interpolated from Kellog's allusion to other cases reported in the press, it seems fairly safe to conclude that a helluva lot more than seven people have been killed by alligators. We'll never know how many, but circumstantial evidence suggests plenty.

Documenting deaths presupposes that someone witnessed and reported the deed, perhaps, or that physical evidence was found after the fact. Human remains as evidence of gator malfeasance tends to become mighty scarce if not discovered immediately. The crocodilian digestive system is extremely efficient: A birdlike gizzard does the grinding, and stomach acids powerful enough to melt down a bulldozer dissolve even the largest bones. Indigestible material is apparently retained indefinitely, not passed in the usual manner. Human jewelry is a staple item in the stomachs of man-eating African crocs, and dog collars show up fairly regularly in American alligators, sometimes with dates still readable on vaccination tags showing them to be quite old. Even if indigestible bits are eventually passed, who's to say that a wristwatch found in the bottom-mud of a gator hole wasn't lost there by a fisherman? On the other hand, if anybody ever dredges up a heart pacemaker or intrauterine contraceptive device, I suspect even Roger A. Caras would have to call that evidence pretty conclusive.

Mr. Caras, in the past a well-known TV animal commentator and now president of the ASPCA, makes an interesting statement in his book *Dangerous to Man* (revised in 1975, two years after Sharon Holmes was killed): "There are no authentic records of man-eating by American alligators." To my knowledge, he has never recanted the statement.

We can only speculate about the probable fates of the many folks who have simply disappeared in swamps and bayous over the years. Such macabre musings are a favorite pastime in gator country, as reflected by country singer Jerry Reed in the song "Amos Moses." Ruminating on the fate of a mythical Louisiana sheriff looking to arrest the alligator poacher named in the title, he wails, "Well, I wonder where the Louisiana sheriff went to? You can sure get lost in a Louisiana bayou!"

3 • Alligators

It has long been rumored that diehard Confederate troops, holed up in the swamps of Georgia, Louisiana, Mississippi, and the Carolinas after the war, amused themselves by feeding captured Yankee soldiers to the alligators. Perhaps this is what Johnny Horton, in the song "Battle of New Orleans," had in mind with "We fired our cannon 'til the barrel melted down, so we grabbed an alligator and we fought another round."

A related area worth examining involves the delicate subject of race. A number of historical writers, including Kellog, specifically mention blacks frequently falling victim to gators. An early French traveler, M. de la Coudreniere, asserted that alligators in Louisiana "feed on men, chiefly negroes [sic]." R. N. Lobdell, of the Mississippi State Plant Board, wrote in 1926 of a black child carried away by an alligator in 1916, snatched from his mother's side as she washed clothes on the shores of Alligator Lake in Bolivar County.

Considering that the alligator's traditional range is located entirely within the borders of what were once slave states, and the conditions in which blacks of that era worked and lived, it naturally follows that their exposure to potential attack would exceed that of whites many times over. Remember that Jack, Dr. Kerr's "waiting boy," was sleeping *outside* the tent. Remember, too, that white men didn't have to get up to their neverminds in alligator-infested water to drain the swamp and create more arable land.

Since slaves were often viewed as little more than cattle, one or two turning up lost or even seen taken by a gator would likely get only passing mention in the LOSSES column of the plantation ledger. Even in post-emancipation times extending well into the twentieth century, the death of a black man was rarely considered newsworthy, even under what we now consider the extraordinary circumstances of alligator attack. The very fact that some records do exist convinces me the actual number may be staggering, possibly hundreds.

Hundreds? Well, if traditional lore is correct and alligators of earlier times behaved with any similarity to their saltwater cousin, the Indo-Pacific crocodile, then, yes, possibly hundreds, maybe even a thousand. The saltwater croc (*Crocodylus porosus*) is reliably reported to have killed and eaten nearly 1,000 men at a single sitting, and in just one night! It happened during World War II on Ramree Island, just off the Burma Coast.

The estimated 1,000 Japanese occupying the island, retreating before allied forces, sought refuge in a mangrove swamp separating the island from the mainland, expecting rescue by the no-show Japanese navy. Bruce Wright, a naturalist and member of the British forces, recorded his impressions of the event from aboard a launch grounded in the swamp by the tide. His description, as reproduced in *Crocodiles and Alligators,* is as follows:

> That night was the most horrible that any member of the M. L. [marine launch] crews ever experienced. The scattered rifle shots in the pitch black swamp punctured by the screams of wounded men crushed in the jaws of huge reptiles, and the blurred worrying sound of spinning crocodiles made a cacophony of hell that has rarely been duplicated on earth. At dawn the vultures arrived to clean up what the crocodiles had left. . . . Of about one thousand Japanese soldiers that entered the swamps of Ramree, only about twenty were found alive.

Though I can find no record of American alligators slaughtering on such a massive scale, Kellog makes one cryptic reference to "Mrs. Trollope's story of the sleeping wife and her five babies killed and mangled by alligators." A case of mass gator attack against a lone individual occurred 3 October 1993 in Lake Serenity (cute name), Sumter County, Florida. Early on Sunday, neighbors spotted in the lake the body of seventy-year-old Grace Eberhart, presided over by a dozen or so alligators. Wildlife officials killed seven of them in efforts to recover all the missing pieces but never did find her right arm. The official cause of death was a broken neck, probably from one of the reptiles trying to twist her head off.

That bit in the Ramree incident about "spinning" crocodiles refers to a habit common to all crocodilians of tearing food into bite-size chunks by gripping what-ever is handy, usually an arm or leg, then spinning until the piece twists off. This behavior, made neces-sary by a lack of shearing or cutting dental hardware, accounts for why some gator and croc victims avoid answering the bell toll only to bid farewell to arms—or arm, as it usually turns out—when the saurian twists it off after failing to drag the body and soul into the drink. Twenty-one-year-old Chris Palumbo came within a tendon's breadth of learning this the hard way in August 1982, courtesy of a ten-foot Florida cutie.

It is entirely logical that an alligator's dietary needs increase proportionally with growth. Cute little baby gators cut their teeth on insects and small aquatic life, graduating to larger fish and frogs as they grow. Some-where around the three- to four-foot mark, they become capable of taking rodent-class mammalian prey. At this point of development, a curious thing happens. With the switch to red meat comes a marked change in temperament, from mild-mannered fish-eater to ferocious, meat-eating predator.

This Wally Gator to Godzilla metamorphosis was first recorded by Louisiana gator gurus Ted Joanen and Larry McNease in a report on alligator farming practices. They noted, "The behavior of alligators fed fish and nutria [sort of a poor-man's otter] showed obvious differences. Animals fed fish were shy and wary, whereas, those fed nutria were aggressive at the feeding sites and were generally more 'active' animals." Diet was also "found to have a significant impact on productivity. Alligators fed nutria consistently produced larger [egg] clutches and had higher nesting, fertility, and hatching rates than those fed fish."

Somehow I find disquieting the thought of a big, scaly lizard that is at its best on a red-meat diet, getting all the while bigger and more aggressive and looking for ever-larger quantities of meat, preferably in one easily caught package to minimize energy expenditure. Obviously, an alligator big enough to need meals as large as deer, pig, dog, or human is also big enough to do something about it. Opinions vary as to how big a gator needs to be for us to consider him a hazard to human health, but general consensus and bloody precedent suggest anything over six feet is capable of reducing me and thee to possession. Of the assembled gang that ate Grace Eberhart, the biggest measured nine feet, seven inches. In September 1977, fifty-two-year-old George Leonard got his cork pulled by a puny seven-foot female. Alligator, that is.

The point I am so delicately trying to make is that even though it doesn't take a big one to kill you, the likelihood of becoming *hors de combat* in the presence of a super-saurian is in general much higher. It therefore stands to reason that the more heavyweights you have lurking about, the more likely you are to be converted into post-digestive swamp muck. I wonder how big those water dragons in the days of yore—the ones observed to "feed on men"—really were. How does twenty feet grab you? Any way it wants to.

According to Louisiana records, two *Nimitz*-class swamp cruisers collected in 1718 measured nineteen and twenty-two feet respectively, and probably weighed close to a ton each. Get out a tape measure and extend it twenty-two inches. The span there represented is, by a happy coincidence, about equal to the width between a twenty-two-foot alligator's eyes, which is a handy reference for hunters to use in sizing gators in advance. Allowing for overhang on either side of the eyes' central location on the skull, that big boy could swallow a wide load like me without even thinking about it.

Twenty feet is mighty big for even a Nile crocodile (*C. niloticus*), let alone an American alligator, and specimens that size are sufficiently rare in both species as to be considered oddities. Nevertheless, quite a few approaching that size have cropped up over the years. One gator killed in 1879 near Avery Island, Louisiana, measured eighteen feet, five inches and was so heavy four mules were needed to drag it out of the water. Another of nineteen feet, two inches was killed in 1890. Considering that seventeen-footers were commonly reported up until the 1940s—yes, *1940s*—and at least one in the twenty-foot class was reported in 1920, the existence of bona-fide swamp monsters is undeniable.

Exaggeration by chest-thumping, smell-like-men gator hunters has been suggested, but that doesn't seem likely. Many of the lengths are recorded in the ledgers of the commercial hide and leather trade, and it was only in 1943 that buyers began paying for hides on a linear-foot basis. Before that, all hides brought a standard price based on an eight-foot maximum length, and even a twenty-footer was worth no more than a wimpy eight. Ergo, no reason to exaggerate. This seems rather odd, big skins being in demand by tanners and all, but since gator hunters of that era were rarely economics majors, the subtler aspects of supply and demand had probably escaped them. Trying to figure out how many of those megalizards were around back then would be little more than an exercise in wild guessing, but let's take a stab at it anyway, just for fun.

The Taylor and Neal size-class frequency chart of 1984 represents graphically the occurrence of alligators in given size classes per 100 adult animals, graduated in one-foot increments. In other words, among every 100 adult alligators, there will be forty-five six-footers, thirteen eight-footers, and so on. The scale cuts off at ten feet, with eight in that class per hundred, so we will have to fudge from eleven feet on up. Since the frequency of occurrence between nine and ten feet differs by a factor of one, we will assume a linear regression by that value for all sizes up to sixteen feet, with anything seventeen feet or longer assumed to have an occurrence frequency of one. And you think *you're* confused. (I know how boring this is, but I want to head off accusations of pulling figures out of thin air, which technically I am, but at least I'm doing it scientifically.) Since we do not know how many gators of any size were alive at the time, dead ones will have to suffice. Some 3.5 million gators of all sizes were killed by hide hunters in Louisiana alone between 1880 and 1933, and 2.5 million more were taken in Florida between 1800 and 1893, for a total of 6 million. Dividing this figure by 100 yields 60,000 hundred-units, and at one gator over sixteen feet per unit, that's 60,000 saurians of the Tokyo-eating class in just two of the states they inhabit.

Anything that big just about has to eat big stuff, up to and including cattle, and the village idiot if he's willing. (R. V. Pierce, reporting to a U.S. Biological Survey team around the turn of the century, said a monster alligator on Florida's St. Vincent Island attempted to take a mule teamed to a wagon as it crossed a small stream, and almost succeeded!) Applying our formula to "small" alligators in the eleven- to sixteen-foot group yields a whopping 1.68 million amply proportioned for man-eating. By the same process, today's population—excluding anything beyond fourteen feet—features roughly 630,000 saurians of unquestionable man-killing size. Pretty dicey odds, wouldn't you say?

Regardless of how many there were, by the time 1950 rolled around most of the really big ones had been trapped and shot out, and leather merchants developed new markets for smaller skins. Consequently, the already beleaguered population went into a nosedive. Not until the 1960s did wildlife managers recognize that the alligator was in trouble, and individual states began implementing protective measures. The feds started sticking their noses in about then too, in spite of which the states' excellent management programs succeeded in bringing populations back to levels only slightly less than they were at the turn of the century, the difference mostly accountable to habitat lost in the interim to condos and shopping malls.

The core of this success story, despite what you heard last night on PBS, was not the ban on trapping and hunting but rather the development of alligator farming, which Louisiana pioneered. With the farms taking pressure off wild populations by forcing hide prices down, all but eliminating the incentive for poaching, by 1972 Louisiana was able to reopen hunting on a strictly regulated, area-specific basis, and by the 1980s statewide seasons were routine.

Why the lecture on alligator economics? Well, remember all those folks we talked about getting eaten

3 • Alligators

back when gators were in their heyday? And how most of the ones big enough to do the eating were killed out by around 1950? Depending on local conditions, it takes anywhere from eight to ten years to grow an alligator to potential man-eating size from infancy, considerably less time if you start out with a fair-size four-footer or so. Isn't it interesting that that nine-year-old boy, whom Florida insists wasn't killed by an alligator, was killed in 1957? And another in 1959? It is no surprise, really, that Florida, with its tropical climate and extended growing season, would be the first state to grow a new crop of man-killers, including a few Hulk Hogan types. In 1956, one measuring seventeen feet, five inches was killed in Lake Apopka. I also find it interesting that the first officially recognized death came in 1973, just four years after federal restrictions under the amended Lacey Act closed down hunting seasons (never mind that gators were doing quite well under state management), and was concurrent with the adoption of what is now called the Endangered Species Act. The death of George Leonard in 1977, the only fatality among fourteen serious attacks recorded that year, coincided perfectly with yet more bureaucratic meddling spawned by U.S. participation in the Convention on International Trade in Endangered Species of Wild Fauna and Flora (CITES).

By no means am I suggesting that we return to the bad old days of unregulated market hunting, or otherwise seek to wipe out the alligator. Far from it. A swamp just wouldn't be a swamp without its spooky presence, bellowing in the night like a bass Valkyrie and making me wonder if there really are such things as Sasquatches. And like most wild things, the alligator fills a very important niche in his proper environment. The problem comes when overprotection blurs the distinction between what is and is not an alligator's "proper" environment; I may not be a wildlife biologist, but I have a hunch it ain't on the kitchen linoleum. . . .

It was 2:30 in the morning of 19 November 1993, and Gail Ennis's pet parrot was screeching like a stiffed waitress. Tiptoeing into the dining room of her Delray Beach,

133

Florida, home, Gail didn't see anything amiss. But that was before she looked out the window. Guess what she saw looking back from less than a foot past the window screen. If you said a seven-foot alligator skulking among the azaleas in the flower bed, you'd be right.

"Howard!" she yelled at her husband as her two small dogs went berserk, "there's a gator out here!" It was about then that the screen popped out and a couple of yards of black, scaly unwelcomeness came slithering into the room. One of the dogs, the smart one, hightailed it into the bedroom. The other one ran into the kitchen with the gator in hot pursuit. Gail tried to grab the frantic dog as it ran past, missed, then fell on her bum knee and couldn't get up. Undaunted, the gator came straight at the woman, the claws on its webbed feet clacking noisily against the tiles. Gail, needless to say, was somewhat unsettled.

About then the cavalry arrived in the form of a very wideawake Howard. He gathered up Gail and the dog and bundled them off into the bedroom. Grabbing his gun, he crept back to confront the home invader. Hissing like a broken steam pipe, it came for him. In a superb Robert Ruark impersonation, Howard coolly shot the saurian right through the eye as it charged, the bullet lucking into the golfball-size brain.

Ed Shea's Tampa floor-care shop got a lot more than an airing out when he propped open the doors one day. Standing near the counter, he turned to see what all the hissing was about and was met by an impending seven-footer inquiring about the leather-cleaning rates. Shea, squatting on the counter top and nursing a headache after smashing his head against the ceiling tiles, dialed 911. A state trapper shortly appeared and lassoed the critter, dragging it out to the parking lot with a vacuum-cleaner hose clamped in it jaws, the appliance rattling along behind.

During the summer of 1994, Toni Stone was swimming in the lake near her central Florida home when a ten-foot bull gator tried to get up close and personal. A strong swimmer, she beat the reptile ashore and scrambled up the beach, only to find it running fast up the grass

3 • Alligators

after her and closing rapidly. She made the house in time, but for several days the gator would come for her every time she stepped outside. It was finally removed by wildlife authorities.

A ten-foot alligator, trapped at a Miami shopping mall after complaints that it was taking up two parking spaces, was tagged, transported, and released twenty-three miles away. It came back in less than a month. Duffers will be interested to know that the term "water hazard" has a very different meaning on Florida's golf courses. Guess why.

Isolated incidents? Hardly. Over the summer of 1995, Florida wildlife authorities responded to over 12,000 complaints, ranging from alligators sunbathing in the middle of freeways to scaly panhandlers mooching backyard handouts and snoozing under parked cars. They regularly turn up in swimming pools, school yards, factories, tollbooths, swanky hotel fountains, and the space shuttle's flame trench at the Kennedy Space Center. Compare '95's complaint total against the slightly less than 2,500 incidents reported in 1982, and there can be little question that Florida's gators are becoming increasingly blase about their "instinctive fear" of man. Further corroboration exists in the hundreds of pets that disappear annually from suburban Florida neighborhoods.

If there is anything of which I am definitely sure, it is that a link exists between dogs and cats becoming furry Swedish meatballs and humans meeting a similar fate. In nearly every modern case of human predation by any species that I have examined, epidemic pet losses in the same area invariably preceded or was concurrent with the festivities. Predators in general have little philosophical difficulty making the transition from eating pets to eating their owners, and it is no different with the alligator. As with cougar, wolf, and bear gourmands with a taste for abundant, easily caught domestic animals, gators adopt Shep and Pussy as preferred fare, even when "natural" prey is readily available:

At first the sound was barely perceptible, a thin, indistinct note quivering at the edge of recognition like a half-forgotten memory. The men listened, their faces lined with concentration as they strained to filter the symphony of night noises riding on the fog that rolled up from the river bottom. Again the sound cut the blackness, closer now and more distinct—a far-off shriek of pure animal savagery echoing hollowly through the forest. An involuntary shudder rippled through the men as a sudden crash of sound assaulted their ears, the throaty squall of a hound in full cry cresting the ridge.

Others soon joined the lead hound as the rest of the pack boiled over the ridge, a primal cacophony of thirty voices echoing through the river bottom. The pleading, knife-edge tenor of a little July bitch, a big Walker's demanding trip-hammer chop, and the booming bass of a leggy, blanket-backed Trigg stood out among the chorus. But none sang with more clarity and distinction than the half-redtick Walker bitch, her voice ringing with the urgency of an excited lover as she led the pack on the trail of a coyote.

Rufus Godwin grinned with pride and satisfaction. The little bitch, named Flojo, belonged to him. He had had her less than a week, but she was already proving to be the best hound he'd ever owned. The second time he hunted her, he had turned down $5,000 offered by another houndsman. Flojo wasn't for sale. She was too good, and her genes would ensure that his pack would become one of the finest in the state. He listened as the pack, aggregated of his and the two other men's hounds, crossed the hardwood bottom and dropped out of earshot after they topped the ridge at the far side. Only Flojo's ringing voice still carried faintly in the still night air, then it too faded from hearing. It was the last time anyone would ever hear her.

Wolf hunters are an odd lot, at least in the traditional sense of what "wolf" and "hunting" mean to most people. They hunt only at night, carry no firearms, rarely stray more than a few yards from the truck, and almost never see the quarry. And they don't really hunt wolves. Coyotes, optimistically called "wolves" by this special breed of houndsmen, are the focal point of the hunt. The hounds do most of the hunting while the men provide moral, logistical, and resupply support from a pickup-truck command post by a campfire. The music of hounds on the chase is what wolf hunting is all about. A typical hunt consists of three parts coyote, two parts assorted hounds, and one part coffee with a slather of fireside bull-session thrown in for seasoning.

Coyotes are not the only object of the houndsman's affection. Both red and gray foxes are chivvied about as well, with the former vastly preferred; a red fox may run all night, but grays have an annoying habit of climbing trees when pressed, evoking colorful and creative cursing as the hunters fumble for flashlights in pickup glove boxes, then stumble out to the tree many shin-barked miles away to "jump him out" and have another go.

The hounds are as interesting as the men who hunt them. Traditional names like redbone, bluetick, and black-and-tan are considered dirty words among dyed-in-the-wool fox and wolf hunters. Monikers like Trigg, July, and Walker grace the pedigrees of the bona fides, with the more recent entry of the English redtick, like Rufus Godwin's Flojo.

That dog's disappearance in September 1995 was only the latest in a string of similar vanishings that had started twenty years earlier in the Blackwater River State Forest on the eastern edge of Florida's panhandle. It is not uncommon for a foxhound to be missing for several days after a hunt. They may run 100 miles in a night, winding up a great distance from the release point. They usually rest up for a day or two before returning to wait, snoozing, under a bush for their owners to pick them up. At any point in the journey, they may fall prey to dog thieves, miscreants who capitalize on the dogs' value on what amounts to a black market. Even unregistered "grade" dogs that are good hunters fetch $500 or more. To battle the thieves, some hunters utilize radio-tracking collars to quickly locate and retrieve hounds that run beyond earshot. Godwin's bitch had been wearing one of the electronic tattletales when she disappeared, but nary a beep registered on Rufus's receiver. At least, not at first.

A couple of nights later, Rufus was hunting along Coldwater Creek in the same area where Flojo had disappeared, and on a whim tuned his receiver to her collar frequency. He got a beep, faint but steady. When he climbed up the creek bank, thinking the reception would improve with elevation, the signal disappeared. Experimentation revealed that only when he stood at a certain spot by the creek was the signal readable, but too weak to pinpoint the source. A couple of weeks later, he asked a friend, who had also lost a dog in the area, to come try his receiver. Sure enough, the second dog's signal came in weakly at the very same spot on the bank of Coldwater Creek. Something weird was afoot, for sure.

The men began working slowly upstream, the signals occasionally fading out but coming back stronger with each passing yard. After half a mile, Rufus spotted something on the creek bank. It was Flojo—or half of her anyway, the markings on the lower legs and torso providing positive identification. The upper half containing the collar was nowhere in sight. According to the direction finder, it lay somewhere farther ahead in the inky blackness. A few hundred yards upstream, the other man's receiver went nuts when they came to a large pool matted with coontail weeds. Raking with a long stick, they dredged off the pool's bottom the empty collar of the other missing dog.

Rufus's receiver still beeped steadily, indicating the transmitter was somewhere even farther upstream in the growing tangle of brush and trees lining the creek. When they came to another large pool, the signal led them to the right and up a small slough. It became increasingly shallow and finally dried up entirely, yet the signal, now stronger than ever, led on deeper into the forest. Another 100 yards brought them to what appeared to be a shallow stand of water some seventy-five yards long and twenty-five yards wide. There was no bank or any apparent depression, just a flat stretch of water like a black mirror laid flat on the forest floor. Rufus's radio receiver went berserk, issuing a nonstop chatter of beeps that made it clear this was the place. Removing the long-range antenna to tighten the receiver's directional cone, Rufus stepped forward into the water. It turned out to be a lot deeper than he thought. After he scrambled out of the

3 • Alligators

knee-deep water at the edge, probing with a sapling showed the pool to be twenty feet deep. He noticed something else too—a little stream of bubbles snaking along the surface, the movement too deliberate to be random. And wherever the bubbles went, the radio signal followed.

I am sure you already know that an alligator was responsible for the bubbles, and that it had Flojo's tracking collar in its stomach. You may be surprised, though, when I tell you the gator contained not just one collar but a whole collection, including one from a dog that had disappeared fourteen years prior! In what may have been some sort of *quid pro quo* arrangement with the local game animals, for twenty years that gator had been killing and eating hounds, crawling out of its hole to wait in ambush where a game trail crossed Coldwater Creek. The spookiest part was that the gator's lair was just a quarter of a mile from a swimming hole favored by the local kids. "Wonder what that gator would have started eating if we had stopped feeding him $5,000 hounds," Rufus later mused. Yeah, I wonder too.

Other than a high incidence of death wishes among the human inhabitants, or the more real epidemic of low-IQ people illegally feeding alligators backyard tidbits, the primary reason for Florida's unparalleled nasty encounter rate owes to its having large populations of both people and gators, the latter numbering over one million and increasing. Sketchy though they are, the attack numbers reflect a clear trend toward getting worse instead of better. The annual rate of attack has increased steadily since 1985, topping out at twenty in 1994, the last year with complete records as of press time. There have been 201 officially acknowledged attacks since 1948 and of these, 191 occurred between 1973 and 1995, most with consequences requiring a lot more than Band-Aids and aspirin.

In August 1984, eleven-year-old Robert Crespi died while swimming in Florida's St. Lucie River when a twelve-foot bull gator pulled him under. "It was terrible," said one witness. "I could see the gator with the boy's hand sticking out of his mouth, and swimming with him down the river." Police summoned to the scene commandeered a boat and found the saurian about 200 yards downriver. It dropped the boy and submerged when they shot at it.

In June 1993, another boy, ten-year-old Bradley Weidenhamer, was wading in shallow water in the Loxahatchee River when a big bull swatted him down with a sideways sweep of its head (a common tactic), then grabbed him by the head and started swimming off. It released the boy after the father and some bystanders attacked it with canoe paddles, but it was too late. The gator's teeth had fatally pierced Bradley's skull.

That none of the five attacks recorded in 1975 resulted in death is purely miraculous. The one involving forty-five-year-old Thomas Chickene, attacked while swimming in a Polk County rock quarry, netted him an open fracture of the sternum, broken ribs, a shattered collarbone, and multiple deep lacerations to his neck, chest, chin, and back. That he wasn't drowned and consumed is attributable to bystander intervention after Chickene had shoved an arm down the reptile's throat, causing it to release its grip just as it was about to pull him under for the third time. Afterward, the gator crawled out on the bank and bellowed, presumably in protest of such rude mealtime interruption.

Thirty-four-year-old wildlife researcher Kent Keenlyne owes his life to a good left jab and a handy boat. Keenlyne was wading waist-deep, checking some turtle traps in a lagoon area of the Oklawaha River, when a gator grabbed him by the right arm and shoulder from behind and below in a sneak attack after first slapping him down with its head. The ensuing, somewhat lengthy disputation culminated in Keenlyne punching and shoving at the saurian's head until his biceps muscle tore free, letting him scramble into his small johnboat before the gator could regroup. The felon in this case remains at large, all efforts at capture having failed.

To be fair, I should point out that other states' gators are equally inclined to demonstrate their dentition on sundry parts of your anatomy. In 1974 Texas game warden Bill Hiles was directing traffic around a road-hit gator when the reptile swiveled around and grabbed him by the hip and started spinning. He got a broken hip and a few hours of surgery out of the deal, not to mention a new-found respect for alligators—even wounded ones high and dry on the asphalt.

In June 1978, eight-year-old Thad Little was wading with two cousins and a friend in a shallow marsh near Hackberry, Louisiana, catching minnows in a hand net. The youths had crossed the same narrow, knee-deep stretch five times, but on the sixth crossing something suddenly yanked Thad under. Fighting furiously, he managed to free himself, but not before his right leg was shredded and his chest deeply lacerated by the gator's clawed feet. It was only afterward that he saw the nine-foot, nine-inch bull gator. Later, hospital staffers commemorated the lad's tough sense of humor by attaching to one his IV bottles a piece of surgical tape on which someone had inscribed, "Gator-Aid for Gator-Bait."

If you live north of the Mason-Dixon line or west of the Mississippi, you are probably reasonably safe from being indirectly converted into an expensive set of luggage complete with matching shoes and handbag. But before you become too smug with "it can't happen to me" ideas, I remind you that alligators are increasing in both number and range, and that they are surprisingly temperature-tolerant, able to survive sub-freezing air temperatures by breathing through blowholes in the ice. While you're chewing on that, consider the following August 1988 Associated Press item:

ALLIGATOR FOUND IN NEW YORK RESERVOIR

New York—After years of debunking stories of alligators living in New York sewer systems, municipal officials were astounded to find a small alligator in the reservoir.

"I couldn't believe it," said Mr. Andrew McCarthy of the Department of Environmental Protection.

Officials began hunting last week when residents near the reservoir began calling to say they had seen an alligator. On Monday two department employees spotted the alligator on a rock. It jumped into the water and swam away before they could get to it. Later that night, accompanied by an expert from the zoo and a Mrs. Myra Watanabe, a university professor who has captured alligators in China, among other places, they succeeded in bagging it. The alligator was taken to the Bronx Zoo, where experts examined it, pronounced it healthy, and placed it in a cage.

And you thought it was safe to go in the water.

WOLVES, DOGS, and COYOTES

If a betting contest were held to determine the terrestrial predator with the greatest numbers and widest distribution on a worldwide basis, the smart money would be on the canines. Don't start up with me, now, about shrews, weasels, domestic cats, and the like; you know what the rules are: Only man-killers need apply.

American Man-Killers

I hope my mailman doesn't sue me over the hernia he is bound to get delivering all the hate-mail generated by this chapter. No matter what I say, somebody is sure to get upset. If the green weenies don't put out a contract on me for implying the wolf might be a man-killer, the cattlemen will for intimating it is anything less than the devil incarnate. The coyote? Who in his right mind would suggest the little song dog of the prairies could do harm? Heck, he can't even catch the Saturday morning Roadrunner (*beep beep*). Old Spot a killer? A pox on you, sir! Oh, well, I guess it just goes with the territory. If only I had been born rich instead of so darn good-looking, I wouldn't have to work for a living and could leave this to someone else. But seeing as how I'm stuck with it, I can at least take some consolation that the facts are on my side.

If you are unfamiliar with the controversy surrounding wolves, it can be safely assumed you probably don't get out much. Once a common fixture from sea to shining sea, the gray wolf's (*Canis lupus*) modern range has been reduced to roughly that of the grizzly, mostly restricted to Alaska, Canada, and a few scattered pockets in the northern border states, Minnesota having the most at an estimated two thousand. All the hubbub centers around recent efforts to reestablish wolves in other traditional U.S. ranges, particularly in the national parks, which is just fine with me. In fact, I sort of like the idea of getting my blood curdled by the haunting song of a genuine, no-fooling wolf harmonizing with whippoorwills and coyotes as I listen from my north Texas back porch. Of course, were I a cattle rancher concerned that my livelihood was about to get eaten, I might see things a bit differently.

Whether wolves eat enough cattle to be justifiably considered a menace is a question not likely to be answered to anyone's reasonable satisfaction. If you ignore history, which modern wolfmen say you must, the only means of proving it one way or the other is by the empirical method: Restore wolves and see just how many Herefords they can eat at a sitting. Which doesn't really seem fair. Admittedly, the

4 • Wolves, Dogs, and Coyotes

wolf program has a provision whereby any rancher who can prove Big Bad and company killed his prize bull will be compensated from a fund provided courtesy of your tax dollars. The problem lies in the proving-it-part. Who's to say Bossy didn't die of natural causes and was merely scavenged by wolves? And it is hard to tell the difference between a wolf kill and one by a pack of dogs out on a lark. Both have been cited as reasons for denying compensation.

Historically, wolves have clearly demonstrated their untrustworthiness in the feedlot. The legendary Custer wolf, working alone in South Dakota and Wyoming in the early part of the twentieth century, killed an estimated $25,000 worth of livestock before getting his card punched in 1920. Twenty-five grand bought a lot of Cheez Whiz back then, and translates to something like $500,000 at today's prices. About the same time, another lone wolf named Snowdrift killed 1,500 head in Montana over a thirteen-year period and, in spite of a $500 bounty on his head, died fat and happy of old age.

Rugged individualism and self-reliance being prerequisites in the cattle business, some understandably upset cattlemen still deal with the matter in the traditional way. When they get caught at it, Legaldom's iron fist slams down hard. In February 1996, some poor inmate had to give up his bunk to a Billings, Montana, man sentenced to six months in prison for killing a wolf, which he initially mistook for a stray dog. The radio-collared *lupus*, one of several recently released in Yellowstone, had obviously not read the fine print restricting him to doing business within park boundaries.

I don't know where all this will lead, but a full-blown range war is not out of the question. Some landowners follow a quiet policy of shoot, shovel, and shut up, with trespassing poachers blamed for any dead wolves accidentally found lying around, but others take a more militant approach. One rancher dealt with federal agents attempting to enter his property to investigate a wolf killing by chasing them off at gunpoint, and was supported and hailed as a hero by local residents. Some state and local governments have resisted federal restocking efforts, the general consensus being "not in my back yard."

The hot topic of whether wolves seriously deplete game herds has hunters falling off both sides of the fence. Some, including Sincerely Yours, like the wilderness-in-a-bottle concept of sharing the woods with a few howling, happy-go-lucky canines. On the other hand, it may just be the *idea* of free-roaming wolves that I find appealing; the reality might be a whole 'nother ball game. Some hunters make the rather salient point that the last thing we need is more competition for the available game, whose habitat and management are paid for by our license fees and special taxes levied on our equipment under the federal Pittman-Robertson and Dingell-Johnson acts.

Whether reintroducing wolves is tantamount to issuing *human* death certificates on a lottery basis doesn't appear to be a significant issue, at least not at the moment. In one phrasing or another, I have read "no record exists of a human killed by wolves" so many times that I fear it is permanently burned into my retinas. And it would seem to be true, at least in North America. Europe is another matter.

The same wolf that stalks our amber waves of grain has racked up quite an impressive record in Poland, Romania, Portugal, France, Yugoslavia (yes, I know all about the Serbs), Italy, Spain, and other far-flung locales. Much of the activity dates back to the 1700s and beyond, but twentieth-century headlines have not remained wolfless. In 1927 wolves besieged and nearly wiped out an entire Russian village before the army came charging over The Steppes to the rescue. In the 1960s wolves attacked 168 people in the Ural Mountains country, killing and eating eleven of them. In 1956 a postman was killed and partially eaten by a lone wolf two miles from Rome, Italy. More recently, an October 1995 newspaper report says thirty-three-year-old Olavi Veikanmaa was attacked by a wolf near Helsinki, Finland. At least I think that's what it says; it's written in Spanish.

Nobody really knows why European wolves are more disposed to unsociable conduct than the American model. Habituation has been suggested as a possible factor, wolves on the Continent having been in close association with humans for a much longer period. If true, it makes me wonder whether stocking wolves in national parks is such a good idea. On the other hand, if familiarity breeds wolfish contempt, you would think an American Indian or two would have gotten the chop somewhere along the line. Some tribal lore suggests they did, but rabid behavior or overt provocation cannot be ruled out.

It certainly seems reasonable that in hard times a wolf would choose human-on-rye—hold the mustard—as preferable to starvation, but unless an attack was witnessed, you would have a hard time proving it. Bones not consumed outright would become scattered and lost almost immediately. There are a few "possibles," like the skeleton of a man found in company with those of three wolves on the Alaskan coast, a .357 magnum revolver with all chambers fired lying nearby. It hardly seems worth the breath to argue whether the old boy got himself into a sticky situation he couldn't get out of or died defending himself against unprovoked attack. My guess would be the former, since Alaska has more wolves than Carter's got little liver pills, and yet not one lonely homesteader or solitary hunter has been killed or eaten unprovoked, at least not that we know of. One other snippet of human remains has turned up in company with wolves, a skull found in a den. Scavenged? Probably. But we'll never know for sure. Wolfdom shall forever remain haunted by the Great Unknown.

That bit about no documented attacks needs some clarification. It is better said that no *authenticated* record exists of a human killed by a *wild, healthy* wolf. I stress "authenticated" because there is no shortage of wild wolf tales whose validity cannot be proven. A good example appeared in letter form in the August 1991 issue of *Montana Farmer and Stockman* magazine. The writer related from memory that sometime around 1930 in Michigan, "one helluva big wolf" killed and ate a baby snatched from its carriage parked outside beneath the kitchen window. He allowed that the case was thoroughly investigated and the wolf hunted down and killed by members of the local sheriff's and state police departments, and proof surely existed if only somebody would research the matter. Well, somebody did.

In October 1992, Dr. Richard A. Santer, professor of geography, department of social sciences, at Ferris State University, Michigan, undertook to authenticate the baby-killer story. He and two research assistants perused area newspaper files dating from 1930 through 1940 for stories referencing the incident—one heck of a pile of reference rocks to turn over. They found five dog-bite articles but no wolf. Next they canvassed the area for people who had lived there at the time and interviewed them. They came up with lots of bear, bobcat, coyote, and dog stories, but the wolf-well again came up dry. Conclusion? If an incident as spectacular as a wolf killing and partially eating someone's baby had occurred—complete with both bodies prominently displayed on the town square—it seems reasonable to expect at least a line or two in the local paper about it. Further, the grapevine news-distribution network, the most efficient in the world, would fairly guarantee at least one or two people remembering the incident. When I asked Dr. Santer why the sheriff and state police files were not checked, he said the absence of corroboration by the other sources made the additional effort seem unnecessary. That may be true, but it does leave a question mark on the incident. It is certainly plausible that a wolf would prey on a defenseless infant if given the opportunity, as they have most certainly done in Europe and parts of Asia, but it doesn't appear to have been so in this case. Two dry holes, dutifully dug and dynamited, pretty well convince me that somebody had a faulty memory or an overactive imagination.

You may be wondering why—in light of my elsewhere tenaciously refuting the defenders of bears, cougars, and other carnivorous miscellany—I am so willing to concede that the wolf as a species has gotten a bum rap. Simple. The bear and cougar huggers rely on obfuscation if not outright lies to uphold their darlings' reputations; the wolfmen do not. They don't have to. Records, observation, and extrapolation from known facts are the stuff from which research is done and opinions are formed, and I come down on the side best supported by the available evidence. Since there is no evidence proving the North American wolf is a business-hours man-killer, no way will I crawl into the quagmire of trying to prove a negative by saying there is no evidence proving he is *not* a man-killer. Innocent until proven guilty and all that.

While verifiable stories of snarling, slathering, wild wolves running amuck and terrorizing the good townsfolk may be in short supply, cases do exist involving rabid, injured, captive, or "tame" animals. Back in 1947, a wolf attacked railroad worker Mike Dusiak near Ontario, Canada, leaping from ambush to knock him off his handcar. In a battle involving two hand axes wielded by Dusiak, the wolf pressed the assault for a full fifteen minutes, even after its head and belly were split open. It was finally killed by a passing train crew who lit into it with picks and shovels. Rabies tests were not routine back then, and the official account does not mention whether rabies was a factor. Nevertheless, an attack persisting for a quarter of an hour against an actively resisting armed man makes the disease a near certainty. Since Dusiak lived to give a full report of the incident, he obviously wasn't bitten.

Around 1985 a six-year-old Canadian boy got his arm mangled and later amputated after climbing into the wolf enclosure at Toronto's Metropolitan Zoo. The lad, who was brain-damaged in a car accident as a toddler, was recently awarded $15 million in a lawsuit filed by his parents, suggesting his condition must be contagious. Zoo officials were genuinely stunned that the wolves had actually attacked somebody, citing the number of times attendants had been in and out of the enclosure over the years with nary a fang bared. Speculation was that the unusual means of entry may have triggered a defensive, territorial response, or the boy's size combined with his unnatural gait incited predatory behavior. The second observation seems the most likely, considering that of two older children with him at the time, only one was slightly injured when he tried to intervene.

Twenty-four-year-old Tricia Wyman was killed in April 1996 by five wolves at an Ontario wildlife reserve. Published reports of the incident were a bit sketchy, but apparently the wolves attacked her when she entered the compound to feed them. No mention was made of whether any flesh was eaten, but the fact that constables had to kill three of the wolves to reclaim the body sure sounds like they were protecting a food source.

A story related by Frank Dobie, introduced elsewhere, about an old fiddler named Uncle Dick doesn't really qualify as an attack, but it sure is interesting. Uncle Dick was walking alone early one evening on his way to a rural home, where he was to provide the music for a couple's postnuptial celebration. As he ambled along the narrow, tree-lined road, he caught snatches of movement from the shadows to either side. He didn't think much of it at first, imagining birds fluttering to roost, but as twilight deepened, the wraiths began slowly edging closer, looking less and less like birds. Uncle Dick started whistling to drive away the willies, his pace quickening each time he glanced back, wide-eyed, at the rapidly closing shadows. Before he knew it, he was in a flat-out run, the sound of rapid footfalls behind prodding him to speeds he thought impossible. Rounding a bend in the road, he saw an abandoned, dilapidated cabin and headed for it. Without knowing how, Uncle Dick was soon perched on the cabin's rotting roof, looking down into a sea of hungry eyes mounted in the business ends of a dozen wolves.

I don't know if "treed" is an appropriate term for Uncle Dick's predicament, but whatever it was, it sure wasn't fun. The roof sagged and creaked alarmingly with the slightest movement, threatening to give way at any moment and deposit him among cruel, slashing fangs. Worse, the wolves were becoming frenzied, their supposed meal so tantalizingly close yet just out of reach. Afraid they might successfully climb the cabin's rough-hewn log walls, Uncle Dick searched for a solution. He knew there was no use running; they would pull him down before he cleared the front yard. If he stayed where he was, the wolves would probably tear the cabin down to get at him, if the roof didn't cave in first. If only he had a weapon, there might be a chance. But other than the little penknife in his pocket, which hardly seemed suitable, the only thing he had with him was the old, beat-up fiddle in its case across his back. He suddenly remembered something he'd once heard about music soothing the savage beast. Had he known how the line really went, Uncle Dick would probably never have thought to try it, but try it he did. Uncasing the fiddle, he rosined up the bow and started playing. The wolves were mesmerized, sitting up and raising their voices in accompaniment to "Yankee Doodle." All night the old fiddler played, repeating his entire repertoire time and again, the beasts below becoming agitated whenever he stopped. He later observed they seemed particularly taken with "Turkey in the Straw" and "Swing Low Sweet Chariot." The wolves finally drifted away with the dawn, just before Uncle Dick's bow arm gave out.

I dearly wanted to work some reference to *Fiddler on the Roof* into this but couldn't find quite the right angle.

In December 1995, a three-year-old boy was snatched off his front porch by a semi-tame wolf near Farmersville, Oregon. The grandmother, Darlene Molina, heard the fracas and ran outside to find the boy gone and sundry articles of his clothing scattered about the yard. She heard screams in the distance and ran to discover the wolf shaking the tot in its jaws. The predator dropped him when Molina screamed, only to pick him up again and run off. It dropped the boy twice more in the ensuing chase before being taken down in a most ungrandmotherly flying tackle. Molina then snatched up the boy and ran for the house. The wolf, a persistent cuss, followed her home in a running battle to reclaim its prey, biting the woman severely on the arm several times before she got inside to safety. It hung around until the ambulance and sheriff arrived, and was finally shot to death when it lunged at a deputy. The boy came mighty close to cashing in—unconscious, eyes fixed, and turning a most unlovely shade of blue from lack of oxygen after being nearly crushed in the massive jaws—but he survived with one hell of a story to tell his own grandchildren.

American Man-Killers

The wolf had been found as a cub and raised by a local man, then released to fend for itself after becoming unruly or the feed bills got too high. (Know what it costs to feed a wolf these days? Neither do I, but it must be plenty.) People raising and keeping wolves as pets is not as uncommon as you might think. Take a look at the classified ads in the back of your favorite outdoor magazine; you can mail-order the genuine article or a hybridized wolf-dog for a few hundred bucks. You could handle one, right? One Alaska woman thought so, and took to raising the things for fun and profit. While introducing her infant child to one of the cuties, it bit the baby to death with a single snap to the head. (Ironically, two years prior her seven-year-old son had disappeared under circumstances suggestive of grizzly predation.) There are between 300,000 and 400,000 hybrid wolves currently in the U.S., raising interesting questions about your own neighborhood. According to the best figures I could find, sixteen people have died of half-wolf bite since 1978, and at least one partially consumed. Dozens more have been merely mangled to one degree or another, Yours Truly among them.

Back in the days when I trained guard dogs for a living (I said I was cute, not smart), I had some experience with hybridized wolves trained to guard a local, minor celebrity who was convinced the Mafia was after him. Though half wild, they were the most intelligent animals I have ever encountered. It took them less than a day to figure out how kennel latches worked, and the countryside was terrorized more than once before I became clever enough to see the utility of padlocks, chosen for their toughness after the wolfies bit a couple of dog leash-type snaps in two.

One of the wolves, named Lucifer, learned he could entice me inside by stashing his feed pan in the doghouse at the back side of his kennel, where I couldn't reach it through the "bean hole" in the gate at feeding time. Once inside, no matter how carefully I watched him, he always somehow managed to slip past me and flip open the gate latch, escaping for a rousing good game of "Ha-ha, you can't catch me" before I could do anything but curse. It was starting to get really embarrassing, going around asking neighbors if they had seen the 150-pound wolf I was training to kill, not to mention the stigma of being outsmarted on a near-daily basis by a dog, wolf hybrid or not. So I came up with the bright idea of padlocking the gate from the inside.

For those of you unfamiliar with guard- and attack-dog training techniques, we used a process known as the Kohler Method. It involves one man handling the dog while a second man, the "agitator," serves as chew-toy and all-round bad guy to the trainee. While guard dogs are trained to make blood pudding out of anyone but the handler who violates their assigned perimeter, attack dogs do so only when instructed. Until he hears *"Blitz!"* "Get 'em!" "Watch!" or other suitable instruction from the handler, a properly trained attack dog can under most circumstances be petted, wrestled with, or have its ears pulled by just about anybody—except its agitator. Attack dogs positively hate agitators, for reasons obvious in the name. It naturally follows that you never want to enter a kennel occupied by a dog (or wolf, as the case may be) that you have personally agitated, let alone lock yourself in with one.

I did.

One day, while making dinner rounds of the dogs I handled (training included accepting food only from the handler), I came to Lucifer's kennel and, naturally, his food bowl was not by the gate. Why we didn't think to wire them in place I'll never know. Anyway, I nonchalantly entered, padlocking the gate behind me. Just as I started to turn around, somebody slammed a 150-pound sledge-hammer into my back. The concrete kennel floor flipped up to smack me in the face with a hollow *thwack!* knocking me not quite out but at least halfway into last week.

With white spots exploding on a black field before my eyes and blood streaming from my nose, I could just hear over the ringing in my ears the distant sound of an enraged animal growling and ripping at something it didn't like. When my head cleared after a few seconds, the sound grew intensely loud and close. When I tried to rise, a heavy weight jackhammered me back to the concrete.

155

American Man-Killers

Squirming furiously, I twisted onto my side, the big jaws clamped and shaking viciously in the collar of my coat preventing me from turning all the way over. I bellowed as many variations of *"Nein!"* "Out!" and other such cease-and-desist commands as I could think of—including quite a few I didn't learn in Sunday school—trying to call the three-quarters wolf off the attack. He was having none of that. Twisting to the left on my stomach, I tried to grab a foot to yank him off balance before he decided to shift his grip to something I considered important. While I reached out for the leg, my heart did a one-and-a-half gainer in full tuck position when I glimpsed the collar around the huge, furry neck. It wasn't green.

It isn't easy keeping sorted a bunch of dogs that all look more or less alike, especially when three of them are near-identical triplet wolves. We had solved the problem by assigning each handler a distinct color scheme; his charges wore collars in the appropriate motif, and matching placards stenciled with the dogs' names were mounted on the kennel gates. I was green; the two other handlers were red and yellow. The thing trying to kill me had a red collar, identifying it as Dan, the biggest and worst-tempered of the wolves, and the one I had most often served as agitator. Somebody, probably the pimply kid we employed as a pooper-scooper after school, had put Dan in the wrong kennel. I made a mental note to chastise the lad when next I saw him, putting off until later the decision of whether to use a cat-o'-nine-tails or thumb-screws. Meanwhile, as President Bush might have put it, I was in deep doo-doo.

I tell you in all modesty that I wasn't frightened by the predicament; I was terrified spitless. I knew what one of those big boys could do, and this one had me right where he wanted me. Encouraged by visions of WOLF EATS LOCAL IDIOT-type headlines, I twisted around until the side of my face buried in the thick neck ruff, stretching back with my left hand to grab the wolf's hind foot near my knee as he stood over me. With strength fueled by panic, I jerked it out and up.

The big predator lost balance, releasing my coat collar and dancing sideways to stay on its feet. I held on,

156

scrambling to get up, and was just to my knees when the wolf contorted around like a snake held by the tail, snapping its jaws on empty air where my hand had held its foot a microsecond earlier. In one continuous sweep it swiveled back, a blur of teeth flashing white straight at my face. The jaws clamped around my right arm, which I'd thrown up instinctively just in time, completely spanning the forearm with the canines almost touching on the side nearest my face. Tensed muscles parted with a crisp *snick* beneath shearing incisors under 600-pounds-per-square-inch pressure, stopping just short of reaching bone.

I will never understand why he didn't crunch right through the relatively small forearm bones, as he was certainly capable of doing. Perhaps the thick cloth of my coat sleeve stickied his wicket a bit. I didn't spend a whole lot of time puzzling over it right then because I knew what was coming next: a shaking that would shred my arm into fajita stuffing if not snap it like a matchstick. Quickly, I grabbed the collar beneath the throat and, with this leverage, pushed my forearm deeper into the jaws, triggering the gag reflex that would loosen his grip. I struggled to my feet while maintaining the hold, forcing the animal to a disadvantaged position on its hind legs.

An observer might have thought I was teaching the wolf to dance, a bloody Tango with me leading, but just barely. (I know you were expecting a reference to *Dances with Wolves*, so there it is.) We waltzed around a bit, how long I am not sure, slipping and sliding in my own blood that had splattered on the concrete after cascading down the wolf's neck and chest. Little by little, he seemed to weaken, gurgling audibly as my juices filled his throat and choked him. I finally forced him into a corner near the gate and, with my knee against his chest, released the collar to fish the keyring from my pants pocket and unlock the gate. Taking hold of the collar again, I backed outside and in one motion yanked my arm free and slammed the gate.

I don't really know how many stitches or inches of silver wire it took to patch me up—the doctor didn't say, and I didn't ask—but it was a helluva lot more than I would have liked. Still, a broken nose, a few feet of silk lacing, and a buttful of penicillin is a bargain compared to the other possibilities. The probable reason I am not a footnote in somebody else's book about man-killers is that the incident occurred when it was cold out. Otherwise I would not have been wearing that heavy coat and the initial bite would have gone somewhere else, fulfilling Dan's greatest ambition. I relate this incident more as a monument to stupidity than a testament to the presumed hairiness of my chest, and to illustrate the destructive powers inherent in any large predator, "domesticated" or otherwise.

Before closing down *The Howling* department, a few words are in order concerning the old tales about orphaned children nurtured and raised by wolves. Now, there's a little gem the rational man should have no trouble dismissing out of hand. Shades of Lon Chaney, Jr.! Wolf-children? The very idea! Well, that's one of the neat things about wolf research: Just when you think you've got 'em figured out, they throw you a slider.

A few years ago, one of the networks aired a short-lived series, I forget the name, about a man raised from infancy by wolves. Named "Lucan," as I recall, he possessed a number of interesting physical traits induced by his abnormal upbringing: accelerated heart rate, glowing yellow eyes giving superb night vision, able to leap speeding Ferraris in a single bound, and so on. I guess it was all too fantastic to be believable, and the show was canceled after one season. The strange part, though, is that the premise was based in fact.

In the mid-1790s, a boy estimated at eleven years old was found running naked in the woods near Aveyron, France. He was wilder than a March hare, requiring four men to subdue after being run down on horseback—and he damn near outran them! Based on his appearance and conduct—which included sleeping curled in a corner on the floor, lapping water with his tongue, howling fit to beat the band, and biting and scratching the Holy Water out of several nuns charged with his care—it was concluded he had been raised by and living among wolves.

4 • Wolves, Dogs, and Coyotes

This, mind you, happened at a time when and location where wolves were eating people by the dozens, and had been for centuries. The wolf-boy, named Victor, was ultimately delivered to a school for the deaf, don't ask me why, and placed under the care of physician Jean-Marc-Gaspard Itard, who later wrote *The Wild Boy of Aveyron* (1801), chronicling his mostly unsuccessful efforts to tame the lad.

Another French case involved a fourteen-year-old boy named Jean Grenier, adjudged a werewolf and sentenced to death in 1603. He was granted clemency and lived for eight years in a Franciscan monastery. He was described as lean and gaunt with clawed, deformed hands, tremendous four-footed agility, and a dietary predilection for rotten meat.

According to an account related by Barry H. Lopez in *Of Wolves and Men,* in October 1920 the Reverend J. A. L. Singh found two small girls living in a wolf den near the village of Godamuri, India, about seventy-five miles southwest of Calcutta. The girls, estimated to be one-and-a-half and eight years old respectively, were captured along with a couple of wolf cubs when the den was excavated several weeks later. Both girls were agile quadrupeds and highly talented biters and howlers, and possessed inhumanly keen ears and noses. They preferred to sleep during the day and eat their raw meat—the only food they would accept—at night. Like most wild things, they did not take well to captivity and the youngest, named Amala, died about a year after capture. Kamala, the eldest, lived to the ripe age of seventeen in Singh's orphanage.

Similar stories about American wolf-children have typically been lumped with giants and hobgoblins as products of rum-jug imagination, but I am not so sure. While I make no definitive claims one way or the other, I believe it is at least a possibility. The psycho-gurus who know about such things say a child's most elemental behaviors—social conduct, language, self-identity, and so forth—are indelibly ingrained during the first eight or so years of life, learned through observation and mimicry of its parents and siblings. Once a child's personal identity has been established, rarely can it be reversed or modified to any meaningful degree unless caught at a very early age, and certainly not after the onset of puberty. It is therefore wholly believable that a child raised by wolves would forever believe it *was* a wolf, complete with behavior appropriate to its identity.

The big wad of gristle most people have trouble choking down is the concept of wolves "adopting" human children in the first place. Actually, if you look at it from the wolf's point of view, it is not as farfetched as it sounds. Wolf behavior is classic pack predator stuff, based on family associations presided over by a matriarch or "Alpha" female, in which responsibility for the raising of young is shared by all pack members. Adoption of orphaned cubs is pretty well standard practice. Though I can find no documented case of interspecies adoption by wolves, the maternal instinct is sufficiently strong to make it not only possible but even probable under the right circumstances. A good example would be the undeniable phenomenon of dogs adopting and suckling kittens and baby pigs.

Human children could come into wolfish possession through any number of means, including kidnapping. There are plenty of examples of wolves, and other predators besides, stealing children from the edges of fields while the mothers worked. Predation is most often blamed, but with wolves, curiosity is a likely factor.

Though I can't prove it, I believe it is possible that wolves may not recognize human infants as such, because they do not smell human; they don't smell like anything. In the same way that deer fawns have little or no body scent for the several days they are most vulnerable to predation after birth, I believe human children may be relatively scentless, a vestigial survival mechanism we no longer need, sort of like an appendix. I doubt anyone who has ever been present at a diaper changing would agree, but that doesn't really count. If, then, an infant or young child winds up in the company of wolves and cannot be identified by scent, I see no reason adoption would not be a possibility. I am therefore willing to accept that at least some accounts of American wolf-children are probably true to some degree.

4 • Wolves, Dogs, and Coyotes

The detailed account a wolf-girl reported operating in the Devil's River region of southwest Texas between 1845 and 1852 rings true, owing to the specificity of date, location, and names of individuals involved. She was born in May 1835 on a homestead at the confluence of Dry Creek and Devil's River. The mother, Mollie Pertul Dent, died giving birth, and the father, John Dent, was simultaneously killed several miles away in a thunderstorm at the ranch he had ridden to for help. The child was never found, but evidence at the isolated cabin led to the assumption that she had been taken and apparently eaten by wolves. Ten years later, near what is now Del Rio, "a creature, with long hair covering its features, that looked like a naked girl" was seen in company with several wolves attacking a herd of goats. Other similar reports were made that same year, and Apache Indians in the region told of finding a child's footprints among those of wolves. Since wolf-girls eating the livestock wasn't considered kosher, a hunt was organized.

On the third day of the hunt, the girl was duly captured, cornered in a box canyon, but only after the large wolf with her was killed when it attacked the hunting party. Hog-tied and muzzled, she was delivered to a nearby ranch and locked in a storage room. That same evening, a pack of wolves, apparently attracted by the girl's incessant howling, surrounded the ranch house and panicked the livestock into a stampede. The girl escaped in the ensuing melee. Seven years later, a crew surveying a new route to El Paso spotted her and two wolf cubs on a sand bar in the Rio Grande, several miles upstream of the Devil's River confluence. She was never seen again after that day.

Other similar cases have been reported which, had they not been prematurely truncated, might have developed into the real deal. One of them involved four-year-old Margaret Schweitzer, recorded in the Duluth *News Tribune* for 4 October 1906; you read right—we are talking twentieth century.

Margaret disappeared one afternoon while gathering nuts in the woods with some other children near Big

American Man-Killers

Rapids, Michigan. A search party was organized to scour the woods, but no sign of the girl could be found. Late on the second day, a volunteer found her bonnet lying beside a narrow trail twisting off through the brush. On hands and knees, he followed it to a clearing littered with animal bones, feathers, and sheep skins—a wolf den, confirming the worst fears held by many as to little Margaret's fate, or so it seemed.

The man was about to leave and report this find when he noticed movement near the den entrance. It was Margaret, alive and well, running to greet him with a big grin on her face. She told the man she had been playing with some "nice little doggies" met in the woods the day before, and was so engaged when his approach spooked them away. During her two days among the wolves, she had eaten nuts and kept warm at night by cozying up with her new-found friends.

Sort of makes you wonder about werewolf stories, doesn't it?

Though you can safely bet Aunt Fanny's corset that wolves are dangerous, it would seem to be so only under circumstances of captivity or extreme provocation. Some of my less-refined acquaintances say the same thing about redheaded ladies. Anyway, I wouldn't lose much sleep worrying about my mortal remains winding up as wolf droppings; there is a far greater danger much closer to home, perhaps sleeping at your feet right now.

*　　*　　*　　*

Man and dogs (*Canis familiaris*) have lived in close symbiosis ever since we learned that wolves hanging around the cave helped keep the saber-toothed tigers at bay—cheap protection for the price of a few mastodon scraps. I don't think it necessary to dwell excessively on the dog's place in modern society in terms of its inestimable value as a servant and companion. Given the lobbying efforts of the American Kennel Club, United Kennel Club, single-breed booster societies, plus the various humane organizations, Fido has a PR team that most politicians can only dream about. And why not?

4 • Wolves, Dogs, and Coyotes

On any given day, some dog somewhere will save a drowning victim, drag a child from a burning house, scare off a burglar, sniff out a six-ton cocaine shipment, or even dial 911 to report a medical emergency for its owner, as one did recently using auto-dial. Even Lassie and Rin Tin Tin would be hard put to keep up. But—you knew there would be a but—for all the good dogs do, it comes at a price. That ebony Labrador stretched sleeping peacefully by the hearth has a darker side. Somewhere deep, or maybe not so deep, inside the shepherd playing ball with your children out in the yard, there lurks a demon. Well, maybe not a demon, but certainly an inbred, instinctive behavior that humans have been able to suppress, but not eliminate, through selective breeding. It is always there, simmering just beneath the surface, waiting to boil over with consequences too horrible to imagine. Any dog, *your* dog, has within it the makings of a man-killer.

It was a Sunday in September 1995. Scott Wilkenson and his wife still glowed with pride in the birth of their daughter, Sara Beth, just two weeks prior. Scott may have been thinking about the future when he went to Sara Beth's room that morning, daydreaming about swinging his little girl in the park, sharing an ice-cream cone, or holding her on his lap and reading a fairy tale. Imagine his horror on entering the infant's room and seeing the floor spattered with blood, his daughter a shapeless lump in the soaking crib. Nearby, placidly licking blood from its muzzle and coat, sat the family chow, looking innocent as ever. "The Wilkensons had no previous trouble with the five-year-old dog," the reports said.

On 14 December 1995, six-year-old Lang Forsyth was playing in the yard of his uncle's farmhouse, frolicking in the snow with a pair of German shepherds while his father, Mark, helped with some chores. When Mark returned about fifteen minutes later, he found Lang face-down in a growing halo of blood from deep gashes and punctures in his head and neck. He bled to death on the way to the hospital. "The boy had played with the dogs continuously for the past year and he was not afraid of them," the reports said.

Another boy, four-year-old Alec Balbachan, died while visiting his uncle, mauled to death on 19 November 1995 by two Rottweilers as he played in the yard. "The dogs [had] played with children before and were usually docile," the reports said. "No one seems to know why the dogs suddenly turned on Alec."

I do. Regardless of the breed, size, temperament, or political leanings of a dog involved in an unprovoked attack, I can tell you precisely why it happened: Dogs are predators.

It is hard to imagine, looking into those deep, soulful eyes, that looking back from behind them is a predatory animal that will, under the right circumstances, kill and possibly eat you, your neighbor, or one of your children. Of course, old Shep won't always eat you. He may be content to just mess you up a bit, perhaps chew your face off, which is what thirty-two-year-old Donnie Brown's pit bull did to him as he lounged in the bathtub. Or he may amuse himself by dragging sundry pieces of you around the yard for a while, possibly burying them for later, and other playful stuff like that. But don't take it personally. He is not being "mean," "cruel," "vicious," or any of the other anthropomorphic labels people use to explain such behavior. He is just being himself, shaking off the facade he is forced to adopt most of the time. Think of it as a vacation, a time when your pet is temporarily freed of the yoke humans use to suppress his normal tendencies to hunt, kill, and roll in the putrefying remains of his prey. He'll be back to what passes for his old self in a little while, even if you won't.

At this point, if you are not cursing, screaming, crying, laughing, or loading the shotgun while trying to decide who to shoot first—me or the dog—you are probably thinking something like, "Maybe so, but not *my* dog." Well, read on, friend. I may make a convert out of you yet.

In a single month, January 1996, a five-year-old boy was rushed into surgery after the family's pet chow bit off most of his face; another five-year-old was found screaming in his backyard as the family Rottweiler dragged him around by the head; a nine-year-old girl almost lost her arm to her brother's pit bull in Bethany Beach, Delaware; and a ten-year-old Texas boy's "best friend," a 150-pound Great Dane, demonstrated its affection by ripping open the boy's face and puncturing his skull in several places.

In November 1995, five-year-old Samantha Blake received a broken jaw and deep lacerations to her face and torso, courtesy of the family's two dogs, a Rhodesian ridgeback and a pit bull, when she went to feed them. In another case that same month, the family pit bull dragged a one-year-old girl off her parents' bed by the head, causing injuries that took seventy stitches to close. I'd bet a post hole against a pan of cornbread that these dogs' owners thought "not *my* dog" at some point too.

Before proceeding, I want to clarify my personal position on dogs in general: I do not hate dogs, despite having been bitten more times than I can remember, and even partially eaten by one of them. It was just one bite, a three-by one-inch chunk torn from my arm, but seeing the big chow-shepherd actually chew and then swallow human flesh—*my* flesh—then lick its lips and look up at me as if expecting more, was purely astonishing.

I grew up on a ranch with an assortment of hunting dogs, border collies, boxers, and Heinz fifty-sevens as constant companions and playmates. It has been my privilege to own quite a few good and some not-so-good hunting dogs, from fox, wolf, and 'coon hounds to retrievers, pointers, setters, and "layers" that slept on the porch all day. In my household, Pekingese, schnauzer, Lhasa apso, and cocker spaniel pets have slept on my hearth and, when I wasn't looking, my bed. And I dearly loved all of them.

The best dog—no, make that the best friend—I ever had was a female golden retriever, my beloved Sandy. She looks down from a picture on the wall behind me as I type this. When she died in my arms a few years ago, I wept unashamedly before men who considered me a tough *hombre*. I buried her on a hill out in the pasture, marking the grave with a stone in which I chiseled the words, "Sandy, My Friend." For weeks I wandered around in a daze, weeping quietly whenever her name was mentioned or when I walked past her special place on the porch. Sometimes, after all these years, when chill winds carry news of faraway secret places and the sky turns the color of ducks, I sit alone on the back steps and bawl like a baby.

If a man can truly love a dog, I loved Sandy. But you know what? I never fully trusted her. Regardless of my emotions, common sense told me that beneath that beautiful, silky coat I so loved to caress, there beat the heart of a predator—wild, and given to acts of mayhem on a whim. And them, folks, is the cold, hard facts.

I know how hard it is to accept the idea of your dog harboring anything but purest benevolence toward all. What most people fail to realize is that the things we characterize as affection, loyalty, or nobility are nothing more than instinctive behaviors pre-programmed into every member of the canine family, behaviors designed by nature to ensure survival. The behavior we see most of the time is what the dog knows will bring it food, a scratch behind the ears, or a romp in the yard.

As anyone who has spent time observing wild canine predators can tell you, when a dog wags its tail, rolls over onto its back, or "smiles" at you, it is communicating through body language that it recognizes your dominance as leader of the pack and does not intend to challenge you or make trouble. When it shuffles up shyly at your side, head low and "smiling," it is offering its neck to the slash of your fangs, demonstrating obeisance in acknowledgment of its position in the pack's pecking order. When it crawls, cringing on its belly, up to your feet, looking up with pitiful eyes, it is not apologizing for peeing on the rug; it is just sorry that it got caught, and hopes to forestall punishment with a display of submission.

In all but the rarest circumstances, your dog's behavior is rooted in absolute selfishness: whatever will bring it the most benefit at the moment. In other words, it does what it must to survive, and if that means "begging" for food (a natural behavior) instead of chasing it down and killing it, the dog doesn't really give a damn.

4 • Wolves, Dogs, and Coyotes

If you want a real eye-opener into your dog's true personality, spend some time watching it when it thinks no one is around. You may notice that it comports itself quite differently, ears at half-mast semaphoring that it is in charge now, the leader (that's you) having gone off to hunt in some downtown office. Watch how it moves more aggressively than usual, an air of arrogant dominance in what it considers its territory, saluting with an upraised hind leg at each signpost. It flows from here to there in spurts, pausing to work out scents of possible prey or interlopers from another pack, which may come in quadruped or bipedal form. Pay particular attention to the eyes. Is that the look of your dear little Fluffy, or of a predator on the prowl? Now, step out so it can see you and notice the instant change. The facade descends, and the predator becomes the bouncy bundle of good intentions that you love.

Dogs' instincts follow a distinct order of progression in which some behaviors take priority over others. Food takes precedence over social rituals, mating urges supersede food procurement, and competitive aggression swamps out darn near everything. A gang of males competing for a bitch in heat, for instance, will fight each other standing in the back of a meat wagon while the female broils up a sirloin and wonders what all the fuss is about.

The class of breeds known as "working" dogs exemplify predatory skills and instincts honed to a fine edge through selective breeding. Hounds represent the pinnacle of scenting and trailing skills. Bird dogs combine scenting ability with exaggerated stalking talents. (Pointers do not really point but rather stalk with extreme caution to sneak up and grab a meal before the flush, which is why dogs steady to wing and shot are so hard to train and so highly valued.) Retrievers combine chasing instincts with the practice of bringing food back to the den. Shepherds and collies are engineered to accentuate territorial, defensive, and prey herding instincts. The mastiff breeds—which include bulldogs, Rottweilers (from which Dobermans were derived), and American Staffordshire terriers (pit bulls)—were developed centuries ago to maximize size, strength, and predatory aggressiveness, the purpose illustrated in Shakespeare's Mark Antony exclaiming, "Cry havoc and let slip the dogs of war." Almost any breed you care to name represents a refinement of some trait or traits rooted in predatory instinct and related behavior.

Some instincts are more subtle and take a bit of coaxing before they become noticeable. Most dogs do not like being hugged around the neck, for instance, their survival subroutine rebelling against being held down with your fangs so close to their jugular. The reason passing trains or emergency sirens evoke howling is more darkly primal than mere discomfort in the ears.

Here's a little experiment you might try, although I wouldn't recommend it with anything larger than a miniature poodle: Wait until your dog is looking at you, then stare it right in the eye. Try not to move, blink, or smile, and do not speak or look away for even a second. Sustained eye contact makes most dogs extremely nervous. Some dissolve into submissive heaps, others run off and hide, and some do both. If it has ideas about usurping the pack-leadership position, it may return the stare, punctuated with growls and an openly aggressive posture. A dog that does this bears watching, but in a very different way.

Most animals are sensitive to eye contact to a degree that's almost psychic in extent, as if they can actually feel the touch of a gaze over surprising distances. To prey animals, sensing a predator's probing eyes can spell the difference between another day on the plains and a twelve-hour trip down the alimentary canal. Predators use eye contact among themselves to issue challenges and signal aggression. You may have noticed that when two dogs square off, neither spends much time looking at its feet. Further, dogs that get along well with one another constantly shift their eyes to avoid contact. You see the same thing in people, who generally get nervous when someone stares at them, especially if one or more members of the local predator pack are involved, staring balefully from across the street while picking their teeth with a switchblade. Many a bar fight has erupted when stare met stare, the challenge issued, understood, and answered with nary a word spoken.

I am convinced that many dog attacks result from staring on the victim's part. On encountering a strange dog, the first thing most people do is stare at it, especially if they are afraid. If the dog leans to the submissive side, such eye contact may send it packing or bring it cringing to your feet. Others consider it a challenge or a sign of predatory intentions on your part, in which case preemptive defense of self or honor is inevitable, and dogs are not known for observing the rules of gentlemanly engagement.

A good chunk of attacks are exercises in dominance, particularly those against children; dogs are quite astute at sizing up rivals to decide if they can take them. Infants killed in their cribs are fairly common, and generally reflect the dogs' observing the time-honored tradition of eliminating the competition's offspring, heirs-apparent to the pack throne. Dogs attack postmen, burglars, and vacuum-cleaner salesmen out of a sense of territory, or defense of the pack den area. Predatory attacks are frequently characterized by the dog's assaulting or threatening those coming to aid the victim, a competitive response to prey pilferage by other predators.

Predation by dogs is both common and natural, profiling closely the methodology of any other carnivore, and is little understood by most people. For instance, we have always heard that wild predators take only the old and weak, but that's not necessarily true. It often works out that old or infirm prey is slower and therefore easier to catch, but healthy adult specimens are taken regularly as necessity or opportunity dictates. There is an instinctive attraction, however, to prey exhibiting some abnormality, such as an odd gait or apparent clumsiness. Examples would be the top-heavy toddling of a small child, the shuffling gait of the aged, and locomotion by bicycle, roller skates, crutches, or a wheelchair.

In October 1995, seventy-five-year-old Walter Feser was sitting quietly in his back yard near Yakima, Washington. He did a lot of that, sitting quietly, since it is hard to do much else when you are confined to a wheelchair. Without warning, two pit bulls bounded over the

American Man-Killers

back fence and boiled straight at him in a flat-out charge. There was nothing to do but wait for death, which came rather quickly as the predators savaged the helpless man, killing his pet dachshund for good measure. Moments later, a neighbor who came to get the dogs off Feser got severely mauled for his trouble, the intervention interpreted as a competitive bid for the prey. Less than a month later, two pit bull-Rottweiler crosses in nearby Wapato chased down and mauled eleven-year-old Corey Cooley as he walked home from school. He was lucky to get by with just stitches when a passerby drove the dogs off. In January 1996, a chow dragged three-year-old Shumaine Comer off his tricycle, puncturing his head in several places and ripping off half his nose and one ear. In December 1995, two pit bulls attacked ninety-year-old Hattie McDonald when she stepped outside to get her newspaper. Officials said she probably would have been killed had a passerby not come to her aid.

Random drive-by maulings are a growth industry among enterprising canines, involving either individual animals or bona-fide packs on the hunt (more on that later). A few other examples:

In September 1995, two dogs of unknown breed attacked an eight-month-old boy in Juarez, Mexico, just across the border from El Paso, Texas. While the babysitting father slept, the dogs tore out the boy's genitals and part of his rectum on the family patio. At last report, U.S. doctors were attempting reconstruction with financial aid from the Shriners. The father hasn't been seen since the attack. A month earlier, two Rottweilers jumped nine-year-old Kamesia M. Parker as she walked to a friend's house; the last report I read said she would probably lose her left arm.

When two Baytown, Texas, men went to investigate a pair of pit bull-Rottweiler crosses shaking and dragging something across a city park playground, they found the object of interest was six-year-old Jennifer Perez, torn and bleeding from cranium to metatarsus after being ambushed at the swing set. After the men kicked and beat the dogs off her, she was helicoptered to a hospital in critical condition. In August 1995, six-year-old

4 • Wolves, Dogs, and Coyotes

Jesse Espinosa was mauled in his own driveway when a pit bull showed up unexpectedly. In January 1996, two-year-old Kayla Baumgardner received 200 stitches in her face during seven hours of surgery to repair damage inflicted by a neighbor's Labrador retriever.

In September 1995, two Rottweilers mauled nine-year-old Misti Ryan as she walked to her school-bus stop in Odessa, Texas. Her injuries included scalping, a fractured skull, a broken nose, and numerous tears to other parts of her body. The dogs dragged her 200 feet down the street before neighborhood adults could beat them off. When police arrived, they had to pepper-spray the dogs repeatedly to keep them off the girl and from attacking her seven-year-old brother. According to the report, "The dogs remained aggressive until the victim was removed from the scene by ambulance."

In December 1995, sixty-four-year-old Il Chang of Pasadena, California, was attacked by three 100-pound Rottweilers as he walked along the street near his home. When sheriff's deputies arrived, the dogs were dragging Chang around the street while trying to pull him apart in an obvious predatory attack. The deputies emptied a can of pepper spray trying to get the dogs off the man; they finally succeeded by clubbing the beasts with the butt of a shotgun.

I dearly wish somebody would explain to me the rationale behind police using pepper spray and such nonsense against a dog attempting to savage a human. In most states, deadly force can be used legally to stop one person from committing deadly assault against another, and police have most certainly done so on more than a few occasions. So why the hell don't they just shoot the dog? There may be several reasons, none of them rational.

As pointed out earlier, dogs as a species have their very own lobbying machines, and one or another group of idiots inevitably comes forward to defend dogs involved in attacks and even deaths, protesting loudly when the felons are killed. Police may be reticent about busting Fido's chops for fear of lawsuits, or the beating they would take in the media. In some cases, they may even be trying to avoid prosecution. Recently, a man was charged and tried for killing the dog that mauled his little girl. A jury acquitted him, but I will always wonder where they found a prosecutor idiot enough to file the case. Since I am protected by the statute of limitations, I'll go ahead and confess to a similar crime and let you decide if it was justified.

More years ago than I care to remember, my youngest daughter, Crystal, was playing in the big yard that separated our house from my parents' next door. I was outside with her, fooling around with a fly rod while babysitting as my wife did laundry. Nearby, a black half-pit bull my father owned—why, I'll never know—was chained along the wall of a large outbuilding. It had dug a deep hole beneath the foundation, making a sort of den in which to lurk before boiling out to ambush passing cats. My daughter, about two years old, came bobbing toward me on unsteady legs, squealing in delight at the colorful loops of fly line piling gracefully on my head as I practiced. I didn't really notice she was passing within chain length of the dog, and probably wouldn't have thought much of it if I had. I had fallen into the "he's never tried to bite anybody before" trap, an error that almost cost my daughter a trip to the hospital, if not her life.

I had just looked down to work on a wind knot in my leader when I heard Crystal's screams, washed over by the deep, guttural growls of a dog that means business. Looking up, I saw her running, terrified, away from a black blur erupting out of the hole. As in a nightmare where everything moves in slow motion, the blur resolved into the image of the pit bull, rushing forward with hind legs rising above its ears, snarling obscenities and popping its teeth like bass castanets. I dropped the fly rod and started running, trying to reach my daughter before it did. I was almost too late. I dived on top of him just as the teeth snapped, deflecting them down and away from the back of Crystal's head at the last microsecond. The teeth closed on her shorts, harmlessly tearing a hole in them as I rolled to one side, taking the dog with me.

4 • Wolves, Dogs, and Coyotes

That was one of the few times in my life when I have literally seen red, a crimson diffusion of insane rage pumping into my retinas—I had not yet realized Crystal was unhurt. Screaming like a mad thing, I seized the dog by its collar and swung it bodily over my head, crashing it across the top of the doghouse again and again, stopping only when I realized I had killed the son of bitch, beaten it into a skin bag of bone-splintered mush. I tossed the limp carcass aside and ran to my daughter, my dominance firmly established. I do not regret one whit killing that dog, or the means whereby it was accomplished. Under the same circumstances, I would do it again. I have no compunction about eliminating a child-killer, accomplished or not.

To give some idea about how ridiculous animal protectionism has gotten, in 1995 a New Jersey man was charged with animal cruelty after killing a rat. That's right, a big, ugly, property-destroying, disease-spreading, Norwegian brown rat, the same kind that infests homes and businesses by the millions from one end of North America to the other. The man had set a trap to catch rats that were eating tomatoes from his backyard garden. It must have been a live trap, because the rat was still alive when he found it. It squeaked a couple of times when he whacked it with a broom handle to kill it, prompting a do-gooder neighbor to call and report barbaric animal cruelty at the house next door. The humane people came out, looked at the scene, took the man's statement, and charged him with animal cruelty. Fortunately, New Jersey judges are wise, and the case was thrown out.

In Oklahoma, you are legally better off beating your wife than wrestling with a declawed bear. Under a 1996 law, the fine for bear wrestling is $5,000, but only $2,000 for spousal abuse. I wonder what the future holds: the death penalty for swatting flies? Twenty-five-to-life for gargling with Listerine? Germs have rights too, you know.

According to a report in the September 1989 issue of the *Journal of the American Medical Association*, 183 people were killed by dogs in the ten years leading up to

1988, most of them children. That's nearly double the number of acknowledged deaths by alligators, bears, and cougars combined, and in just ten years! Dogs kill an average of something like ten people per year in this country. I am frankly a bit surprised that the number is so low, considering that the rate of attack is somewhere between two million and five million per year. In 1994, for instance, 4.5 million dog attacks resulted in 800,000 injuries serious enough to require medical attention, fifteen fatal. The insurance industry estimates it annually pays $1 billion in dog-bite liability claims. And you wondered why your premiums were so high. I don't think there can be any debate that the nomination for Number One American man-killer should go to the dogs.

When dangerous dogs are mentioned, most people automatically think of pit bulls, Rottweilers, huskies, or one of the other large, aggressive breeds, and with ample justification. (When I heard, in the initial reports about the O. J. Simpson murders, that a bloody Akita was seen lurking about, guess what I immediately suspected.) But size alone does not a man-killer make. All dogs can be dangerous, even the "toy" breeds. As soon as you stop laughing, see if your library has a copy of the *Journal of Pediatrics*, 1982 edition, and read the account of the child-killing Yorkshire terrier. Another example involved a dachshund killing a seven-month-old boy when the mother stepped out of the room. Sort of makes you look at your Chihuahua in a whole new way, doesn't it?

People who own the larger breeds may do so for a variety of reasons. With few exceptions, hunting dogs come only in the large economy sizes, so there isn't a whole lot of choice. Don't be fooled by their seeming good nature, though; of the 183 deaths cited earlier, assorted retrievers, hounds, and spaniels numbered among the responsible. Depending on their purpose, cattle dogs range from midsize collies and heelers used for herding to protection dogs like the Great Pyrenees, on a par with St. Bernards in size. Though not ordinarily overtly aggressive as breeds, individual animals have been responsible for more than a few injuries, and some deaths.

4 • Wolves, Dogs, and Coyotes

I have been easing up on the most dangerous breeds, preparing myself to deal with the far more dangerous species on the other end of the leash. Frankly, I have less problem with pit bulls, Rottweilers, Dobermans, the various husky types, and whatnot than with the people who own them. I guess it is because I understand all too well why certain people want such dogs, even though they have no practical use for them. It is the same mentality that makes people buy "muscle" cars or 4x4 trucks jacked up so high you get a nose bleed every time you shift gears. It is a "macho" thing, external trappings that serve the owner's need to be recognized. In principle, I don't have a real problem with that; if you want to drive a Corvette, it's fine with me—as long as you don't try to find out if it will really go 140 miles an hour while I'm driving on the same freeway. The dogs are another matter. Your big, macho 4x4 is unlikely to come into my yard on its own initiative and assault me, but the same cannot be said of your Rottweiler, wolf hybrid, Rhodesian ridgeback, or pit bull.

Frequently, the mentality of people suffering from My-Dog's-Bad-and-So-Am-I syndrome is reflected in the names chosen for their pets. The dog that mauled Jesse Espinosa was named "Rock." A boxer that bit its owner's ears off was named "Mugsy Malone." "Sinbad," a ninety-five-pound malamute, mauled and nearly killed an El Segundo, California, man in his own driveway. (The city council later commuted the dog's death sentence to banishment from the city and mandatory counseling by a dog psychologist. No joke.) "Satan" is a pretty common name, and I know a couple named "Badass." Here's a cute one: After a 180-pound (that's no typo) Rottweiler attacked a three-year-old girl in Aberdeen, Washington, inflicting injuries that required over 100 stitches to her face alone, its owner hid the animal for five days from police and animal-control officers. At a court hearing to determine whether the dog should be destroyed, the woman got into a shouting match with the judge and later threw a fit outside the courtroom, stomping on a piece of paper she had wanted to introduce as evidence proving her dog was not vicious. The dog's name was "Motherf---er."

In 1996, after a sixty-pound pit bull was impounded and sentenced to death for mauling a three-year-old girl, animal-control officials had to hide the animal, fearing its owner would burglarize the shelter to save it. The man, who already had a two-page rap sheet that included assault on a police officer, was placed under a restraining order after he threatened animal-control officials. He later vowed, "If anything happens to my dog, somebody will pay, somebody severely will pay, I will make sure."

To further illustrate the phenomenon of people living vicariously through their dogs, I remember once talking with a man involved in dogfighting. He was a pit-bull man through and through, decrying the bad rap the breed was getting in the press and saying that people just didn't understand the dogs or appreciate their nobility. When I asked him why he was willing to risk his beloved dog's life in the pit, he said, "When that dog goes out there, it is like I'm going out there. When he is fighting, I feel like it is me tearing into the other dog's neck. It's exciting in a way you can't get any other way."

While it cannot be questioned that all dogs are potentially dangerous, some breeds are clearly more so than others. Pit bulls—which officers with the Los Angeles County gang unit say are the breed most favored by the Cruds and Wimps, or whatever it is gang members call themselves—accounted for forty-two percent of the fatalities in the 1989 study. (In at least two unrelated incidents reported in 1996, gang members used attack-trained pits as offensive weapons to commit one robbery and a murder.) The rest break down to German shepherds at nine percent; huskies at seven; malamutes, six; Dobermans, Rottweilers, and wolf hybrids, five; Great Danes and St. Bernards, four; with the remaining twenty-seven percent shared by hounds, bulldogs, chows, cocker spaniels, retrievers, boxers, and English sheep dogs.

Considering the Rotty's increased popularity in recent years, making it the second most favorite breed, I suspect they now share equal billing with pits as the most dangerous animals in America. And I am

4 • Wolves, Dogs, and Coyotes

apparently not alone in the opinion. State and city governments across the country have enacted or are considering laws banning the breeds outright within their borders. Others mandate "dangerous animal" registration of these and other aggressive breeds, which is about as effective as registering guns; no street trash would dare rob a liquor store with an unregistered gun. I wonder if the dogs know they are registered?

In some cases, laws have been drafted enabling prosecutors to charge owners with murder when their dogs kill. If you view these measures as extreme, consider that in most states a dog that attacks or even kills a human can be executed only after its owner gives permission, or following a protracted legal process paid for by taxpayers.

In addition to "He's never done anything like this before," one of the most common things you hear from people who own dangerous dogs is some paraphrase of "I can handle *my* dog. He is well trained and always under control." I have met quite a few people of this ilk, and frankly always wondered just who was controlling whom. Nevertheless, giving the benefit of the doubt, let's look at some genuinely well-trained and under-control dogs.

You'd have to burn a couple of barrels of witching-hour oil to find a class of dogs more intensely trained and strictly controlled than police dogs. Not only does the handler's life depend on immediate and unwavering obedience, but the public's safety must be protected as well. To assure that man and dog operate like a well-oiled machine and that there are no "accidents" on the streets, the dogs remain with the officers continually, both on the job and at home. At intervals, they go through refresher courses together to keep the edge honed fine. The dogs themselves are the cream of the crop, carefully screened for proper temperament, breeding, and intelligence before selection. Every plausible precaution is taken.

In November 1995, a K-9 officer was dispatched to the scene of a residential burglary, where a suspect had fled on foot after being shot by another officer during a struggle. The dog, a German shepherd, was supposed to track and subdue the fleeing felon. Instead, it doubled back to chase down and attack a seventeen-year-old girl, one of the burglary victims who lived at the residence. In November 1990, a police dog in Ft. Myers, Florida, killed its handler's two-week-old daughter in her crib. The child died of multiple bites to the head, chest, and abdomen.

Dogs whose owners cannot or do not control them are bad enough, but another group goes far beyond mayhem unleashed, having never been leashed in the first place. Commonly referred to as "strays," they are more properly called feral dogs, animals that developed into truly wild predators after being dumped in rural areas by well-meaning but extremely ignorant urbanites who didn't want them anymore.

I will never understand why people assume that releasing an unwanted dog "out in the country" is some-how more humane than turning it in at the pound. Perhaps they think all rural residents are animal lovers eager to take in every itinerant dog that shows up on the doorstep. Nothing could be further from the truth. Assuming the dog does not get run over and killed or is injured and dies after many days of suffering beneath a bridge or culvert, it may be killed by some farmer's own dogs when it comes around seeking food. The lucky ones die quickly from bullets to the brain when spotted skulking around chicken coops or stalking newborn calves. The last one I had to kill was a little white mongrel female, found half-dead out in the barn. She might have weighed twenty-five pounds healthy, but the bag of bones I buried scarcely weighed fifteen. I ended her suffering with a .22 bullet just behind the ear, quick, painless, and cheap. Newborn pups similarly discovered are usually eliminated with a few hundred grains of applied claw hammer to the head—equally quick and painless.

That's how the ones that don't starve to death—their stealing, scavenging, and hunting skills not up to rural survival standards—usually end up. A few will adapt, learning to live on road-kill and tidbits stolen from back-porch feeding bowls or hog pens until they learn how to stalk and kill prey, which usually includes sheep, calves, goats, and other livestock. To give some idea of the scope of this problem, one study estimated feral dogs kill an average of 175,000 head of livestock annually for a loss of $7 million—and that's at 1977 prices. These days the numbers are at least tripled, with losses variously estimated at anywhere from $15 million to $75 million annually. This does not take into account the impact that wild-dog predation has on local ecosystems. The state of Georgia alone documented 5,000 white-tailed deer killed by dogs in a single year.

Though individual specimens are often responsible, much of the carnage involves group activity by dogs ganged up in retro-evolutionary packs. Fortunately, most rural folks have the knowhow to deal with them when things turn nasty. In October 1995, a pack of five feral dogs attacked sixth-grader Justin McQuire while he fished in a small creek near Buna, Texas. Justin took a helluva lacing before a relative saw his predicament and came to the rescue. He survived by balling up and using his arms to protect his head and neck during the attack, something he had learned in a hunter-education program at his school. It hardly seems worth dwelling on the obvious ramifications of gang assault "in the country," two or more biting heads being worse than one in just about any setting, but the phenomenon of pack activity in urban areas deserves a word or two.

Feral packs operating in cities are a well-documented fact, particularly in the inner-city areas that we used to call "slums," with their overdose of abandoned buildings that make perfect hiding and denning habitat. A few years ago, a pack led by a pair of German shepherds terrorized an entire neighborhood in the Queens borough of New York City for several months, attacking people on a near-daily basis and prompting mothers to keep children indoors lest they become victims. Adults armed themselves to walk to the corner store, while others patrolled the streets with axes and clubs, hoping to find and kill the marauders, something animal control was apparently unable to do. The dogs were finally killed after being traced to their den in an abandoned building.

American Man-Killers

Similar scenarios have played out in New Haven, Connecticut; St. Louis, Missouri; and Paterson, New Jersey, to name just a few. And death was no stranger. In one case, a pack consisting of a beagle, a dachshund, and several small terrier breeds killed and ate an eighty-one-year-old woman. In another, a five-year-old boy was killed from ambush on his front lawn by several large dogs that included collies and at least one Labrador. It is certainly conceivable that a child walking alone on some secluded street could be killed, dragged away, and eaten (bones and all, as is common among canine predators) without leaving a trace, and my money says it has already happened.

Big fun, these feral dog packs.

In addition to helping quite a few funeral directors achieve early retirement, dogs have in recent years been traced as the source of a new predator emerging on the American scene: the coydog. The result of illicit affairs between dogs and coyotes, coydogs can get as big as timber wolves and equally smart. While their appearance on the livestock scene has been met with justifiable trepidation, their impact as human predators remains to be seen.

*   *   *   *

With studied stealth, the predator crept forward, head low, its eyes locked like targeting lasers on its prey. It had been watching from cover for over half-an-hour, calculating, waiting for one of the younger animals to drift away from the safety of the herd. At last a young male had moved, running off to one side in the odd, top-heavy manner of its kind, then sat down with its back foolishly exposed as it dug in the ground, apparently seeking food. Ignoring the rest of the oblivious herd, the predator began its stalk, the hollow ache of hunger throbbing in its belly.

The two-year-old boy giggled with delight as the sugary white grains of the sand box filtered through his fingers. He looked up, grinning, at his mother standing a short distance away with some other adults around a barbecue grill, hoping she would come share in the fun. He started to call out to her, but the sound was strangled into silence when something seized him by the throat from behind. He felt himself being dragged farther away from his mother. He reached out for her, trying to scream.

The coyote stopped after dragging the boy a good two hundred yards into the brush that surrounded the park. He was still alive when the predator started feeding. Six weeks later, his picture started popping up on milk cartons and chip packages under a MISSING heading, as had two other children from the same area in the preceding weeks. The few scattered bones constituting their collective remains were never found.

The foregoing account is unique among the other shenanigans recorded in this book, for it is the only one that is purely fictional. It is more than a made-up story, though; I think of it as a kind of prophecy. Maybe "prediction" would be more apropos, a forecast of things to come based on extant conditions and comparable precedents. In other words, it's going to happen sooner or later, if it hasn't already.

In August 1995, a coyote grabbed a sixteen-month-old boy from the yard of a Los Alamos, New Mexico, home and started dragging him off. The boy's mother heard him screaming and ran outside to drive the animal off. In June a three-year-old girl had been similarly attacked in the same neighborhood. In July 1995, a coyote stalked and attacked fifteen-month-old Erica Galvin while she played in Griffith Park, Los Angeles, California. The girl's mother, Dana Galvin, told *Los Angeles Daily News* reporter Keith Stone, "Her body was flip-flopping on the ground. He was trying to eat her; he was trying to kill her." The same coyote had been involved in three other attacks against adults. Of thirteen known attacks in Los Angeles County since 1975, six occurred in that park. In 1981 a coyote killed a two-year-old girl near Glendale; we can only assume that preemptive intervention prevented consumption.

It's the same old story: Put people and predators together, protect the latter, and habituation leads to people becoming prey with their pets as appetizers. Further proof of the connection between habituation, protection, and predatory attacks by coyotes can be found in the files of the national parks, where such events have been common for decades.

In October 1959, a coyote attacked a group of Boy Scouts hiking near Slough Creek in Yellowstone Park. Living up to the Scout motto "Always Be Prepared," one of the boys lit into the critter with a pocketknife and drove it off. In November 1974, a coyote attacked a man named Rick Hutchison after stalking him while he was filming a geyser eruption. The predator lunged from a distance of ten feet but was knocked back when Hutchison kicked it in the head. Undaunted, the animal came at him several more times before giving up after a kick to the lower jaw caused it to painfully bite its own tongue. Hutchison later learned that the same coyote had attacked his partner when he was unloading some equipment from their truck.

Maybe Yellowstone's coyotes learned something from the tongue-biting episode. Gerry Bateson was walking along a snowplowed road when a coyote leaped from one of the snowbanks and tore his lower lip half off. Another coyote was seen similarly stalking a boy from the cover of a plowed snowbank, but the boy's father chased it off before any serious lip biting occurred—by the coyote, I mean.

Several incidents have occurred outside but nearby the park. Sometime around 1967 near Mammoth, Montana, a coyote attacked nine-year-old Cara Lee Nuss as she was walking to school, knocking her down and biting her severely on the leg before being driven off. A few years prior, a coyote tried to snatch one-and-one-half-year-old Martha Biastock from her carrier on the front porch of her home. The mother had placed the child there while she unloaded groceries from the car. She heard a commotion and looked up to see a neighbor beating the coyote with a broom. After she joined the fracas, it took them several minutes to drive the determined predator away from its meal. The child suffered bruises and a bad tear in her lip that took twenty-one stitches to close.

4 • Wolves, Dogs, and Coyotes

More recently, in 1995, a pack of coyotes was seen following a group of California children walking home from school. In January 1990, twenty-seven-year-old Brian Dean was attacked while skiing in Yellowstone. The animal lunged when Dean swished by it, knocking him off his feet and attacking his face as he lay on the ground. After a protracted battle that netted him numerous cuts and puncture wounds severe enough to later land him in the hospital, Dean escaped when he stunned the predator with a blow to the head from one of his skis.

In 1988 a coyote attacked and was preparing to eat an eighteen-month-old infant in British Columbia, but some adults chased it off before it could sample the main course. The child was hospitalized and received over 250 stitches. That same year, a coyote attempted to drag a teenager out of a tent in Banff National Park, Canada.

Once considered a denizen of the prairies, the coyote's range now extends from sea to shining sea. In 1995 coyotes were reported eating pets in Seekonk, Rhode Island; the Texas cities of Carrollton, Dallas, and Ft. Worth; Cadillac, Dowagiac, and St. Joseph, Michigan; plus a host of other cities from Acton, Massachusetts, to Long Beach, California. And we know what's next on the menu, don't we? In 1992 two hunters were attacked in separate incidents by coyotes in Vermont. In 1994 a Barnstable, Massachusetts, woman was bitten severely on the leg while taking her morning constitutional on a road near her home. In March 1995, two hikers managed to kill a coyote after it attacked them near Mt. Sunapee, New Hampshire.

If you want to blame someone for this unprecedented explosion in coyote numbers, distribution, and bad conduct, lay it at the feet of Carol Burnett, Mary Tyler Moore, Bob Barker, Ricki Lake, Robert Redford, Betty White, Ellen DeGeneres, and the rest of the Hollywood illuminati who know better than anyone else what is good for wildlife, for it was they who launched the 1980s anti-fur campaign that dropped the bottom out of the fur market. It used to be that a prime coyote hide could swell a trapper's coffers by as much as $75.00. These days you can hardly give them away, so why bother?

183

American Man-Killers

What more can I say? The darling of suburbia is a killer, and seems to be getting better at it. Call me a romantic, but I find it comforting to know there is an option to being eaten by cougars, bears, alligators, or my own dog. I always try to look on the bright side of things.

DEER, ELK, and MOOSE

Run, man, it's Bambi!

Whether you are one of the millions of Americans who annually stoke up the larder with venison personally collected in the woods, or an animal lover laboring under the delusion that all those darling little deer just need a big, warm hug, you are in for what may be the crowning surprise of your life. I don't want to put anyone into a state of terminal shock, so let's ease into this gently with a less-than-fatal, albeit bloody account of Bambi the man-killer.

American Man-Killers

In the extreme northwestern reaches of Tarrant County, Texas, where the Trinity River flows from Eagle Mountain Reservoir, traverses the Ft. Worth Nature Center, and empties into Lake Worth, a surprising diversity of wild creatures live in relative secrecy from prying eyes. Ancient trees stand sentinel over a shadowy world where owls and whippoorwills haunt the night. The river has carved for itself places to rest during the dry-season ebb—shallow backwaters and deep, dark holes that have evolved into marshes and swamps, where hawser-thick moccasins drape the trees like black tinsel and where beavers, nutria, and raccoons make their homes on the banks. Bats and chuck-will's-widows swoop above the still waters in the twilight, feasting on an insect smorgasbord. Though few in number, alligators ghost the shadowy waters, ever watchful for the opportunity to take in a meal from those incautious enough to stray close to the banks of their watery domain. And, naturally, a few white-tailed deer hang their hats in this urban wilderness, located practically in the shadow of Ft. Worth's skyline.

Deer weren't on the minds of Ron Smith and Aric Alvarez in October of 1993 as they trudged along the riverbank. They were looking for a place to fish and while away a Sunday free from urban struggles. The men had set out early from Vance's Camp, a fishing camp some five miles downriver from Eagle Mountain Reservoir, and had walked roughly two miles upriver toward the lake. They came to a brush-shrouded bend, just the kind of crappie hole they were looking for. Smith baited up and settled back in the grass, more interested in solitude than fishing, while Alvarez, Smith's nephew, moved a bit farther upstream to cast for bass.

A half-hour had passed when Smith was startled out of a half-doze by the sound of something moving in the brush. Thinking that Alvarez had returned, Smith sat up and was surprised to see a nine-point white-tailed buck eying him from scarcely twenty yards away on the far side of the river. The man sat still so as not to spook the deer. He watched it and it watched him for a while; then the deer stepped into the river and began to swim. Smith

5 • Deer, Elk, and Moose

was fascinated. He had never seen a deer at such close quarters in the wild, and hoped the animal would swim closer and give him an even better look. He didn't realize just how close a look he was about to get.

The deer traversed the river and clambered out, shaking itself like a dog. Just ten yards from Smith, the deer turned and looked straight at the man as if seeing him for the first time. Smith remained still, to see what the buck would do next. It stretched its nose toward the man, sniffing the air. Suddenly, its demeanor changed from simple curiosity to pure malevolence. Previously cupped ears swiveled back to lay flat along the neck, every hair on its body bristling. The head dropped slightly, cocking to one side as the buck stared balefully through half-slitted eyelids. Smith sensed that he was in danger, and oddly thought of the date, October 31— Halloween Day. Trick or treat. The buck pawed the ground once, dropped its head low, and charged with astonishing speed.

Smith knew the buck wasn't bluffing, and tried to get up to run. He was halfway to his feet when the animal smashed into him. He fell backward into the river, reflexively grabbing the antlers and pulling the buck in after him. Momentum carried man and deer deep beneath the surface. Smith clawed to the top, sputtering muddy water out of his lungs as the buck bobbed up scant feet away. Smith gained the shore first and clambered out. He figured the impromptu dunking might have taken the wind out of the buck's sails, but no such luck. The deer climbed out seconds behind the shivering man and was on him again in a flicker.

The impact of the second charge slammed Smith to the ground onto his back, knocking the wind out of him. The buck pressed the charge, stabbing at the man's face with the brush-honed pitchforks on its head. Smith grabbed a double fistful of horns and hung on for literal dear life. He didn't realize until it was too late that he had seized the tip of an antler. The buck's next lunge drove the point of the right main beam completely through the palm of his left hand and into the ground. Since this didn't feel very good, Smith tore his hand off the crucifying spike and wormed out from under the buck. Gaining his feet, he shifted his grip and somehow managed to bulldog the nine-pointer to the ground. To paraphrase the obvious, he now had a buck by the horns and couldn't let go.

Alvarez had been out of sight around the bend when he heard his uncle's cries, followed by a loud splash. Figuring Smith had accidentally fallen into the river, the lad dropped his pole and ran to help. It was a wonderful collection of flying dust and wildly flailing arms, legs, horns, and hooves that greeted Alvarez when he crashed out of the brush. He sized up the situation and ran in to deliver the hardest kick he could muster to the buck's ribs. The deer didn't even flinch. The lad looked around for a weapon and found a large tree limb with which he intended to brain the deer. Smith looked up just as Alvarez was about to swing the club down on the buck's head, which was within inches of his own. "For God's sake, don't kill me!" he screamed.

Realizing that he might further injure his already bleeding uncle, Alvarez cast the limb aside. Frantic with concern that Smith was about to get his insides hooked outside, Alvarez tried to pry the buck off. He'd have had more luck separating a miser from his bankbook. He was about to give the club idea another try when he remembered the long fillet knife Smith had on his belt. Careful to avoid the slashing hooves and antlers, Alvarez reached beneath the embattled man for the knife. Smith held on while Alvarez cut the buck's throat. It took nearly twenty minutes for the animal to bleed to death.

Smith held on until the last quiver, then collapsed, heaving like a bellows on the trampled grass. He didn't know how badly he might be injured—covered in blood and experiencing severe pain in his hand, ribs, and abdomen, he feared the worst. Just as the first waves of shock began to wash over him, Smith instructed Alvarez to go back to the camp for help and lapsed into semiconsciousness.

At the hospital, Smith learned what a lucky man he was. Other than considerable blood loss, his most

5 • Deer, Elk, and Moose

serious injuries were the hole in his left hand and a few bruised ribs. Doctors credited the down vest Smith had been wearing against the morning chill with saving his life. Without the padding, Smith would likely have received an impressive new set of optional navels.

If you think you know me well enough by now to conclude this was no isolated incident and that I am going to launch an extended, violent dissertation about the dozens of people who annually get hammered by deer, you are mistaken. Actually, I am about to launch an extended, violent dissertation about the *hundreds* of people who annually get hammered by deer.

As success stories go, the white-tailed deer (*Odocoileus virginianus*) is an all-American classic. At the turn of the twentieth century, there were something less than 500,000 whitetails in all of the U.S. Today, thanks to the efforts of various states' wildlife-management programs, a similar number is annually killed by hunters in Texas alone. Population estimates vary widely, but even the most conservative put 18 million deer within U.S. borders, not counting the vast Canadian herds or those in Mexico and Central and South America. Yet there are people out there who will try to convince you otherwise, frequently propagandizing school children with the notion that whitetails are in imminent peril of extinction.

I once read in a major metropolitan newspaper a letter to the editor written by an eleven-year-old boy expressing his wish that people would stop killing animals, especially white-tailed deer. He said that unless hunting was stopped, whitetails would be extinct by the year 2000. I used to have a copy of the letter, but darned if I can find it. You'll have to trust me on this one, but make no mistake that the letter and the organized brainwashing it evidences are very real.

Be that as it may, anyone with a lick of sense knows there is one whole passel of deer in these here Yewnited States—more, in fact, than when Christopher Columbus missed that left turn to the West Indies. Except for Alaska, Hawaii, and where prohibited by law, every state

American Man-Killers

hosts a sizable population of whitetails. Which is great news, really. Problem is, they are not always content to live in the woods.

A junior high school teacher in Lakewood, Michigan, got an unexpected opportunity to demonstrate the creative use of adjectives when a white-tailed doe crashed into her language-arts classroom through a plate-glass window. It landed on top of two students, miraculously without injuring them, then scrambled to its feet and calmly looked around to consider its options. A hasty exit seemed in order, which it made through another closed window in the principal's office, adding some spice to the hall monitor's life along the way. In one of those odd coincidences common to man-animal interactions, the father of one of the students who got landed on had been trampled by a deer the previous year.

At another junior high school a few miles away in Ostego, authorities suspected some awful crime when they arrived one morning to find blood and broken window glass on the floor. Investigation revealed a case of vandalism, perpetrated by a white-tailed buck found trashing one of the classrooms. Sheriff's deputies killed the injured deer after lassoing it and dragging it outside.

At yet another Michigan institution of higher learning, some preschool students had their afternoon naps interrupted by a buck attempting to crash through the picture window of their classroom. Fortunately, the window was tougher than the buck (the latter broke and the former didn't) and the deer was the only casualty.

Coincidence? Not really. The same sort of thing happens on a near-daily basis all across the country. It is interesting, though, that all three of the above schoolhouse parties happened within days of each other in the same month, November of 1995. Of course, not all deer are interested in elementary book-learning; some prefer to shop 'til they drop.

After a white-tailed buck made its characteristic entrance through a window at the Montgomery Ward store in a Lansing, Michigan, shopping mall, it gamboled down the mall's center aisle to Sibley's Shoe Store. The store

5 • Deer, Elk, and Moose

was full of customers, but the deer made no attempt to charge, possibly because its credit cards had been canceled, and took refuge in a storage room after an alert security guard foiled its escape. It was later tranquilized and removed by wildlife officials.

No shopping trip would be complete without a lunch break, which may explain why a buck crashed through the front glass of Miguel's Pizza Queen Restaurant in downtown Newaygo, Michigan, but I suspect robbery as the real motive. According to Miguel, the deer slammed into the pop cooler several times in an apparent attempt to access the coin box. When confronted, the deer made threatening gestures but decided to call the whole thing off after Miguel went for his gun. It exited by breaking out the store's other front window, and was last seen headed toward the river, pursued by a local dog. Another robbery attempt took place in Owosso, Michigan, at the Tractor Supply Company farm store. Again, entry was made through a front window and the buck fled after failing to find the cash box.

Okay, so you don't buy the robbery bit. How about home invasion?

Two weeks after the bungled farm-store burglary, a deer crashed through the front window of an Owosso home, galloped through the living room, broke through a sliding glass door onto the patio, vaulted a stone wall, and disappeared into the woods along the Shiawassee River. The next day, a buck broke through the French doors of a home in Holt, upended a La-Z-Boy recliner, smashed an antique coffee table, and leaped over a loveseat before exiting the way it had come.

Though tragedy was averted in these cases, serious injuries and even deaths have occurred in others. It came mighty close in the recliner-chair incident; moments before, an infant had been lying in the exact spot where the mangled window frame came to rest. Fortunately, the child had been taken to another room for a diaper change.

Technically, incidents like these are more akin to accidents than actual attacks. I use the "technically" qualifier because, according to some theories, deer that launch

American Man-Killers

themselves through windows are most likely attacking their own reflections out of a sense of territory or competition. This is probably true in most cases, especially if hormone-crazed rutting bucks are involved. Each of the above window jobs—a tiny sampling from my files—occurred in November, a peak month for rutting activity.

Rutting bucks or bulls of just about any species will attack nearly anything, moving or otherwise, and it is particularly true of whitetails. Hunters know to look for "rubs" where bucks have vented their aggression against saplings and brush. A buck in Chippewa Falls, Wisconsin, destroyed a concrete lawn ornament made in the image of a deer.

There are inconsistencies in the nihilistic Narcissus theory, namely that bucks are not the only practitioners and that the timing is sometimes wrong. An example of both occurred in May 1995—well before the autumn onset of rut—when a doe jumped through the window of a home in East Lansing's Pine Forest subdivision. In June of that same year, a buck broke through a window in the city's airport terminal.

I have my own pet theory about the whys of non-rut-related window-bashing. I believe it is a wholly natural behavior, rooted in instinct and closely linked to the phenomenon of deer running toward car headlights on the highway at night, but I don't think an in-depth exploration is justified here. Knowing why deer leap through windows is not as important as knowing *that* they do, sometimes with tragic results.

I suppose I am obligated to mention that an average of 140 people are killed every year by deer crashing through car windshields in highway collisions. But since we are in the homicide business and not accident investigation, these types of deaths don't really count. Let's get back to the real deal.

In the fall of 1990, police in central Texas were dispatched to investigate the report of a pickup parked beside the road for two days with its driver-side door open. As the police arrived, a large white-tailed buck was spotted in the brush about ten yards from the vehicle, thrashing a sapling with its antlers. It charged the

194

officers when they tried to approach the vehicle. It backed off when they did but would come for them each time they moved near the truck. At some point in the festivities, the police figured out it wasn't the pickup the buck was guarding but rather a body lying in the ditch near the open driver-side door.

They finally killed the buck after it repeatedly fought off their attempts to reach the body of sixty-one-year-old Buddy Coleman. The official cause of death was a crushed skull, but he probably would have bled to death anyway from the more than 100 puncture wounds inflicted to his back, stomach, and face by the deer's hooves and antlers.

It is impossible to say whether Coleman fought with his assailant or died instantly at the outset when attacked from behind. My guess would be the latter, based on the fact that no "defensive" wounds were evident on the arms. And there's no telling how long the buck might have ravaged the body after death. The attack, incidentally, was unprovoked. Coleman was practically within sight of his home at the time, picking up aluminum cans along the road. The buck, a monster by Texas standards at 160 pounds, was healthy and tested negative for any disease that might account for its behavior.

This incident is not unusual for having happened in the first place—people-bashing is a relatively common whitetail pastime—but why on earth a deer would want to guard a body at all, let alone do so for two full days after the fact, is beyond me. Nobody, including the few dozen wildlife biologists I asked about this, seems to know. This presumably emergent aspect of whitetail behavior has gone unnoticed until very recently by just about everybody. Aberrant though it may be, it happens often enough to make me suspect it may be inherent to the species, a behavioral parallel to nontypical antler growth among bucks, or does birthing quadruplet fawns.

In June 1994, near Possum Kingdom Reservoir, a couple of hundred miles from where the Coleman incident occurred, a Texas woman was almost killed in her own driveway by a velvet-antlered buck as she collected her mail. A passerby saw the unconscious woman within minutes of the attack and called authorities. This buck stood guard over its victim too, taking up station beneath a mesquite tree about thirty yards distant. It charged Brazos River Authority chief ranger Mike Cox when he arrived on the scene and tried to approach the woman. Cox had to kill the buck before paramedics could tend to her. She survived with multiple lacerations, bruises, a concussion, and several broken bones.

Darned if I know, guys. Until somebody comes up with credible proof of whitetail man-eating, I guess we'll have to write it off to racial tensions or just bad karma.

Exactly why whitetails attack humans without provocation is an equally slippery question. As already mentioned, lust-induced dementia in bucks is frequently blamed, and I do not question that this is certainly a factor in many instances. But it cannot account for the large number of attacks that occur in the off-season. Obviously, a buck still in velvet in June can hardly be considered a sex maniac. Then there is the interesting dilemma posed when does commit acts of overt aggression. My friend Mike Biggs, a professional wildlife photographer who specializes in whitetails, told me that one of the closest shaves he's ever had was when a little 100-pound doe "beat him up" with her flailing front hooves. That she didn't smash in his skull is accountable to his extensive experience with the species and a very fleet pair of feet.

The provocation aspect, or more properly the lack of it, would seem to be the most enigmatic. Predators attacking unprovoked is easy to figure out with the formula EB + AH = SP. For the uninitiated, this translates to Empty Belly + Available Human = Satiated Predator. Things aren't quite so pat where normally inoffensive herbivores are concerned. Though it is completely logical that a deer would attack defensively to protect itself from predators or its territory against other ungulate interlopers, I cannot see the rationale behind playing kickball with a human for no apparent purpose other than just for the sheer hell of it.

Since free-roaming deer are now standard features in many suburban parks and neighborhoods, habituation would appear to be an obvious factor in those areas.

5 • Deer, Elk, and Moose

Deer accustomed to being literally hand-fed in the back yard would have no fear of humans, and the likelihood of attack would certainly be magnified.

In November 1995, a woman feeding apples to a group of does in Wallowa Lake campground near Enterprise, Oregon, got the bad news when a buck slammed in from her blind side and tossed her ten feet into the air, her tailbone breaking upon reentry. Considering the time of year, and that deer are not very astute at determining a human's sex or orientation thereof, the buck may have taken her mingling with his harem as a competitive bid for the attentions of the ladies fair. A few days later, a woman in Bethany, Pennsylvania, noticed a white-tailed buck watching her as she puttered in her garden. She went inside and retrieved an apple, which she offered to the buck. It came forward, sniffed, and promptly gored her. She was lucky to survive with only a few bruised ribs.

A woman in Spring Branch, Texas, had a stimulating experience in her back yard with a "tame" deer, actually a wild animal named "Cedar" by neighborhood residents after it adopted a suburban lifestyle. Early one morning, the lady entered her yard and saw the deer standing nearby. She walked over to pet him and politely said, "Good morning, Cedar." That did it! Cedar, obviously insulted, lit into the woman and tried his best to place her *en brochette*. Being a tough Texan, the woman grabbed a couple of fistfuls of antler and started wrestling for her life. It was nip and tuck for a full forty minutes before the buck became distracted when it backed into a tree, giving the woman a chance to bolt for the house and safety.

Besides disliking ladies bearing apples or cordial greetings, deer seem to harbor some sort of grudge against runners. A competitor in the Maryland College Championship cross-country event was knocked out of the competition—as well as literally out—when a buck ambushed him from cover. A competitor in the 1993 Collegiate Peaks Trail Run received four broken ribs, a punctured lung, a concussion, and several holes in his head when a buck blind-sided him. A witness described it as "something like you'd see in an NFL highlight film."

American Man-Killers

I don't know if Charles Stuart's encounter really qualifies as an "attack." He was most certainly injured, receiving several gashes in his head, a concussion, and a sprained right knee that kept him on crutches for several days. Technically, though, Stuart just got in the way of a deer stampede while walking his dog in Mary Quinlan Park about fifteen miles northwest of downtown Austin, Texas. A total of eight whitetails ran over, stepped on, and otherwise abused Stuart before leaving him bleeding and unconscious in the middle of the road. Sounds like a drive-by to me.

Among the amazing variety of unpleasant white-tail encounters that people have, hunting incidents are the ones I find most interesting. This is partly because that as a hunter I can more closely identify with them. To be completely honest, though, I mostly appreciate them for their entertainment value. When hunters and white-tailed bucks get together under nontraditional circumstances, the results can be purely spectacular.

Gary Tidwell, a friend from Springtown, Texas, had an experience sufficiently unique to qualify as Ripley's material. Hunting from an elevated box blind just a few miles from home, Gary spotted a heavy-bodied deer moving through the brush about one hundred yards off. Closer eight-power inspection revealed that the buck's antlers didn't measure up to its body proportions. The animal was something of a freak, sporting two very long, heavy spikes in lieu of the preferred multi-pointed con-figuration. Figuring "You can't eat antlers anyway," Gary settled the cross hairs on the buck's chest and squeezed off. The deer dropped as if dynamited.

Using one of the long spikes as a lever, Gary turned the deer this way and that, looking to see if his bullet had gone where directed. Strangely, the buck didn't seem to have a mark on it. Puzzlement changed to fear when the deer suddenly sprang up, issued a bleat-like grunt, and charged with murder in its eyes. Having considerable regard for his anatomical nether regions, the astonished hunter fought down the impulse to run, realizing the tight grip he still had on the antler was all that stood between him and a one-way trip to oblivion, courtesy of those brush-honed daggers. Thinking quickly, with his free hand he extracted his hunting knife from its belt sheath and began practicing a bit of unlicensed surgery on the deer. After several minutes of playing "king of the mountain" for keeps, the deer succumbed from blood loss and lay still.

After his heart rate got back on scale, Gary tried to piece together the circumstances that had placed him in hand-to-antler combat with a presumably dead deer. As previously observed, the deer bore no mark save that inflicted by the hunting knife. Looking around, Gary noticed a large, dead tree limb on the ground near where the deer had initially fallen. The limb looked somehow out of place, the more-weathered side down and the grass beneath still green. Close inspection of the freshly broken end revealed the unmistakable mark of a bullet strike. The hunter hadn't noticed the deer-colored limb interposing across the buck's chest. The shot had hit the limb, causing it to fall and knocking the buck cold temporarily—until it came to and asked Gary to dance.

Another acquaintance, Jason Earp, a distant relation to the marshal of Tombstone, got his overdose of whitetail on Halloween Day in 1991 near Eagle Mountain Lake (spookily coincidental with Ron Smith's riverbank dance detailed at the beginning of this chapter). While he and a friend, Bill Tinney, were bowhunting a small area of private land bordering the lake, Jason put two arrows into a big, derrick-racked buck from his tree stand, just moments before the dying sun was engulfed in the maw of a thunderstorm. By Coleman lantern light, the hunters followed the rain-washed, bubbly-pink trail of lung blood for nearly an hour until it disappeared at the edge of the lake. With no blood trail to follow, Jason feared the buck was lost. Just then a blue lash of lightning illuminated the gale-whipped surface of the lake, and there, seventy-five yards out and swimming strongly for the opposite shore, was his buck.

Jason had worked hard for that buck, the best one he'd ever shot. He wasn't about to give it up that easily. Living up to his legendary name, Earp shucked his boots and heavy outer clothes, clamped his knife in his teeth just like John Wayne would have done it, and dived into the chilly water.

A strong swimmer, Jason closed with the buck in rapid fashion, grabbed an antler, and swung the buck up onto its back. He was just drawing back to deliver the *coup de grâce* with his knife when the buck decided to assume a less passive role, sweeping back with its unusually long antlers to knock Jason off into the white-caps and causing him to lose his knife. The deer then reversed direction and started swimming back toward the shore where Tinney waited.

Tinney had no weapon except his own knife (both hunters had left their bows back at the road), but he did have a rope that was intended for dragging the buck out of the woods. When the deer drew close, Tinney tried several times to lasso it, but the gale-force winds kept blowing the noose off course. Distracted by Tinney, the buck didn't see Jason creeping up from behind, using the heavy swells and whitecaps as cover. When he thought he was close enough, Jason lunged and boarded the deer again.

In a lightning-illuminated scene right out of a *Twilight Zone* episode, Jason took a ride among the white-caps that would do any bronc-buster proud. When the deer began to tire, Jason slid off into the knee-deep water and bulldogged it, holding its head beneath the waves until the twitching stopped.

A hunter in Rhode Island got a double treat in October 1995: the chance to witness a genuine buck fight in the wild, and a free nose job. The man was hunting during the muzzleloader season when a pair of bucks started fighting near his blind. He shot one of them when the fight ended, and the other one ran off. He had climbed down out of his stand and was going to inspect his trophy when the other deer came back. You guessed it. The second buck charged, smashing into the man's chest and knocking him flat on his back preliminary to the application of some hoof therapy. At some point in the melee, an antler tine somehow got up the man's nose and, when the buck tossed, ripped the nostril right up to the cartilage. With this new motivation, the man made use of the couple of quarts of adrenaline charging through his system to fight the buck off, whereupon it ran before another hunter's blind and was shot.

The attack was provoked, by the way, but not in the way you probably think. The hunter was wearing on his person a liberal application of doe-in-heat scent, made from urine collected from captive does in estrus. Another hunter was similarly scented when a buck attacked him in the same week and just a few miles from where Buddy Coleman was killed.

I don't suppose it is necessary to point out how dangerous—not to mention stupid—it is to wear a sex attractant/stimulant in the woods. The only real surprise is the nature of the injuries these men sustained. Several of my acquaintances and I have frequently debated what would happen if a buck caught up with a hunter who smelled like a willing doe in heat. There was always some disagreement as to specific details, but general consensus ran to consequences consistent with what you'd expect from dropping your soap in the shower of the sex offenders' ward at a men's prison.

It is, if you'll pardon the expression, painfully obvious that it is the hunters themselves who provoke exercises in heightened blood pressure between themselves and wounded game. Sometimes, though, deer take the initiative in what appears to be some sort of preemptive strike. A good recent example involved Raymond Rebels, who was hunting near Garrison, Texas, when a buck boiled out of the brush and nailed him in a sneak attack from behind. Rebels wrestled with the deer for some time, his gun lost, and finally climbed a tree to get away.

Odd as it may seem, I believe it is entirely possible that deer may account for some missing persons. One case that came close is that of fifty-year-old Douglas Moore, whose body was found lying near his pickup truck in the woods of Cherokee County, Texas, in November 1995. He had bled to death from a single puncture wound that pierced an artery in his leg. On the ground several yards away, investigators found more blood that lab tests later proved had come from a deer. A gun, unloaded, was found near the body, and there were no spent casings around. Apparently, Moore had shot the deer and, thinking it dead, unloaded his gun before beginning the job of field-dressing. Big mistake. Had the incident occurred in a more remote setting, chances are the man's fate never would have been known. Incidentally, despite diligent search and tracking efforts extending over several weeks, the deer was never found and is assumed to have survived.

I honestly do not know how many stories I have heard over the years about "dead" deer unexpectedly coming alive. One fellow I know shot a big buck and actually had dragged it several hundred yards when it came to. Fortunately, the deer was effectively hogtied by the drag rope and the man was able to shoot it again with more definitive results before it could do anything unsavory. In another case, a Texas game warden had stopped some suspected poachers, not realizing they had an out-of-season spike buck hidden beneath a tarp in the pickup bed. While he questioned the men, the tarp became animated as the spike scrambled to its feet and leaped over the warden's head to disappear, frolicking, around the bend. I wonder if he gave them a ticket?

Mule deer also suffer from the Lazarus syndrome, and are equally inclined to ill manners. Jack Hughes was kneeling over a big muley he had shot near Winston, Oregon, preparatory to field-dressing, when the deer suddenly sprang up for a game of belly-button roulette. Hughes tried to back off, but one of the buck's flailing front legs hooked through the binocular strap around his neck, effectively tethering the man to the animal. With escape impossible and his knife lost in the initial lunge, Hughes had no choice but to grab some antler and hope for the best. He thought Kismet was going to get the last word when the buck suddenly wrenched free of his grip, but the strap fortunately broke about then and the deer opted for the discretion of greener pastures.

Silly as it sounds, I can't help but think that American deer hunters would be wise to adopt the old African hunter's philosophy: If it bites or gores, you can't make it too dead. Any big-game animal, regardless of size or sex, can be dangerous as typhoid, especially if wounded. Even a brown-eyed white-tailed doe is capable of a most convincing Lizzie Borden impersonation, giving you a lot more than forty whacks with her axe-edged hooves. The last time I checked, rifle ammo was still considerably cheaper than emergency-room rates, so an insurance shot applied to something that is big and well armed seems like a real bargain. And please don't start up about not wanting to ruin any more meat. If you shoot a deer where you are supposed to, in the chest, you'll ruin darn little meat. Yeah, I know—you always shoot 'em in the neck, using that same excuse about wanting to preserve meat from bullet damage. I hope you'll pardon me if I suggest that philosophy smells distastefully similar to something one would be better off not stepping in.

Now that I have your attention, let's talk about neck shots.

First off, anyone who claims to shoot deer or other game in the neck to avoid ruining meat is obviously unfamiliar with neck roast. If the truth be known, this dubious concern for culinary propriety is often a smoke screen to hide the shooter's penchant for lily-gilding. Since the neck is such a small and therefore difficult target to hit, some gun-toting bozos (I do not honor them with the title "hunter") choose it by way of demonstrating their presumed marksmanship talents with "a running neck shot at 200 yards."

I've heard quite a few variations of this tale in hunting camps over the years, and more often than not, the speaker would later prove unable to hit the inside of his hat if it were propped over the gun's muzzle. There's nothing wrong with making a good shot under difficult conditions and being proud of it. But to deliberately handicap yourself by choosing the smallest, most difficult vital area in which to place a shot at live game is at best irresponsible and in some cases downright criminal—for reasons we'll explore shortly.

The other reason people opt for neck shots is their sincere belief that it is the only way to guarantee a quick, clean kill. And you know what? They are right. Sort of.

American Man-Killers

A number of hunters have told me they started shooting for the neck after losing one or more deer that escaped after being shot in the chest. To a man, their preferences in guns ran to .22-250s, .243s, .270s, 6mms, or some other puny caliber. Of the dozens of wounded animals I have helped track down, all but two had been shot with one of these powder puffs.

I can hear the hue and cry of Jack O'Connor's disciples now, storming the castle gates with flaming torches and demanding my head on a bloody post. Please do not tell me about all the deer, elk, moose, bears, and woolly mammoths that have been killed with these or other small-caliber rifles. And yes, I know all about Walter Bell killing several boxcar loads of elephants with a .256 Mannlicher. Nevertheless, the fact remains that killing big game with a souped-up BB gun is not hunting; it is a stunt. A competent marksman could probably kill a Cape buffalo with a .22 rimfire under the right circumstances. Lord knows enough deer have been poached with that caliber, and I know two instances of full-grown bears, one of them a grizzly, being killed with brain shots through the ear. Yet you don't see a lot of people in deer camps with .22s slung over their shoulders, legalities notwithstanding. Why, then, are some people so enamored with the idea of deflating deer with what were originally designed as varmint-hunting calibers? Several reasons.

Rifles tend to get mighty heavy by the end of a long, mud-slogging, rock-climbing, ankle-twisting day in the field, so the noticeable reduction in overall weight afforded by a magazine full of small, lightweight cartridges is greatly appreciated. Gunmakers haven't managed to remain in business by being stupid, however, and most now produce extremely lightweight rifles in even the largest of calibers. At the 1996 SHOT show in Dallas, Texas, a lady tried to sell me a rifle weighing only six pounds and chambered in .458 Winchester Magnum! Thanks, but no thanks.

Another reason frequently cited for choosing a hamster gun is the flat trajectory afforded by high-bullet velocity. But how important is that, really? Even the venerable .30-30 Winchester has a point-blank

5 • Deer, Elk, and Moose

trajectory that will print inside six inches at 200 yards. Be honest, and think of how many shots you've taken at game beyond that range. Okay, so you do all your hunting on the Midwestern plains and most shots are at 300 yards or more. How much remaining energy does a .270 bullet possess at that range? Not enough, I can tell you. If you really do need a flat-shooter and want to be sure of delivering a potent pill, spend a little time perusing the ballistics tables. You'll find some truly marvelous flat-shooting, hard-hitting gems shining among the pages, like the .300 Winchester and Weatherby Magnums and 7mm Remington Magnum, among others. For that matter, the .30-06 ain't no slouch, even if it is a bit long in the tooth.

The last reason for using too-light guns is one most people won't admit: recoil. Recoil sensitivity is nothing to be ashamed of, yet many people are because some chest-thumping, smell-like-leather idiot in a safari jacket convinced them it is somehow "unmanly." That being the case, Your Obedient Servant must henceforth sit at the back of the bus with the rest of the sissies.

I do not like recoil. It hurts like hell and gives me a headache to boot. Yet the lightest center-fire rifle I own is a .300 Weatherby Magnum, which cranks out roughly twice the kick of a .30-06 at something like forty foot-pounds of free recoil in an eight-pound gun. Furthermore, I have on more than one occasion scared the living daylights out of half the county by cutting loose with a shoulder-fired rifle chambered for the .50-caliber Browning machine-gun round, a nifty little tank-stopper that is spectacularly effective for following up wounded, water-filled oil drums.

Don't get the idea here that I am bragging or otherwise erecting a monument to my manhood. I am not as stupid as I look and long ago came to appreciate such technological marvels as recoil pads and muzzle brakes. So equipped, I can gleefully capitalize on the .300's universal utility and ventilate anything from prairie dogs to mule deer in complete comfort, reserving my heavier armament for the bigger stuff. Overgunned? Hardly. I do not care if my prairie dogs get blown to bits by those

110-grain hollowpoints hustling along at 3,800 feet per second. And I have never sacrificed more than half a pound of meat from a deer punctured with a 220-grain softpoint due to bullet damage. The best part is, I have never had anything walk off or try to bite me after being shot with it either—and it is surely not because I shoot them in the neck.

Admittedly, a well-placed neck shot can be splendidly effective. I have used the shot myself on two occasions, both of them at close range under circumstances where no other shot was available and the deer was already wounded (not by me). A bullet through that tight bundle of blood vessels and nerves will unquestionably make anything from a rabbit to a Cape buffalo go *floomph* in one mighty impressive hurry. The problem lies in the necessity for placing the shot not merely *in* the neck but *precisely* in the neck.

As I said, the neck is a small target anyway, allowing a vertical margin for error of only three inches or so, six at the outside on big animals like elk or moose. If the shot goes a bit high, the bullet may pass close enough to the cervical column to stun but not kill, which could later lead to a very handy and wideawake critter with revenge on its mind. Depending on the angle, a shot that goes wide or low may blow out the esophagus or lower jaw, resulting in a wounded animal doomed to death by inches from starvation. I have twice found the carcasses of deer that met this fate.

The neck shot becomes even less a winning proposition when you factor in considerations like unknown range to the target, wind, improper rest (for the gun, I mean, or even for yourself after tarrying too long around the campfire the night before), being winded from climbing that last ridge, altitude variations, sunspots, or any other of the multitude of things that can affect bullet placement under field conditions. On the other hand, by the simple expedient of moving the cross hairs a bit to the right (I always shoot my deer in the left side at precisely one hundred yards, just like they do it in the hunting magazines) and shooting for the chest, the target area as well as your horizons are expanded considerably.

5 • Deer, Elk, and Moose

One other neurosis that afflicts some hunters bears mentioning, since it very well could account for the death of Douglas Moore. You will recall that Moore's gun was unloaded and no empty casing was found at the scene, but neither was any ammo found on his person or in his vehicle. It is extremely doubtful that he would intentionally go hunting without *any* bullets, so, unless he just stumbled onto a deer shot by someone else, it seems reasonable that he must have had at least one cartridge at some point. For what reason, other than economics, would a man go hunting with only one bullet? Though I did not know Moore personally and am not privy to any of his philosophies, it is quite possible that he suffered from the rather common affliction of the One-Shot Syndrome.

The notion that it is somehow "unsporting" to use more than one bullet to put an animal down is most likely a carryover from the days when single-shot muzzleloaders were the only game in town. If you didn't make the first shot count, you went hungry. With modern magazine rifles, there is absolutely no reason to let an animal run off wounded when the first shot fails to deflate it, yet I have seen men do just that, watch a deer get up and stagger off without making any attempt at a follow-up shot.

Somehow the idea has developed that a one-shot kill is the mark of a true sportsman. Horse dumplings. A real sportsman's interests are in a quick, clean kill, and if it takes two or even three shots to do it, then that's just life in the real world. By no means do I advocate spraying bullets willy-nilly at an animal until you ring its gong, as I have seen done on a few occasions. Every effort should be made to put that first bullet where it belongs, but there should be no hesitation to swat him again if full cooperation is not immediately forthcoming.

I recall reading somewhere about a club comprised of hunters who gained acceptance by going afield with just one bullet and returning with game. I think it was called the One-Shot Club or something like that, and its members routinely demonstrated their predatory prowess by going hunting with only one bullet. I can't say whether Douglas Moore belonged to such an organization, but he may have been of a similar mindset. I have

American Man-Killers

met a few other people who were so inclined. There is nothing wrong with testing or even showing off your shooting skills—I would, if I had any—but the game fields are not the place to do it. That's what shooting ranges are for.

Boy, do I know how to digress or what?

In closing down on the white-tailed division of the Hemlock Society, roughly ten people per annum get all their life memberships canceled after having run-ins with Bambi, and I expect the number will rise appreciably over the next few years. With an ever-increasing number of people living side-by-side with an ever-increasing number of deer, what other conclusion could there be?

*　　*　　*　　*

As my hero Popeye might have put it, "Eye yam depresked." I had been looking forward with nothing less than giddy anticipation to chronicling all the gory carnage visited on my own species by what should be the granddaddy of all non-carnivorous, mammalian man-killers. What else could you expect of something that is ten feet long, weighs a thousand pounds, and has the animal equivalent of a pair of multi-bladed, claymore battle swords on its head? Hot damn! Now, there's a man-killer if I ever saw one! Alas. After many months of diligent research and even some rather fervent praying, I was forced to the inescapable conclusion that the American elk does not kill people. It was sort of like finding out all in the same day that there wasn't really a Santa Claus or an Easter Bunny and that Dolly Parton was actually Cleveland Amory in drag.

Darn it, I just *know* somebody somewhere has gotten the chop from an unprovoked elk, but marinate me in sheep dip if I can prove it. There are bound to be some incidents I've missed, and somebody is sure to write and tell me about one, complete with insinuations that I am woefully inadequate. That's okay, I'm used to it. My wife tells me the same thing all the time.

I am not certain why elk (*Cervus elaphus*) are not card-carrying man-killers. Perhaps they are too busy

5 • Deer, Elk, and Moose

being majestic. You know, bugling majestically in the mountains, posing majestically on ridges against the sunset, leaping majestically through insurance advertisements, stuff like that. It could also be that they suffer from some sort of identity crisis and are too distracted with researching family trees to be bothered with fatally pounding people. You see, elk are not actually elk, which is what moose are called in Europe, but are more properly called wapiti, the same species as the European red stag and the extinct Irish elk, all of which are considered members of the deer family. Now you know why elk hunters always have that confused look.

Do not get the impression that elkish ire is beyond bestirring. Quite a few people have gotten their anatomies nonfatally redecorated by elk. In 1991 a woman in Banff National Park, Canada, got her face kicked in by a pregnant cow, and in 1978 a seven-year-old girl came close to the same fate in Yellowstone. In these and other similar cases, the animals were reacting defensively to people who got too close to them, the intent undoubtedly being to drive away rather than kill, or else somebody would be dead for sure. Nice guy or not, anything that big and formidably armed is nothing to fool around with.

The same conditions discussed elsewhere about bears, cougars, and deer assuming an urban lifestyle apply equally to elk. Elk in back yards and city parks are a sure formula for death, and I expect it will boil over any day now. Watch this space for future developments.

*　　*　　*　　*

Here now comes a herbivore with its act sufficiently together to get an American political party named in its honor: Teddy Roosevelt's Bull Moose Party. Standing as tall as seven and one-half feet at the shoulder, weighing between 900 and 1,400 pounds, and armed with a set of antlers you could swing a hammock from, the moose (*Alces alces*) is a formidable-looking chap from just about any angle. When you add in a face right out of "Star Trek" decorated with a matching set of genuine, murderous-red eyes, the overall effect is astonishingly reminiscent of something Stephen King might choose for the title role in his next novel.

That evolution has bestowed Bullwinkle and company with an overdose of ugly that probably accounts for the astounding variety of "sea stories" and mythological beliefs that envelope the species. Julius Caesar was of the opinion that moose had no antlers, and could rest only when leaning against a tree because they had no knees and hence could not lie down. Logically concluding that a kneeless moose, once down, would be unable to get back up, some enterprising Germans took to going around sawing trees halfway through, with the idea of returning later and collecting the fallen moose that had leaned against the compromised boles.

Around 100 A.D. the Roman scholar Pliny reinforced the kneeless-moose theory and further alluded to the existence of a subspecies that had to walk backward when grazing to avoid tripping over its prodigious upper lip, a belief that persisted well into the nineteenth century in this country.

There is nothing mythological in a general sense about the moose's reputation as a bad actor toward man, but some of the techniques credited to old Limp Lip may have been slight exaggerations. One common tale from early times held that a moose would kill you as a natural consequence of blowing off steam—literally. The bulbous upper lip was believed to contain water that became superheated into steam when the moose was pursued. Once cornered, it would vent this steam through its nose and scald its antagonist to death. A variation of this whopper had chemically produced fire spewing from the antlers with similar consequences; tales of hunters burned beyond recognition were common until the mid-eighteenth century. Another reported technique involved the moose crushing its victim mosquito-fashion with a clapping motion of the palmated antlers.

The self-evident reality is that *Alces alces* is governed by the same laws of physics as the rest of us and must be content to merely stomp, gore, and toss those who displease him, with results no less definitive for being unglamorous.

I don't think it's necessary to extensively dwell on the violence an irritated moose is capable of dishing out to a human; a mere glimpse is usually sufficient to establish its qualifications to kill just about anybody or anything it wants to. There are at least two reliable records of bulls killing full-grown grizzlies in disputes over the evening's dinner plans. Moose have also been known to disembowel motor vehicles when in a less-than-jolly frame of mind. Recently, an eighteen-wheeler had to be towed away after it was trashed by one of two irate moose (or is it meese?) that were fighting in the middle of a Wisconsin freeway. One of them got upset when the truck driver suggested with a toot of his air horn that they should take their dispute elsewhere, and the rest is history.

One of the more curious ways people have managed to get themselves killed involves a unique calling method employed by European moose hunters. As you may know, rutting moose will come running toward any sound even remotely resembling a love-sick cow or a bellicose rival. The simple expedient of slowly pouring water into a lake from your hunting boot will get you besieged by bulls that interpret the sound as her ladyship taking a seductively suggestive tinkle. Cartoon depictions of snorting bulls charging headlong into locomotives are rooted in fact, the train's horn or whistle interpreted as the bellowing of a rival. Well, in Europe, the established mecca of classical music and the composers thereof, hunters long ago learned to capitalize on such moosey misunderstanding with the application of judiciously selected musical selections as they issue from a violin.

Since it is hard to aim and fire a rifle while sawing out the *allegro* movement of Bach's Concerto No. 2 in E Major, a second man, usually a guide, assumes the role of fiddler. That the technique works is illustrated by at least one account of a situation in which both guide and hunter were killed in their blind by a responsive moose. It was in Finland, as I recall, and they picked up what was left of the men with spoons and blotting paper. Sadly, I can find no record of what musical selection was being played.

For what it's worth, I understand that a similar technique is employed by deer hunters in some parts of Arkansas, the fundamental difference being the intent to drive rather than attract. According to the report I received, a beginner fiddle player with an untuned instrument is the most effective.

If you are genuinely curious to see just how thorough a thrashing can be administered in a matter of seconds by an incensed moose, I suggest turning to your TV set. I was truly amazed when nearly all of the major networks began airing "animal attack" specials roughly six months after I started researching this book. There may not be a connection, but such is my conceit that I secretly suspect word got around that some guy in Texas was calling up every state and federal agency in the country and asking embarrassing questions about homicidal wildlife, and the network boys figured they might as well get a piece of it too.

Most of the TV renderings have been redundant, showing the same clips of a muzzled Eurasian brown bear swatting a woman around in a Polish television studio, and the famous 1960s Craighead brothers film of a rapidly detranquilizing grizzly mauling their old, red station wagon, plus a few other "caught on tape" episodes. Most also showed the actual killing of a seventy-one-year-old man who was stomped to death in January 1995 in front of the administration building at the University of Alaska by a cow moose, the whole thing captured on amateur videotape.

If you missed it, I suspect the networks will be running their respective versions again—probably about a month after this book appears on the shelves. If you are willing to fork over $19.95, you can mail-order your own personal copy to view at your convenience. But I won't tell you from whom. The producer is one of those pabulum-puking sentimentalists whose pockets I'd just as soon not help line.

5 • Deer, Elk, and Moose

I find it interesting but not surprising that a moose would be the first American animal to kill somebody in full, living color on national TV. With the simultaneous proliferation throughout suburbia of personal video cameras and big, bad-tempered wildlife, the only surprise is that it took this long to get an actual death on film. Nevertheless, the moose as a species is to be commended for accomplishing a move of this magnitude at such a late stage in its screen career. After all, it is quite a step up from playing stooge and sidekick to Captain Kangaroo and Rocky the Flying Squirrel.

MISCELLANEOUS
KILLERS

Throughout the various contemplative stages of preparing this book, I was increasingly astonished by the staggering variety of creatures that at one time or another have firmly established themselves as man-killers. The various Carnivora and antlered herbivores that aggregate the general class of "big stuff" came as no more of a surprise than did the smaller reptiles with their notoriously lethal poisons. I was fully prepared to accept and deal with the fact that sometimes it is the little things that get you, death from a black widow's neurotoxic bite being no less permanent than getting your head bitten off by something big and toothy. But I was taken aback when dozens of reports started turning up about people getting killed by weasels, raccoons, frogs, and a wide assortment of exotic animals from iguanas to elephants, plus a whole bevy of other things that many people do not even know exists.

American Man-Killers

When the dust settled and I examined the resulting reference pile, it became abundantly clear there was no way to include it all in a single literary work short of a twelve-volume set. I realized too that the total man-hours I'd have to expend to research and document each species' mayhem-related history would exceed that required for building a space shuttle.

I mention all of this by way of explaining why you are not apt to see much in the way of in-depth analysis or causal speculation pertaining to the contents of this catch-all chapter. There just wasn't enough time or space for more than cursory treatment, and the best I could do was to drag the bloody, twitching corpses into the room and leave the analysis to you.

I guess the most logical place to start is at the bottom, down where it's nice and damp and dark and spooky and all sorts of creepy-crawly things live. Things like (ugh) spiders. At the risk of sounding like a chest-thumping moron, I tell you in all modesty that not many things frighten me. Despite having been spindled, folded, and mutilated by a dizzying assortment of malevolent fauna, I do not fear them. I have been burned, shot, infected, stabbed, scalded, acidized, poisoned, and impaled through the crotch on a spear without developing the slightest trepidation about reinserting myself into the same types of circumstances that precipitated those events.

I offer these revelations to preface my confession that there is one thing that undeniably does scare me: I am absolutely, positively, pants-wetting, screaming, run-blindly-through-the-forest terrified of spiders—not just the dangerous ones but *any* spider. Yes, I know it is irrational. Yes, I know that 99.9 percent of spiders are harmless, even beneficial to man. I don't care. I hate the nasty little buggers and try my best to stomp, swat, or shoot every one that I see.

I have no idea why I suffer from such virulent arachniphobia. Perhaps as a child I had some experience that has been blocked from my memory, something like what happened to twelve-year-old John Thomas Dillard in 1995 at his home in Brownwood, Texas. One night while John slept, he was gang-assaulted by a family of black-widow spiders that had hatched under his bed, receiving a total of thirteen bites before his parents responded to his screams. That he survived I can only attribute to the skill of his doctors or, as is more likely, direct intervention by God. From his hospital bed he told reporters, "I've never liked spiders before, and I hate them even worse now." Yeah and amen, Johnny!

It was a banner year for the not-so-merry widow. In December of '95, Japan's entire main island was terrorized by reports of thousands of *Latrodectus mactans* found infesting an Osaka shipping port, where they had presumably arrived in a lumber shipment. No bites were reported, but that didn't stop Japanese health officials from stocking up on antivenin. The furor died down after the authorities figured out that widows are more inclined to hide in dark, secluded corners than run amuck through the countryside.

A black widow's bite is reported to be extremely painful, described by those who have experienced it as "a sharp, stabbing sensation." I'll take their word for it. Follow-up symptoms include weakness, partial localized paralysis, severe cramps, and in some cases coma. The bite is not *usually* fatal to a healthy adult, but it has killed children.

The gurus say we outdoorsy types are most at risk because we spend more time poking around the kind of dark, dank places widows like to haunt. They also say two-thirds of bites are to the thighs, buttocks, and genitals, whatever that indicates.

The other dangerous American spider (there are only two, or so they claim) is the brown recluse, *Loxosceles reclusa*. Its charms are well illustrated by a recent string of California incidents, the latest being what I like to call The Case of the Recluse Widow.

In January 1996, eighty-five-year-old Audrey Needham, a widow who lived alone, swatted some spiders she found crawling around her Orange County home, and later noticed a small, red bite mark on her left hand. Twenty-four hours later, her entire arm was black and blue, horribly swollen and sporting what looked like a huge blood blister. At the hospital, her fingers became gangrenous while doctors struggled to save her life. They didn't succeed. She died two days after admission.

In 1993 a Moren Valley man had chunks of decaying flesh surgically removed from his stomach to help stanch the spread of gangrene and prevent secondary infection after being bitten by a recluse. The year before, a Mira Loma woman had her feet, hands, and part of her nose similarly amputated. In 1989 another woman died from a *Loxosceles* bite, and in 1995 a Boy Scout leader suffered brain damage.

Since there are officially no brown-recluse spiders in California, I wonder what it was that bit all those folks. Even if there are none in California, there sure are just about everywhere else. Though the recluse by and large prefers the temperate climes of the South, it has capitalized on our societal mobility to expand its range as far north as New England by hitching rides in moving boxes. Charming.

Despite my feelings about spiders, I am strangely not so disposed toward the other group of arachnids: scorpions. I have been stung dozens of times, and frankly consider getting stuck by prickly-pear spines to be far more uncomfortable. On the other hand, I have seen some people put flat on their backs after a single strike from that hypodermic tail. Chalk it up to individuality, I guess.

Though not as diverse subspecies-wise as the spiders, American scorpions come in a variety of flavors, most of which are relatively innocuous. There is one species that can be lethal: *Centruroides sculpturatus*, the straw-colored bark scorpion of the American Southwest and northern Mexico, among the deadliest of the world's 1,500 scorpion species. Though its sting is not usually fatal to an adult, children are at grave risk. The venom is neurotoxic, a deadly mixture of two dozen toxins that can shut down heart and respiratory functions in a matter of hours.

In May 1994, one-year-old Ross Brown was stung by a bark scorpion near the edge of the Sonoran Desert along the Arizona-Mexico border. Within minutes he was vomiting uncontrollably and screaming in pain. In an hour he was foaming at the mouth and convulsing violently, skin pale and sweaty, his breathing labored. Fortunately, an antidote was readily available from a Phoenix hospital, and the boy lived.

I could not find any current data on the number of deaths attributable to *sculpturatus*, but figures collected between 1929 and 1951 indicate sixty-nine people were fatally stung by it.

✳   ✳   ✳   ✳

In all of the TV cartoons I used to watch as a kid— heck, I still do—bees were always depicted as living in one of those bulbous paper hives and swarming out to attack *en masse* anyone who disturbed them. Actually, those fictional portrayals of bees attacking and relentlessly chasing Elmer Fudd over great distances were right on the money as it pertains to killer bees.

The story of the killer bee, also known as the Africanized bee, itself reads like a work of pulp fiction. It started in 1957, when some African bees imported for crossbreeding experiments escaped from a Brazilian laboratory. The highly aggressive Africans interbred with the locally established European bee colonies to create a strain of super bees, which may or may not have inspired the Dodge muscle-car designers of yore.

If anything, the new bees were more aggressive than their African ancestors, attacking in massive swarms to deliver hundreds and even thousands of stings to whoever or whatever disturbed them. As far back as 1975, hundreds of horses, cattle, and dogs had been reported stung to death, with over three hundred human victims reported in Central and South America. By now the human tally in that region must be well into the thousands. Ominous reports of the bees' northward spread were at the time pooh-poohed by some U.S. officials, but now the pooh is on the other foot—the killer bees are here.

In August 1995, a man named Ascencion Hernandez was swarmed by killer bees in—I kid you not—Beeville, Texas, after he accidentally disturbed their hive while mowing. Hernandez avoided the brunt of the attack by covering himself with a sheet of plastic, but still received more than 250 stings. Bee County firemen had to hose Hernandez down with fire-retardant foam to get the bees off before paramedics could treat him. He was later hospitalized in stable condition at Bee County Regional Medical Center, which was fairly buzzing with news of the attack.

In April 1996, a swarm of killer bees attacked and killed two emus (similar to ostriches) at a home near La Coste, Texas, and severely stung two children as well. In May of that same year, an attack near D'Hanis, Texas, killed fifty-six-year-old John Nuckles and hospitalized his son. California got its first confirmed killer-bee attack in December 1995 when a swarm of the little nasties lit into a couple of men who were trimming trees.

These are just a few of the more recent attacks I know of, and there are probably a lot more than anybody realizes. There is an organized effort to downplay and even deny killer-bee attacks. Don't want to put people in a panic, you understand, or incite the ignorant, unwashed masses to acts of insecticide against any misidentified harmless bees. A bee lobby? What next!

I don't see any need to examine extensively the various forms of wasps, yellow jackets, and hornets. Their stings are unquestionably painful but not fatal, except in individual cases involving extreme allergic reaction. One unexplored behavioral aspect of wasps deserves a word or two, though, since it just might wind up getting somebody killed. It almost got me.

A few years ago, I was hunting in the off-season out of a deer blind for coyotes, having reasoned there was no point in camouflaging myself uncomfortably among the prickly pears when a nice, spacious blind was available. While scanning the open *sendero* for activity, I caught out of the corner of my eye a glimpse of something moving *inside* the blind. Praying fervently that it wasn't a rattlesnake, I eased my head around until I could see what it was.

I was relieved to see it was just a mud-dauber wasp, scooting around nervously in search of a nest-building site. I watched it for a couple of seconds, and was astonished when it disappeared down the upright muzzle of my rifle! I was looking for a piece of bailing wire to swab him out with when he suddenly extracted himself and buzzed out the blind's window.

As I sat there pondering whether the rifle would have blown up had I shot while the bore was plugged by a wasp, it came buzzing back through the window and headed straight for the rifle's muzzle. It was carrying a great big wad of mud under its belly, obviously intent on building a mud nest inside my rifle barrel. I eliminated any future possibility for such shenanigans by that particular wasp and, after making sure the bore was clear, immediately placed a piece of tape over the gun's muzzle to protect against coconspirators; a practice I have followed religiously since.

*   *   *   *

At least two people have been stung to death in the U.S. by fire ants, another gift from South America, and I expect there will be a lot more as the useless little arthropods continue expanding their range. I can find no record of anyone killed, other than through allergic reaction, by our native red ant, the only insect I know of to whose venom I am violently susceptible; one bite anywhere on my body sets my lymph nodes on fire and makes me as nauseous as a coyote with a carrion hangover.

*   *   *   *

Another insect that is not likely to kill you outright but will sure eat you alive is the mosquito. Mosquitoes kill with an indirect approach, reminiscent of biological warfare, by infecting you with some fatal disease. Americans are generally aware of the untold deaths from mosquito-spread malaria, sleeping sickness, and whatnot in Third World tropical regions, but most people have no idea of the number of deaths that occur in this country from mosquito-borne plagues.

American Man-Killers

In the state of Texas in 1995, there were twenty confirmed cases of hemorrhagic dengue fever, a quaint tropical illness that produces severe muscular pain, inferno-class stomach inflammation, headaches that a truckload of Excedrin wouldn't put a dent in, and death from internal hemorrhage. That same year, health officials in Reynosa, Mexico, just across the border from McAllen, Texas, reported over 900 cases, with an additional 150,000 confirmed cases reported in Central and South America. Not all dengue victims die, but somewhere along the line, most wish that they would.

Several localized outbreaks of malaria and the St. Louis encephalitis strain have been reported recently, with twenty-seven deaths attributed to the latter. And regardless of what they say, I am not convinced the HIV or AIDS virus cannot be transmitted by mosquitoes or other insect vectors.

*   *   *   *

Another little bloodsucker, the deer tick (*Ixodes scapularis*), is the last insect we will herein step on. Most outdoorsmen are familiar with the danger posed by tick-borne Rocky Mountain spotted fever. My late friend Weldon Moss survived the disease after contracting it during a Colorado elk hunt in 1988, even though he received no medical treatment. In fact, he didn't even know he had it until told so after the fact when a routine blood test picked up lingering telltale signs. Weldon always was a tough character. It took a massive heart attack to kill him a few years ago. I still miss him.

Nobody knows how long ticks have been infecting Americans with Lyme disease. Most people think the disease is something relatively new, but the actual fact is we only recently learned to recognize it. The initial symptoms are flu-like, which is what most Lyme-infected people initially assume they have. An estimated 10,000 are infected yearly.

Left untreated, the disease can persist for years if not indefinitely, producing irreversible arthritic complications and liver damage, plus a grab bag of other unpleasant symptoms too extensive to list here. Believe me, I know. I've got it. Or I think I do. I've had several "bad" bites over the years and display many of the late-stage symptoms, but my doctor said the test for Lyme is so unreliable there is no way to be 100 percent sure. The antibiotic treatments she prescribed seemed to alleviate some of the milder symptoms for a while, but relapses are common, and I'm stuck with the arthritic complications in any event. Oh, well, it could be worse. Lyme makes you miserable, but it won't kill you—at least the run-of-the-mill version won't.

There is a new Lymelike disease, also transmitted by ticks, that has so far killed four people. Called *human granulocytic ehrlichdiosis,* or HGE, its symptoms are virtually indistinguishable from those of Lyme. HGE is curable but responds to only one specific antibiotic. Lyme responds to several, some of which can actually accelerate HGE and hasten death, so knowing which type you have is crucial. Doctors are working on improved tests for detecting the diseases as well as a reliable way to distinguish between the two, but haven't come up with anything so far.

*   *   *   *

One other disease, which comes via a different type of vector organism, bears mentioning. In 1995 Nicaragua, health officials were stymied for months by an infectious illness that wound up killing twenty-seven people before they could get a handle on it. It turned out to be leptospirosis. Sound familiar? If so, it is probably because you recently had your dog vaccinated for it.

I wish I had the time and the talent to relate the indescribable terror one feels upon encountering an animal operating under the insane influence of rabies. Lacking both, my best suggestion is to rent the movie *Old Yeller.* The savageness therein portrayed is right on the money, even if a bit on the light side.

The incidence of rabies has been increasing steadily all across the U.S. for a number of years now. In 1995 dozens of people were treated after encounters with confirmed rabid skunks, foxes, raccoons, otters, cats, dogs, and bats. Bats are notorious rabies vectors, yet some bat lovers say the species is no more or less likely to carry the disease than any other animal. Bull cookies. Casual observation of their communal lifestyle makes it clear how the disease can spread through a colony faster than bad news at the stock exchange. Anecdotal evidence indicates you don't even have to be bitten to be infected by a bat; all it takes is breathing the same air.

At least two cases have been reported of people contracting rabies after merely visiting bat caves, with no bite involved, leading health officials to conclude that air-borne transmission was the only possible cause. In October 1995, thirteen-year-old Maria Fareri died of rabies contracted from a bat that flew into her house; she never touched it, or it her. In March of that same year, a four-year-old girl died under similar circumstances after a bat was found in her room. Since the girl was unbitten, no medical treatment was sought and the bat was killed and buried in the back yard. After the girl became ill, the bat was exhumed and tested positive for rabies. A California man died in September after a bat brushed against him in a shed without biting or otherwise breaking the skin.

If so inclined, we could stir up quite a soup of both old and new infectious diseases that have begun cropping up with depressing frequency in recent years: cholera, yellow fever, bubonic plague, anthrax, the dreaded "flesh-eating" bacteria, plus a whole host of new "mystery" diseases that have yet to be identified. Topped off with a few "death cap" mushrooms, it makes a rather full plate.

*   *   *   *

If there is an animal more universally loathed and feared on a worldwide basis than snakes in general, I don't know what it is. Of the hundreds of snake species indigenous to North America, only four basic types are considered dangerous: rattlesnakes, water moccasins, copperheads, and coral snakes.

6 • Miscellaneous Killers

Note that there is no emphatic proclamation that these are the only *poisonous* snakes, for we are continually dismayed to find that many snakes once considered nonvenomous actually do possess poison glands and fangs. They remain in the "not considered dangerous" category because their poison-delivery mechanisms are located sufficiently far back in the mouth to make human envenomation *almost* impossible. Species in this category include the lyre, Texas cat-eyed, black-banded, and Mexican vine snakes, plus—get this—the ubiquitous garter snake! Yep, the ones you played with as a kid.

In November 1975, an eleven-year-old California boy was bitten on the hand by a garter snake he found on the playground at his school. A short time later, his arm began to swell, his shoulder turning black. He and the snake were flown to the Los Angeles County/University of Southern California Medical Center, where Dr. Findlay E. Russell, a leading authority on the treatment of venomous bites, verified that the boy had indeed been poisoned by the snake. Within days, Russell received nine additional reports of venomous garter-snake bites from doctors around the country.

As far as my research indicates, no human deaths have been attributed to the bite of a "harmless" snake, but the same cannot be said of the genuine article. In this country, ten to fifteen people are annually killed and hundreds more are less-definitively bitten by rattlesnakes alone, mostly the Eastern and Western diamondback varieties. A discussion of the normal circumstances under which most bites occur seems unnecessary, but here are a few nontypical episodes you might find interesting:

In 1996 a jury awarded a San Antonio, Texas, man $6,000 for medical expenses after he was bitten by a rattlesnake while shopping in the automotive department at Wal-Mart. The man was reaching for an air filter when a twenty-four-inch rattler struck him on the right hand from the shelf. This was the store's second rattlesnake incident; an employee narrowly avoided being bitten when another snake struck her plastic name tag—and you know where they are worn.

American Man-Killers

That it is unwise to make fun of a rattlesnake was illustrated by the 1995 experience of an Arizona man. While showing off with his "pet" rattlesnake, the man in mockery stuck out his tongue, which the snake promptly bit. Within minutes his throat swelled nearly shut, and only prompt medical attention saved his life.

Anyone skeptical of stories about people bitten by "dead" snakes needs to talk to thirty-six-year-old Texas resident Paul Russo, who in October 1995 was bitten on the arm by the decapitated head of a diamondback rattler. On the way to the hospital, ambulance attendants twice had to resuscitate Russo when he stopped breathing. He remained on life support for several days but eventually recovered.

There is at least one case on record of a rattler putting a man in the hospital without laying a fang on him. Five minutes after killing one huge rattlesnake, a Thomasville, Alabama, turkey hunter nearly stepped on a second one he hadn't seen. It didn't bite him, but it frightened him so badly that he swallowed the rubber diaphragm turkey call he had in his mouth, and was hospitalized for two weeks after it was extracted. If they can't get you one way. . . .

Space prohibits a detailed discussion of the effects rattlesnake venom have on the body. The viscous, amber juice is composed of a variety of toxins, including neuro-toxins, but is mostly hemotoxic, which simply means that it digests your tissues from the inside out, a less than pleasant sensation.

Although I have never had a rattler catch up with my rapidly retreating backside, a few years ago I did have a close encounter with a copperhead, whose venom is similar to a rattler's but not as virulent. The snake latched onto my left hand when I picked up the log it was coiled under. The initial sensation was exactly like the sting of a yellow jacket, which is what I thought it was until I saw the orange and coppery-brown reptile dangling from my index finger, one fang embedded to the hilt between the second and third knuckle.

Rather than bore you with all the gory details, let it suffice to say that I had a rather interesting time of it for a couple of weeks, without benefit of medical treatment. (Antivenin costs $200 a vial, and my body size would have required at least twelve vials. I knew death or serious complications were unlikely, so I opted to tough it out and save a few bucks.) One aspect of the experience bears telling, a curious phenomenon I have never seen alluded to elsewhere: People who spend a lot of time in copperhead country are familiar with the serpent's "musty" smell, and can frequently detect a snake's presence by scent alone without seeing it. When the swelling in my arm began to go down, I started smelling copperhead.

At first I thought it was all in my head, but the phenomenon was confirmed as real when I got within nose-range of an acquaintance who recognized the scent. "Damn! You stink like a copperhead," I believe were his exact words. Anyway, the more the swelling subsided, the stronger the smell became, oozing out with my sweat and permeating my clothes with the acrid odor. Toward the last, my wife (who has also been bitten, as has her nephew) made me undress outside each day so I wouldn't stink up the house. It was nearly three weeks before all the poison processed out of my system and I once again smelled more or less human.

That more people are not killed by cottonmouths probably owes to the watery inaccessibility of their preferred habitat, otherwise cemetery-plot futures would be on the S & P Top 10 list. Besides being big and possessing a most virulent hemotoxic poison, the cottonmouth is of a decidedly nasty disposition. Given half a chance, rattlers and copperheads will avoid you. Not a cottonmouth. Bestir his ire, and he'll come for you. His ire is easily bestirred.

When I was a kid, the other ranch urchins and I used to amuse ourselves by catching cottonmouths alive, then releasing them out by the barn to watch the dogs fight them. We accomplished this feat by arming ourselves with sticks and burlap feed sacks (we always called them "tow sacks") and wading down the creek until a big moccasin was spotted sunning on an overhanging limb. When prodded with a stick, nine out of ten would launch themselves into the water and swim faster than most people can believe straight at us, the lining of their open mouths bright white against the mottled-brown to dirty-black background of the undulating body. At the last second, we'd scoop it up in one of the tow sacks, then go looking for another one. Why none of us got bitten remains one of the great mysteries of our times.

About the only way to get bitten by a coral snake is to pick it up and fool with it, and even then you'll probably have to stick your finger in its mouth—which is purely delightful news, considering that its venom is a paralyzing neurotoxin quite similar to a cobra's.

Back in the 1980s, one of the members of a hunting party I was part of came close to finding out what it is like to die of coral-snake bite. We had arrived late the evening before opening day and immediately started setting up camp. Several of us scoured the forest by flashlight for firewood to prepare the evening meal. The next morning, I was stoking up the breakfast fire when I spotted the unburned half of a coral snake sticking out of the ashes. Somebody had accidentally picked it up and carried it into camp with an armload of wood. We never did figure out who, but knowing my luck. . . .

Though it is beyond the geographic purview of this work, there are a couple of things you might like to know about giant snakes—you know, man-eating pythons and such. As you probably already suspect, I am not about to waste any pulp rehashing other writers' strenuous attempts to debunk such beliefs; I'd rather prove them as fact. According to a September 1995 Associated Press report, a twenty-three-foot python in Malaysia killed and was in the process of eating twenty-nine-year-old rubber-plantation worker E. Heng Chuan when its meal got rudely interrupted by some other workers. The snake had already swallowed the man's head and crushed some of his bones when discovered. Another AP story, dated 30 April 1969, recounts the death and subsequent consumption of an eight-year-old Pakistani boy by a python of unspecified size. I rest my case.

*   *   *   *

6 • Miscellaneous Killers

Snakes being reptiles, this is as good a place as any to interject a few other cold-blooded man-killers. Now, I make no claims one way or the other about turtles killing people, although there are several species of both fresh-water and saltwater persuasion that are capable, and they can fatally infect you with salmonella (more on that shortly), which is why you no longer see bowls containing baby turtles for sale at the checkout counter. The fresh-water alligator snapping turtle has frequently been re-ported to lop off the fingers, toes, and, if you believe the "fish stories," the hands of the incautious. Since a really big one can weigh up to 200 pounds and possess jaws of human-head-spanning size, use your imagination.

Whether or not you believe snapping turtles are dangerous is entirely up to you. But one man sure thought so, and coughed up the cash to prove it. In July 1990, about the same time as the Teenage Mutant Ninja chaps were in their heyday, a Dallas, Texas, pizza-delivery man reported to police that he was robbed of $50 at turtle-point. Two bandits wielding a vicious-looking snapping turtle cornered the hapless man in a phone booth and held the turtle near his face, demanding money. He complied forthwith, whereupon the bandits hauled shell with the cash.

*　　*　　*　　*

Another reptilian menace, the iguana, more properly belongs in the later section on exotic animals, but we don't stand on formalities here. Iguanas have been the "in" thing as pets for some years now. Though not overtly dangerous, they have nevertheless succeeded in kill-ing or hospitalizing quite a few people. In October 1995, a three-week-old infant in South Bend, Indiana, died after contracting salmonella poisoning from the family's pet iguana. That same year, the health departments of thirteen states reported encountering unusual salmo-nella strains that were later traced to the reptiles. According to U.S. Fish & Wildlife Service records, 798,405 iguanas were imported into this country in 1993 alone. The problem is apparently not exclusive to iguanas but includes all reptiles. In March 1996, fifty people contracted salmonella poisoning after visiting a traveling Komodo dragon exhibit at the Denver Zoo.

There is never a dull moment in the wacky world of reptiles. In 1995 four New York men died after ingesting a dried-toad secretion sold as an aphrodisiac in traditional Chinese medicine shops. The toad juice came without instructions, so the men didn't know it was supposed to be applied, uh, topically, and not swallowed. The things we do for love.

Since reptiles are the distant ancestors of birds, I am obligated to point out that hundreds of human deaths have been caused by birds colliding with airplanes. U.S. House Speaker Newt Gingrich, who you may recall was bitten by a cougar cub, came close to sacrificing all future political aspirations when two geese crashed into his small private plane on takeoff. At about the same time, an Air Force AWACS plane crashed near Anchorage, Alaska, after flying into a flock of geese, killing all twenty-four persons on board.

I can sum up sharks and how to avoid the dangers associated therewith in six words: They will kill you. Don't swim. There isn't space to even list, let alone detail, all the other saltwater nasties that will forcibly eject you from the dance floor if you step on their toes. Besides, everybody knows about all the stuff in the ocean that will kill you. On the other hand, most people are unaware of the freshwater biggies that can enrich and possibly shorten your life, even if by accident.

It was the dead of winter, cold as an executioner's heart and twice as dreary, the day Texas game warden J. C. Romines dredged up and started taking in an illegal trotline. He didn't know at the time that it was occupied, one of the hooks buried in the back of a 67-pound flathead catfish. The fish offered no resistance at first, having "sulked" in frustration from fighting the unyielding line, but it was very much alive. Romines became aware of the fish when its yard-and-a-half of mottled-brown and dirty-yellow hide rose slowly into view, roiling the surface in a muddy slick. Man and fish saw one another in the same instant. In a flicker, it lunged for the bottom, yanking Romines overboard when a hook snagged his right arm.

At 200 pounds of work-hardened muscle, Romines is no pantywaist. But in the water he was no match for the big fish. It dragged him inexorably downward, skidding him along the muddy bottom toward ever deeper water. He thought of the knife in his right front pants pocket but couldn't reach it with his left hand, the right stretched out and away by the fish. The warden thought it was all over, but his progress toward oblivion suddenly halted when the trailing line grew taught. A hook had snagged on the gunwale as the line paid out of the boat. With his free hand, he began pulling himself back to the surface.

Romines thought his lungs would burst before he could reach the surface, but he made it. Gasping for air, he held himself up with one hand against the fish struggling just five feet away. Wouldn't you know it, the overstressed hook hung on the boat straightened and Romines was dragged down again, something that happened three more times during the ordeal. Exhausted and snarled in even more hooks and line, the man used his remaining strength to fight to the surface for what he knew would be the last time, one way or the other. Thankfully, three hooks had caught this time and Romines was able to lever himself into the boat and safety. It's funny, he used to really enjoy a nice, big plate of fried catfish; these days he won't touch the stuff.

*   *   *   *

What has bad breath, big teeth, a shaggy coat of coarse hair, a leg at each corner, weighs up to 600 pounds, and likes to eat people? Before you waste a lot of time trying to figure out if it's your mother-in-law, consider the following:

In October 1993, seventy-nine-year-old Willie Heinen was working outdoors around his home when he noticed his dogs had been strangely absent all day. He whistled for them and heard a commotion of feet running toward him from behind the house, but it sure wasn't his dogs. A sounder of twelve wild hogs came boiling around the corner of the house, running straight for him in a flat-out charge.

Being an old southern-Texas bush hand, Heinen was well familiar with hogs and knew he was in trouble. Unarmed and effectively cut off from the house by the rapidly closing gang of killers, he looked around for a refuge and spotted his pickup truck parked some twenty-five yards away. "Relief" is too mild a word to describe Heinen's emotions when his hand closed on the pickup's door handle. Relief melted into terror, however, when he tried the latch—locked! The hogs were almost on him, leaving no time for other options. Resigning himself to the inevitable, he raised his heavy mesquite walking stick and turned to face the rushing conglomerate of hooves, tusks, and death.

The first hog rushed in and was met with Heinen's cane crashing over its head. Three-inch tusks crunched around the stick, snapping it in half and ripping it from Heinen's grasp with a violent jerk. Electric fingers of pain gripped him as a second hog ripped at his thigh while a third savaged his ankle, yanking him down flat on his back on the ground. The rest of the pack swarmed him, powerful jaws splintering bones and shredding flesh in his right hand, a 200-pound boar hooking at his left leg and tearing away flesh with a soggy *thwop*. Willie Heinen literally was being eaten alive.

Deciding to go down swinging, Heinen threw a fist at the nearest hog. He wasn't certain where the punch landed, but for sure it was the right place. The hog screamed in surprise and pain and ran off toward the brush, the others following with cannibalistic intentions. Heinen struggled through the pain to his feet, then hurriedly hobbled inside before the hogs came back. He somehow managed to telephone a neighbor before passing out.

Six months later, he was still recovering from wounds painfully infected by the pathogens in the rotting meat on the hogs' tusks. If it hadn't been for that lucky punch, Willie Heinen would today be fertilizing the grasses of some *sendero* as hog droppings.

Man-eating hog stories have been circulating for years, reflected in such macabrely humorous colloquialisms as "So-and-so went to the outhouse and the hogs ate him" and "I haven't had this much fun since the hogs ate my little brother." Hogs feeding on human corpses is a confirmed fact, but no verifiable case of man-killing has ever been documented. There's probably a good reason for that: When hogs kill you unwitnessed in the woods and eat you, they eat *all* of you, bones and all. With no witnesses and no body, what is there to document? I once found a boot, a tattered, chewed-on hunting boot, bearing vestiges of what *might* have been bloodstains. Nearby lay the broken half of a broadhead-tipped aluminum hunting arrow. Contemplating the possibilities of how the two objects came to be found together in a dense thicket crawling with wild hogs is an exercise I try to avoid, especially when I am bowhunting.

It may comfort you to know that wild hogs (*Sus scrofa*) do not inhabit all of the U.S., just most of it, in numbers estimated at two million strong.

Beyond pointing out that the American Southwest's javelina or collared peccary (*Tayassu tajacu*) is not actually a pig and has never been known to kill or severely injure anyone, I see little point in discussing him.

*   *   *   *

Since we elsewhere seriously maligned the character of dogs, it only seems fair to give house cats an airing. I know what you're thinking: Zaidle's finally gone off the steep end. Trust me, cats are not only capable of killing, as they have bloodily demonstrated on a number of human infants, they will also happily eat you if given the chance.

In March 1995, authorities discovered what was left of the body of sixty-nine-year-old Frans Heemskerk inside his house in Leiden, the Netherlands. According to the report, the corpse had been "almost totally eaten up" by the man's fifteen pet cats. There wasn't enough left to determine the cause of death, and natural causes were presumed. While I do not claim the cats killed the man, it is interesting that they *chose* to eat him. During the two-week period in which the body was consumed, the pussies came and went as they pleased through a pet door, having ample opportunity to catch prey or filch snacks from neighbors at will. I don't think we're in Kansas anymore, Toto.

Back on this side of the Atlantic, in April 1996 a Texas City couple was severely injured in an attack by their nineteen-pound (!) pet cat. The feline had taken exception to being confined in the living room, which it expressed by ripping a large gash in the woman's wrist and making confetti of the man's legs. When police called animal control to take charge of the animal, the owners refused, saying they were worried about what might happen to their beloved feline in the hands of strangers.

One more: In February 1996, authorities at the Southern California Edison Company nuclear power plant reported the birth of four radioactive kittens. The report did not mention how many rads the felines were putting off, saying only that the glow was "below levels considered dangerous." At last word, the kittens—dubbed Alpha, Beta, Gamma, and Neutron—were doing fine, evidencing no signs of sprouting any extra appendages. Imagine trying to give those things away! Teenage Mutant Kung Fu Kittens, anyone?

There are pets and then there are pets. In October 1978, twenty-six-year-old Margaret Haynie was killed by her husband's pet lioness near Tallahassee, Florida. The cat broke its chain and grabbed the woman when she walked past its shelter, dragging her, screaming, into the woods. The husband fired five pistol shots into the lion without effect. In October 1995, thirty-year-old Diana Renner was killed by a female African lion in Fennville, Michigan. The big tabby was one of several kept by a friend she was visiting. In September 1995, police in Lava Hot Springs, Idaho, issued warnings to "keep children indoors" after fifteen African lions escaped into the countryside. The all-clear was sounded after law officers killed fourteen of the beasts and the last one was shot by a farmer who caught it stalking his cattle. Interestingly, the timing of the last two events coincided almost perfectly with network TV's revival in updated format of the old "Born Free" series.

Eight people were mauled by pet or captive tigers in separate incidents between November 1995 and May 1996. In the May incident, six-year-old Katie Baxter was hospitalized in critical condition after being mauled by one of five tigers kept illegally at a home in Midlothian, Texas. The incident was only the latest in a string of attacks by those particular tigers going back several years.

Lord forbid that any leopards miss out on the fun. Twenty-five-year-old Leeda Brownell had her throat torn out by a 100-pound leopard belonging to a Palm Harbor, Florida, musician. The woman barely survived after receiving a tracheotomy but is unlikely ever to speak normally again. Near Lafayette Township, New Jersey, four-year-old Scott Diego was petting a leopard when it grabbed him by the head and started chewing. He survived with a few extra holes in his skull and stitches in his throat. I once met a man in a hunting camp whose face looked as if somebody in the past had gone over it with a lawn mower. Leopard, his uncle's.

*   *   *   *

In Laguna Hills, California, a three-ton elephant broke loose from its chains at Lion Country Safari, killed the park's game warden, and was charging off for some jollies on the San Diego Freeway when it was finally tranquilized and recaptured. A circus elephant went berserk in Palm Bay, Florida, wrecking bleachers, disemboweling a couple of trucks, playing body-badminton with its trainers, and injuring a dozen people before being killed by police gunfire. Another circus elephant met a near-identical fate after it killed its trainer and badly injured three other men during a live performance.

*   *   *   *

American Man-Killers

Lest we forget that size is irrelevant in the man-killing business, in 1991 a couple in Hillsboro, Oregon, woke up one morning to find their two-and-one-half-month-old baby girl dead in her crib, killed in the night with multiple bites to the neck, face, and chest by the family's pet ferret, a weasel-like animal that might weigh three pounds soaking wet. In November 1995, a two-month-old child in Melrose, Wisconsin, narrowly avoided the same fate when her mother found the family ferret chewing on the infant's face. A number of other similar cases are on record. A total of 425 ferret attacks were reported in California, Oregon, and Arizona between 1978 and 1987.

*　　*　　*　　*

I can't believe that readership interest in the number of people killed by livestock would be worth the ink to include them, though you can sure bet the farm that it happens, and on a fairly regular basis. I suppose exotics, like the various African and Asian antelopes stocked on hunting ranches, could be considered "livestock" in the sense that they are similarly sold and traded. Like any wild critter, some of them can be quite nasty. I know of one man who got severely unlaced by a bull nilgai, the huge, spike-horned antelope of India, and another who almost bled to death after getting skewered on the horns of a springbok.

The American bison or "buffalo," with the exception of a few free-ranging herds in Canada and some of the Midwestern states, has been mostly reduced to the status of livestock, though it hardly can be considered "domesticated." Each year several people learn the hard way that a ton of bull bison is nothing to fool around with. Captive animals account for most deaths, but in 1971 one man had the privilege of seeing his life pulled out on the glistening, pink ropes of his own intestines through a horn hole, courtesy of one of Yellowstone Park's 4,000 free-roaming bison. On average, ten people a year get stomped, gored, tossed, or otherwise abused in Yellowstone while attempting to pet or get their picture taken with bison. Maybe there should be a chapter somewhere devoted to stupidity, the greatest American man-killer of all.

✳   ✳   ✳   ✳

Let's talk about monkeys. Many people keep monkeys as pets, but I am sure I don't know why. Having a monkey around the house is sort of like sharing accommodations with Uncle Fester from "The Addams Family." They are mean as hell and invariably bite the hand that feeds them. They stink to high heaven, cannot be housebroken, think throwing their own feces in your face is high comedy, and are the worst sort of thieves and vandals.

Beyond a penchant for thoroughly disgusting behavior, primates in general have clearly demonstrated both the willingness and the ability to kill grown men. In their native lands, chimpanzees, baboons, and most of the larger monkeys regularly steal, kill, and eat human infants. Yes, I said *eat*. That simians are anything but strict banana-eating vegetarians was established years ago by Dr. Jane van Lawick-Goodall, the chimp lady, whom you may know from the PBS channel. Of course, old African hands had known this all along, but who would take the word of a man whose livelihood and very survival depends on observing and knowing the habits of animals? Anyway, in a thirty-year study of the chimps and baboons of Tanzania's Gombe district, Goodall documented case upon case of the species engaging in both opportunistic and organized hunts for meat, including intraspecies cannibalism. In the book *In The Shadow of Man* Goodall writes:

> During the ten years that have passed since I began work at the Gombe Stream, we have recorded chimpanzees feeding on the young of bushbucks, bushpigs, and baboons, as well as both young and small adult colobus monkeys, redtail monkeys, and blue monkeys. And there are two cases on record of chimpanzees in the area actually taking off African babies—presumably as prey, since when recovered

237

from an adult male chimpanzee one infant had had its limbs partially eaten.

Now, that's pretty clear-cut, and from an avowed monkey-lover at that. I was prepared to pledge allegiance to Goodall's frankness and scientific pragmatism and, were I not already married, might have considered capitalizing on her current state of marital disenchantment and asked for her hand, when I came across the following observation:

> Many people are horrified when they hear that a chimpanzee might eat a human baby, but after all, so far as the chimpanzee is concerned, men are only another kind of primate, not so very different from baboons in *their* eyes. Surely it should be equally horrifying to reflect on the fact that in a great many places throughout their range chimpanzees are considered a delicacy by humans? [sic]

Oh, well. So much for my dream girl.

With the primates' credentials as card-carrying man-killers thus established, I can now offer the following without risking a one-way ride in the back of a rubber-lined truck:

In July 1975, a pet monkey in Jersey City, New Jersey, escaped confinement on the second floor of its owner's house, whereupon it entered the downstairs living quarters and attacked a four-month-old infant boy asleep on the couch. When the child's mother tried to beat it off with a broom, the monkey took the weapon by force and turned it against the woman, chasing her out of the house. Neighbors alerted by the woman's screams attempted to entice the monkey outside with an offer of cherries. When that didn't work, one man tried to shoot it but missed. The police didn't do much better, held at bay by the monkey's fierceness and afraid to shoot lest the child be hit. By the time the husband, the only person who could control the beast, arrived, the boy was dead, big hunks of his flesh bitten out and presumably eaten.

6 • Miscellaneous Killers

The monkey in this case was a macaque, a typically aggressive species of which there are several varieties. The report didn't specify which variety this one was but did say it weighed about thirty pounds, placing it in the size-class of rhesus monkeys (*Macaca mulatta*) and Japanese macaques or snow monkeys (*Macaca fuscata*). Why am I telling you all this? Well, it seems the monkey menace is not limited to just pets. At least three states have large, established populations of free-ranging monkeys, and there could be more.

Large troops of rhesus monkeys roam the Silver River region of central Florida, leftovers from the days when they filmed the old Tarzan movies, and squirrel monkeys (*Saimiri sciureus*) inhabit the junglelike environs around Miami. A troop of Japanese macaques terrorized Branson, Missouri, a few years ago, establishing themselves in the surrounding hardwoods after escaping from an animal park, but I think game-department sharpshooters have pretty much eliminated them by now. The spookiest bunch is the one in Texas. Japanese macaques have been a well-established feature of the arid, southern-Texas landscape for some years now, escapees from a dilapidated primate research center near Dilley. Nobody really knows how many there are, but they seem to be everywhere.

Even though there have been no reported attacks, the monkeys have invaded homes and barns, wreaking havoc on farm equipment, fouling livestock food, and stealing anything not tied down, not to mention invading hunters' blinds, destroying wildlife feeders, and generally disrupting the region's ecological balance. The concern over whether the monkeys will begin demonstrating their talents for mayhem against people pales in comparison to their disease-spreading potential.

The same physiological similarity to humans that makes monkeys valuable for medical research also makes them potential carriers, spreaders, and breeders of human infectious diseases. The Texas colony has been known to carry the herpes B virus (try catching *that* from a monkey!) and the potentially deadly hepatitis B, but the potential for tuberculosis, shigellosis, and a whole host of other osises is very real—even the deadly ebola virus.

In April 1996 at the Texas Primate Center located in Alice—well within the range of the far-wandering Dilley colony—fifty imported monkeys were destroyed after they were found to be infected with the primate strain of ebola. Since the human strain is a mutation of the primate version, I wonder what would have happened had one of those infected monkeys escaped and joined up with the free-ranging colony. Indeed, I wonder.